Adobe® Acrobat® 6 TIPS and TRICKS
THE 100 BEST

Donna L. Baker

Adobe Press

Adobe Acrobat 6 Tips and Tricks
The 100 Best

Donna L. Baker

Adobe Press books are published by Peachpit Press
Peachpit Press
1249 Eighth Street
Berkeley, CA 94710
510/524-2178
800/283-9444
510/524-2221 (fax)

Peachpit Press is a division of Pearson Education

To report errors, please send a note to errata@peachpit.com

For the latest on Adobe Press books go to www.adobepress.com

Editor: Becky Morgan
Production Editor: Gloria Marquez
Copyeditor: Liz Welch
Compositor: David Van Ness, Diana Van Winkle
Indexer: FireCrystal Communications
Cover design: Maureen Forys
Interior design: Maureen Forys

ISBN 0-321-22392-6

9 8 7 6 5 4 3 2 1

Printed and bound in the United States of America

For Deena and the boys.

Acknowledgements

I would like to thank the editorial and development team at Peachpit, with a most special thanks to my editor, Becky Morgan. I would like to thank my agent Matt Wagner at Waterside Productions for bringing me this most interesting opportunity.

Thanks to my husband Terry for exhibiting his usual level of patience and humor, and to our daughter Erin for being who she is. Thanks to Deena for our daily chats, and to Bev and Barb for support and encouragement.

Thanks to Adobe for the software which continues to grow and develop in amazing new ways. Finally, thanks to Tom Waits for musically accompanying me during the long days and nights of writing.

Contents

CHAPTER ONE

Getting Started

Several years ago Adobe Systems introduced a new file format called PDF (Portable Document Format). PDF was revolutionary—what you wanted the reader to see was what the reader generally saw. No longer were you required to balance the design and appearance of a page against the capabilities of the recipient's computer to open and display your work.

Adobe continues to use the format in the ever-expanding world of Acrobat. From its humble beginnings in 1992 to the present day, this program has undergone several incarnations. The latest is the Acrobat 6 family of products. If you are reading this, you are the proud owner of Acrobat 6 Standard. Acrobat 6's versions, including Standard, Professional, and Elements, offer various subsets of functionality.

As you learn to use the program, you become aware of two important facts:

- There is nothing "standard" about Acrobat Standard.

- Acrobat does a lot more than display PDF files.

In this first chapter, you'll see what makes up the program. After a short tour, you'll learn some ways to make the interface work for you. The default layout shows several toolbars and options, but it isn't necessary for you to see them all at the same time.

TIP 1 A Place for Everything

When you first open Acrobat 6 Standard, you see the program spread out before you, as shown in **Figure 1.1** (with the exception of the image of the rose, of course). Here's a breakdown of the opening window:

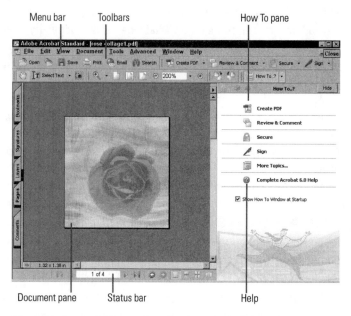

Figure 1.1 Acrobat's program interface is made up of several sections.

- **The Main menu.** The Main menu items range across the top of the window (**Figure 1.2**). Many of the categories—File, Edit, View, Window, and Help—will be familiar to you. The others—Document, Tools, and Advanced—provide specialized program features.

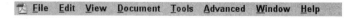

Figure 1.2 Some of the Main menu items are common to other programs.

- **Toolbars.** Acrobat 6 has a large number of toolbars. The default toolbar arrangement is shown in **Figure 1.3**. Most items found in toolbars are available as menu commands as well. An icon with a pull-down arrow to the right indicates that a subtoolbar is available. You simply click the arrow to display the hidden options.

Figure 1.3 The default toolbar and Task Bar arrangement includes several components.

- **The Navigation pane.** You'll see a set of tabs down the left side of the window. Collectively, the tabs are referred to as the Navigation pane (**Figure 1.4**). The options on these tabs let you manage and control the content in a PDF file in various ways. The figure shows the default set of tabs.

Figure 1.4 The Navigation pane displays at the left side of the program window.

- **The Document pane.** Open files display in the Document pane (**Figure 1.5**). Acrobat displays the page size below the open document. Vertical and horizontal scroll bars allow you to reposition the content as desired.

Look Before You Touch

You can modify the screen display—toolbars, Navigation pane tabs, and so on. But before you do, familiarize yourself with the contents. Click the pull-down arrows to see what options are listed in a subtoolbar, for example. Click a tab in the Navigation pane and see what options become available to you. Checking out Acrobat's default offerings may help you as you learn to work with the program.

TIP 1: A Place for Everything

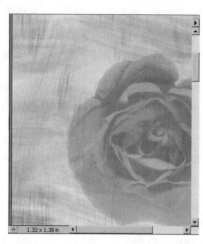

Figure 1.5 Use the Document pane to control your location in the document.

- **The status bar.** The status bar displays below the Document pane (**Figure 1.6**). You see the current page number and total page count, as well as the viewing layout, such as single or continuous page, indicated by an icon. Use the navigation controls to move backward and forward through your document.

Figure 1.6 The status bar displays page information and viewing layout.

- **How To.** The How To pane (**Figure 1.7**) at the right of the screen displays a set of links to common tasks. It is separate from the full Help menu and is intended as a quick reference. You cannot resize this pane but you can hide it.

Figure 1.7 Use the How To pane for quick reference.

TIP 2 Getting Assistance

The How To pane contains a list of the most common tasks you are likely to perform in Acrobat 6 (**Figure 1.8**). Follow these pointers to make your way through the How To topics:

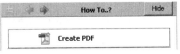

Figure 1.8 Click one of the main topic areas on the How To pane to open a list of topics.

- A list of the main topics appears in the How To pane (**Figure 1.9**). Use the scroll bars to access the entire list. Click a link to the particular task you are trying to accomplish.

Figure 1.9 Each major task lists a number of topic choices.

- Instructions for performing the task or activity appear in the How To pane (**Figure 1.10**). Scroll down the pane to read the entire list.

Figure 1.10 Read the list of instructions for completing a task.

(Continued)

How To...or Not

Some people are comfortable working on screens crowded with menus and dialogs; others prefer the maximum amount of working space. Acrobat displays the How To pane on the initial screen by default. Use the pane as necessary, but if you prefer, you can hide it and use other options to access the information when you need to:

- Close the window if you are working on a task you are familiar with. Click Hide to close the pane.

- In the default toolbar setup, click How To in the toolbar to reopen the pane. The pane reopens in the same screen location.

- Leave the How To pane active until you are comfortable with the program. When you find you can work without having to use reference material, deselect Show How To Window at Startup in the General Preferences. From that point, your program opens without the pane displayed, and you can open it as required using the toolbar command.

TIP 2: Getting Assistance

- At the end of the tasks' instructions, you find further links (**Figure 1.11**). Use these links to locate information on similar types of tasks, as well as links to the main Help menu.

You may also want to:

Create a PDF from multiple documents

Create PDF Topics

Conversion settings for image files in complete Help

Conversion settings for non-image files in complete Help

Figure 1.11 Don't have enough information? Click a link for more information or to open the complete Help file.

- Use the navigation buttons at the top of the How To pane to control your view (**Figure 1.12**). Clicking the active arrow (it is blue in the program) moves you back and forth between pages you have viewed; click to return to the How To pane's main page.

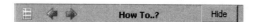

Figure 1.12 Control your location in the How To pane using the navigation buttons.

How To How To...

If you modify the toolbar layout, you probably won't include the How To toolbar. You can still access the contents using the Help menu. Click Help > How To Window and choose one of the options from the list.

TIP 3 Using the Help Menu

The How To pane is fine for step-by-step instructions on basic program functions and tasks. If you need more in-depth information, use
the main Help feature:

1. Choose Help > Complete Acrobat 6.0 Help (**Figure 1.13**). The
   Help program opens in a separate window.

Figure 1.13 The Complete Acrobat 6
Help file opens in a separate window.

2. Use the navigation options at the top left of the window to
   make your way through the file (**Figure 1.14**). The blue arrows
   take you back and forth between pages you've visited. Click the
   Printer icon to print the topic displayed in the main pane of the
   Help window. The plus (+) and minus (-) icons let you zoom in
   or zoom out of the document window.

Figure 1.14 Use navigation controls
to move through the Help file.

3. You can choose from three types of search options—Contents,
   Search, or Index—depending on what you are looking for and
   on your preferred method of working:

   • The Help menu opens to the Contents tab (**Figure 1.15**).
     Each + next to a topic name means subtopics are avail-
     able. Click + to open a nested list of items. If a topic name
     displays a - sign, that means it has nested content that is
     already displayed. Click an item to display its contents in
     the main pane of the Help window.

(Continued)

TIP 3: Using the Help Menu

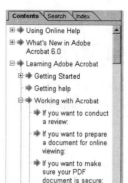

Figure 1.15 Specific topics are nested within larger topics in the left pane.

- Click Search to open the Search tab. Type the search word, and then click Search. The topics that contain the search term appear in the left pane of the Help window (**Figure 1.16**). Click a topic in the list in the left pane to display its contents in the main pane of the Help window; Acrobat highlights each instance of the search term.

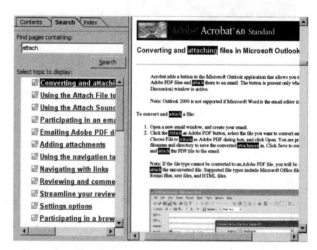

Figure 1.16 Use the Search feature to find a particular term in the Help file.

Note
If the highlighted terms are distracting, click the page with the Hand tool to remove the highlighting.

- Click the Index tab, and then click All to open a pull-down alphabetical menu (**Figure 1.17**). Select an individual letter to display from the Index, or leave All selected. Scroll through the list in the left pane of the Help window. Again, the content is listed in nested topics. Click to open subsequent levels. Clicking a topic in the Index displays its contents in the main Help window.

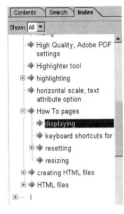

Figure 1.17 Search the Index for topics alphabetically.

Note

Sometimes you need to refer to a page in the Help file over and over. Instead of closing the window and then reopening and finding the page again, minimize the window. The content stays as you last viewed it, and you can switch between the Acrobat document and Help file easily (Figure 1.18). You can also resize the windows and display them both on the desktop, but if you aren't using the information word by word, minimize the window to save screen space.

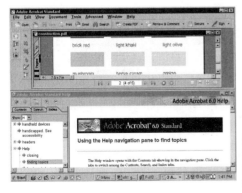

Figure 1.18 Display both your document and the Help document simultaneously.

TIP 3: Using the Help Menu

TIP 4 Making Room on the Screen

One of the best ways to save space, and your eyesight, is to control what tools you display on the screen. **Figure 1.19** shows a most illogical use of the program. Nearly all the toolbars and task buttons available in the program are open. At the full screen size, very little room is left for the actual document. Not only that, but trying to find a particular tool from so many, attractive as they are, is time consuming. These tips help you "unclutter" your screen.

You Can Go Back Again

If you have opened a number of toolbars and want to return to the default set, choose View > Toolbars > Reset Toolbars. Acrobat closes the extras and the layout reverts to the default toolbars in the default locations.

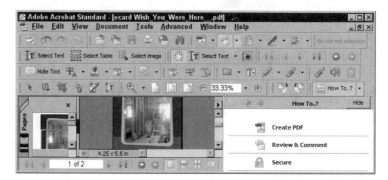

Figure 1.19 With all the toolbars open, there's no room left to work.

- Even using only the default toolbars and task buttons, you may find it confusing to figure out what you have to work with. Move your pointer over the hatched vertical line at the left edge of a toolbar to display the toolbar's name (**Figure 1.20**).

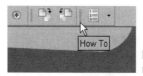

Figure 1.20 Display the name of the toolbar in a tip.

- Tool tips can show you task button names. If the button is large enough to display both the icon and text, you don't learn anything new. However, if you move your pointer over the icon, you see the task button's name (**Figure 1.21**).

Figure 1.21 Display the name of a button in a tip.

- Move your pointer over the hatched vertical line and drag to pull a toolbar from its docked position. When you release the mouse, the toolbar is floating on the screen (**Figure 1.22**).

Figure 1.22 Toolbars may be docked at the top of the window or float on the screen.

- Task buttons work slightly differently. You can't drag an individual task button off the Task Bar (as you can with individual tools on toolbars); if you try, you'll remove the entire Task Button toolbar. Choose View > Task Buttons, and select or deselect the buttons as you require (**Figure 1.23**).

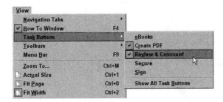

Figure 1.23 Control task buttons from the View menu.

- You often change toolbars when you are working. Save one step by using the shortcut menu. Right-click or Control-click the separator bar to display the same options available from the Toolbars submenu (**Figure 1.24**).

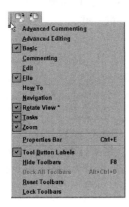

Figure 1.24 Use the shortcut menu to display many of the commands available from the View menu.

TIP 4: Making Room on the Screen

TIP 5

Starting to Work at High Speed

You can set a number of preferences that help you get to work faster, either by getting into the program more quickly or by showing what you are working with more quickly:

1. Choose Edit > Preferences. The Preferences window opens and displays a long list of options in the left pane. Click Startup to display the Startup options in the right pane of the dialog box (**Figure 1.25**).

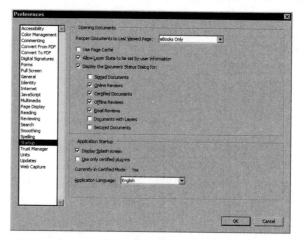

Figure 1.25 Change how the program starts using the Startup preferences.

2. The Opening Documents preferences are listed at the top of the window. For the first control, the default setting is eBooks, which means that only eBooks reopen at the page you last displayed in the Document pane.

Figure 1.26 Use the All Files option when working with multiple files.

Click the arrow and select All Files (**Figure 1.26**). You will find this setting very useful during long sessions when you're working with multiple files. Each time you open a document, the location and page last displayed are shown in the Document pane.

Splash Screen

The lower section of the Startup preferences dialog includes an option for displaying the startup splash screen. Some people like to turn off the splash screen, thinking that the program loads faster. It doesn't. I prefer to keep it displayed, at least until I have fully examined and enjoyed the artwork in the splash screen.

Note

The display feature works only during a single session; if you close and then reopen Acrobat 6, and then the document, it displays according to its document settings, usually showing the top of the first page.

3. Click Use Page Cache (it is deselected by default). The page cache is a buffer area. If you cache the pages, as you display one page the next page in a document is read and placed in a buffer area until you are ready to view it. Pages load faster, and the faster load time is particularly noticeable if you are working with image-intensive or interactive documents.

4. You can leave the other two Opening Documents options selected. The Layer State pertains to documents containing layers; the author of the document defines what layers are displayed when the document opens in Acrobat. The third option, Display the Document Status Dialog For, refers to displaying specialized information about objects such as layers and digital signatures.

5. Click Page Display in the left pane of the Preferences dialog. You can set some page preferences to get to work faster as well.

Figure 1.27 You can hide large images from view if your computer can't draw images quickly.

6. Acrobat displays large images by default. Deselect the Display large images option (**Figure 1.27**) if your computer has a slow redraw speed. If your computer is quite slow images will display eventually, but take a lot time to draw on your screen. Then each time you use the scroll bars or move the document in the Document pane, you have to wait for the image to redraw again.

(Continued)

TIP 5: Starting to Work at High Speed

7. Click the Use Greek Text below xx pixels option to make the text on a page smaller than the value specified (the default value is 6 pixels) appear as gray lines (**Figure 1.28**). Selecting this option speeds up redraw time as well.

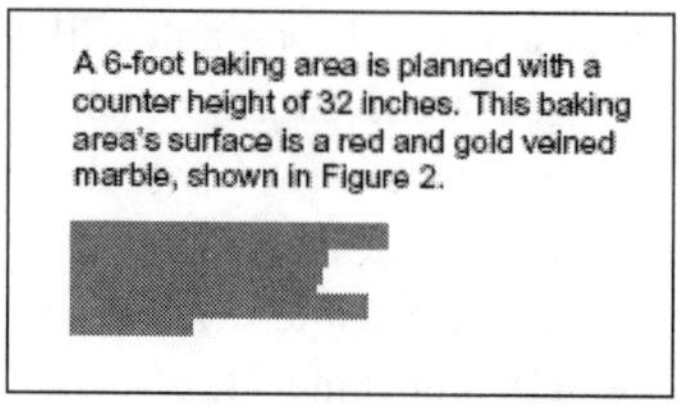

A 6-foot baking area is planned with a counter height of 32 inches. This baking area's surface is a red and gold veined marble, shown in Figure 2.

Figure 1.28 Substitute gray lines for very small text to display pages more quickly.

8. When you have completed setting and changing preferences, click OK to close the Preferences dialog and apply your settings.

Settings For All Seasons

The settings you choose are not specific to a particular document but apply to the program in general. Each time you open Acrobat 6, the program uses your preferences until you change them again.

CHAPTER TWO

Converting Source Documents

You can create PDF files in a number of ways. With earlier versions of Acrobat, you primarily exported PDF files from various source programs or imported Web pages. In Acrobat 6, you can work from within Acrobat and convert files to PDFs, either as a single file or as multiple files, or as content pasted from the clipboard.

Conversions can be controlled by PDFMaker macro settings, by Acrobat Distiller, and by source programs that export PDF-formatted files directly. Regardless of the mechanism, you must consider the same factors. You'll learn how to configure conversion settings according to the material you are working with—and according to what you intend to do with it. You prepare information for *print* use, for example, differently than you prepare information for *online* use.

Acrobat 6 uses an interesting method of presenting work options to you. Rather than manipulating a massive collection of toolbars and menu items (although they certainly do exist!), you can choose to work *functionally*—that is, according to the processes you are attempting to apply to a document.

TIP 6 Creating PDF Files from Source Programs

If you can print a file in a program, you can usually generate a PDF file. The key is the printer driver called *Distiller*. You don't have to install the driver independently; it is included as part of the Acrobat 6 installation process. The Distiller driver and Acrobat Distiller are related, but Acrobat Distiller is a program. To create a PDF file from a source program:

1. Open your program and the document you want to convert to a PDF.

2. Choose File > Print to open the Print dialog box.

3. Click the pull-down arrow and choose Adobe PDF from the printer list (**Figure 2.1**).

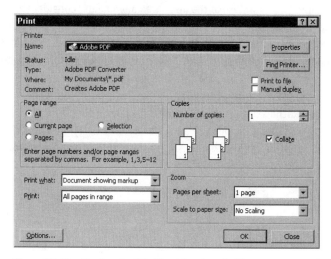

Figure 2.1 Use the Acrobat Distiller driver installed in your programs' Print menus to create PDF files.

4. Click OK. The file is processed, and a Save dialog opens (**Figure 2.2**).

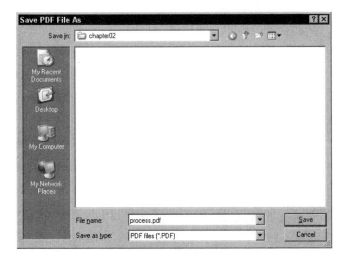

Figure 2.2 Select a location to store your converted file.

5. From the Save in pull-down list, select the location where you want to save the file, change the filename if desired, and click Save. The file prints to PDF, rather than to your printer, and you have a PDF version of the source file.

In some programs, you can save a file directly as a PDF. Here's an example using Adobe Photoshop:

1. Choose File > Save As to open the Save As dialog.

2. Click the Format pull-down arrow and choose Photoshop PDF from the list of file formats (**Figure 2.3**).

(Continued)

Filenames and Formats

Get into the habit of setting up a system of filenames when you are converting files from one format to another. When you print following these steps, by default the folder containing the source document opens and the file is assigned the source document's name and the .pdf extension.

TIP 6: Creating PDF Files from Source Programs

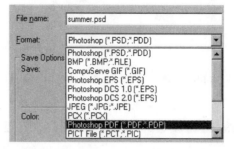

Figure 2.3 Use the Save As command in programs that can export to PDF directly.

3. Click Save. The dialog closes, and Photoshop saves the file and displays it (**Figure 2.4**).

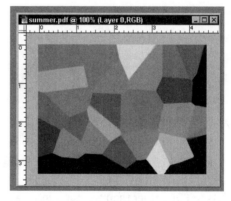

Figure 2.4 Photoshop displays the image saved in the PDF format.

More on Image Compression

There are additional save dialogs based on types of compression. For example, for both JPEG and Zip compression, you can choose image interpolation, or resampling options. For JPEG compression, you can also choose a quality level. Choose a quality level depending on the final use of the image. If you are planning to use the images online, a medium to high quality level is sufficient (5 to 8 on the quality scale). Use a higher quality level for images intended for print.

Choosing Compression Types

You make decisions on compression options in a number of locations—when converting files from source documents, within Distiller, and in Microsoft Office applications. The options available vary depending on the process involved. You use compression to decrease the size of the PDF files; using the correct format decreases the file size without affecting the quality of the file.

How do you choose the best option? Here are some brief notes on each and an example showing when to use each format:

- Use Zip compression for images with large areas of a single color or repeating patterns (**Figure 2.5**).
- Use JPEG compression for grayscale or color images, such as photographs (**Figure 2.6**).
- Use the CCITT compression method for black-and-white images made by paint programs and scans. Acrobat uses CCITT Group 3 and Group 4 (**Figure 2.7**).
- Run-length compression is best for images with large areas of solid black or white (**Figure 2.8**).

Figure 2.5 Zip compression is best for color-blocked or patterned images.

Figure 2.6 Use JPEG compression for grayscale images and photographs.

Figure 2.7 Use CCITT compression for figures like this one.

Figure 2.8 Use run-length compression for images with large black or white areas.

Using the PDFMaker Macro in Word

Microsoft Word has long been a natural partner of Acrobat. You create Word documents, convert them to PDFs, and distribute them to the world. Using Acrobat 6 and the newest version of Word, the conversion process is easier than ever.

New Office Tools

If you install Acrobat 6 on a computer that's running Microsoft Office XP or later, you'll see additional elements added to the Office menus. In Word, the handiest addition is a new toolbar (see Figure 2.9). that contains icons for converting a document to a PDF, converting a document and emailing it, and converting a document and initiating a review cycle.

Two new items are also added to Word's main menu. The Adobe PDF menu contains the three commands just described, as well as a command for changing the conversion settings. The Acrobat Comments menu lets you import comments from a PDF file into Word and proceed with a review cycle.

1. Open the document you want to convert. Click Convert to Adobe PDF in the PDF toolbar (**Figure 2.9**) or choose Adobe PDF > Convert to Adobe PDF (**Figure 2.10**). A dialog opens displaying the progress of the conversion process.

Figure 2.9 A new toolbar is added to Word after you install Acrobat.

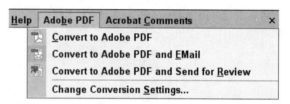

Figure 2.10 Acrobat adds a couple of new menu items to Word.

2. On the status bar, you first see the printer icon and then the red Distiller icon . The Distiller icon rotates as the file is being converted.

3. When the conversion is complete, the dialog closes, and the Distiller and printer icons disappear from the desktop's status bar.

4. The PDF file opens in Acrobat 6 (the default option) or you'll return to the Office document.

Converting Word Files Using Mac OS X

When you install Acrobat 6 on a Mac on which Office X is running, you find a two-button toolbar added to Word, consisting of the Convert to PDF ⬚ and Convert to PDF and email ⬚ icons.

1. Choose the conversion settings you want to use (**Figure 2.11**); the options include Standard, Press Quality, High Quality, and Smallest File Size.

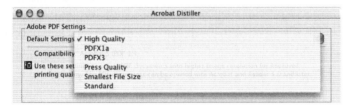

Figure 2.11 Choose your settings directly from Distiller.

The file is saved in the same folder as the source file, using the .pdf extension.

2. Click View File to open the file in Acrobat; click Done to return to the Office program.

Distilling with Mac

The Convert to PDF icons launch Distiller and let you define conversion settings, unlike when you're working in Windows, where the macro maintains the settings within the Office program.

TIP 8 Changing PDFMaker Conversion Settings

As you're converting documents to PDF, you are not restricted to using one set of conversion options. You can use one of several pre-built settings, or you can create custom settings, called *job options*. Choose Adobe PDF > Change Conversion Settings to open a four-tab dialog. In this dialog, you configure your output alternatives and determine the complexity of your PDF file and its file size:

1. You choose basic options on the Settings tab (**Figure 2.12**). Here you'll specify the conversion settings by choosing from a pull-down menu, as well as choosing basic document processing options, such as whether you want to see the resulting PDF file in Acrobat when it's converted.

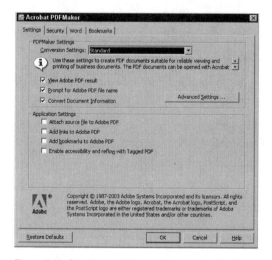

Figure 2.12 Start by modifying settings on the Settings tab.

2. The Conversion Settings pull-down menu offers four options (**Figure 2.13**):

Figure 2.13 You can choose from a selection of preformatted settings.

- Standard—The default set used for basic business document conversion and viewing. Standard settings use a printing resolution of 600 dpi.

- High Quality—Used for high-quality output; prints to a higher image resolution but includes only a limited amount of coded information about the document's fonts. High Quality sets the printing resolution to 2400 dpi.

- Press—Used for high-end print production, such as image setters, and prints at a high resolution. All the information possible is added to the file. This setting includes all coded information about the fonts used in the document.

- Smallest File Size—Creates the smallest file size possible; used for distributing content for the Web, email, or onscreen viewing. Images are compressed and their resolution is decreased.

3. Select options specific to the program. For example, in Word you can add bookmarks and links, and tag the document.

4. Click the Security tab to set passwords for the file (**Figure 2.14**). You can also set permissions for manipulating file content, such as printing, viewing, and extracting.

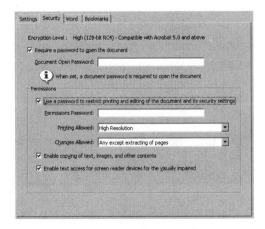

Figure 2.14 The Security tab lets you set permissions.

(Continued)

Acrobat 5 Job Options
Acrobat 5 used a set of five default job options—Screen, Print, Press, CJKScreen, and eBook. In Windows, the Acrobat 5 options are available in Adobe PageMaker and Adobe FrameMaker for backward compatibility.

TIP 8: Changing PDFMaker Conversion Settings

5. Click the Word tab. Change settings to convert Word elements, such as comments and tables of contents into PDF-formatted elements (**Figure 2.15**).

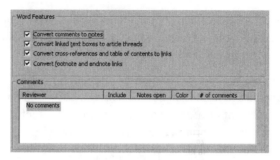

Figure 2.15 Choose Word-specific conversion settings.

6. Click the Bookmarks tab to set bookmark configurations (**Figure 2.16**). You can use either headings or styles as the basis for Acrobat bookmarks. See Tip 62 for more information on this.

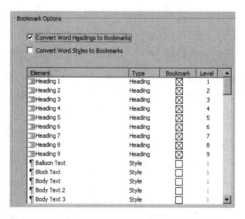

Figure 2.16 Create bookmarks from either headings or styles.

7. Click OK to close the dialog. At any time you can revert the settings to the prebuilt options by clicking the Restore Defaults button at the bottom of each tab (**Figure 2.17**).

Figure 2.17 Use the Restore Defaults button to remove customized settings.

Navigate with Bookmarks

Acrobat uses a number of different navigation processes to make it easier for you to get around a document. One of the most common navigation tools is bookmarking. You identify headings, images, or other important information within the document and Acrobat creates links in the Bookmarks panel. Chapter 7 covers bookmarks.

How the Settings Compare

Let's see what happens when we convert the same file using different prebuilt settings.

Figure 2.18 shows the range of file sizes. The file generated using the Smallest File Size setting is the smallest file (imagine that!) while the Press option generates the largest file size.

Name	Size	Type	Date Modi
tile-small.pdf	48 KB	Adobe Acrobat Document	6/2/2003
tile-standard.pdf	165 KB	Adobe Acrobat Document	6/2/2003
tile choices.doc	176 KB	Microsoft Word Document	4/3/2003
tile-high.pdf	207 KB	Adobe Acrobat Document	6/2/2003
tile-press.pdf	208 KB	Adobe Acrobat Document	6/2/2003

C:\acro6_peachpit\projects\tile choices\settings test

5 objects — 801 KB — My Computer

Figure 2.18 Different settings produce very different file sizes.

Even without printing, you can see the difference between some of the options. In **Figure 2.19**, the page at the left shows a portion of the document converted using the Press option, and the page at the right shows the same area of the document generated with the Smallest File Size option. The difference is clearly visible in the image and letter quality.

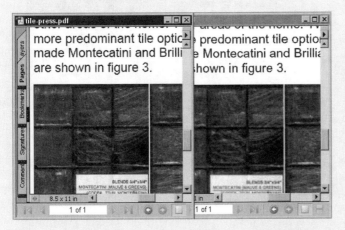

Figure 2.19 Different settings produce very different image qualities.

TIP 9 Converting Excel and PowerPoint Files

Microsoft Excel and PowerPoint both feature PDFMaker macros, so you can quickly and easily convert spreadsheets or presentations into Acrobat documents.

In PowerPoint:

1. After you install Acrobat 6 and open PowerPoint, you'll see both the Adobe PDF toolbar and the Adobe PDF menu.

2. Choose Adobe PDF > Change Conversion Settings to open the conversion dialog.

3. The dialog contains two tabs. **Figure 2.20** shows the Settings tab; the Security tab is the same across the Office programs (see Figure 2.14).

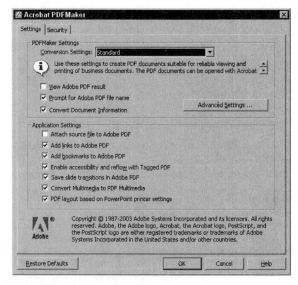

Figure 2.20 Specify options on the Settings and Security tabs in PowerPoint conversions.

4. On the Settings tab, you'll see the same pull-down list of options, as well as the same conversion options, that you saw in Word (see Figure 2.12).

5. Look at the options in the Application Settings section. Some are general Office options, such as the option for adding links. Other options are specific to PowerPoint presentations, including the ones for converting multimedia and for creating transitions.

The process is much the same for Excel:

1. Open Excel. Note the Adobe PDF toolbar and the Adobe PDF menu items, including one that's unique to Excel (**Figure 2.21**).

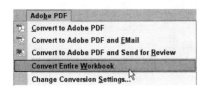

Figure 2.21 You can convert a worksheet or an entire workbook in Excel.

2. Choose Adobe PDF > Change Conversion Settings to open the Acrobat PDFMaker dialog.

This dialog offers the same two tabs as the PowerPoint dialog, and it uses the same application options available to other Office application files.

Converting Excel Workbooks

In Excel's Adobe PDF menu, you see an extra command that lets you convert an entire workbook. Excel spreadsheets are organized as sheets within a workbook; the Convert to PDF command applies to the active sheet only.

TIP 9: Converting Excel and PowerPoint Files

TIP 10 Converting Web Pages through Internet Explorer

The first time you open Microsoft Internet Explorer after installing Acrobat 6, you'll notice the Adobe PDF toolbar. Use it for working with PDF files directly from the Web. Click the pull-down arrow to the right of the Adobe PDF icon on the toolbar to display the menu options (**Figure 2.22**):

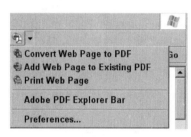

Figure 2.22 A set of menu options are added to Internet Explorer.

- To convert the file, click the icon itself, or select Convert Web Page to PDF. A dialog opens that lets you name the file and define its storage location. Click Save to convert the file.

- Click Add Web Page to Existing PDF to attach the content of the Web page to another file. In the resulting Open dialog, select the file you want to attach and click Save.

- Click Print Web Page to convert the page to a PDF file and send it to your printer. A printer dialog opens that lets you select printer settings.

- Click Adobe PDF Explorer Bar to open an Explorer window at the left side of the Internet Explorer interface (**Figure 2.23**). When you have located a file, click the X at the top right of the pane to close it.

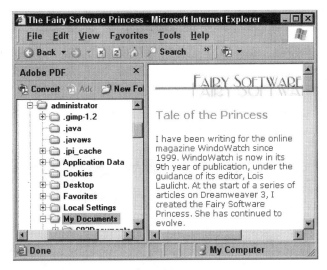

Figure 2.23 Use the Adobe PDF Explorer Bar to locate files.

- Click Preferences to open a small dialog containing three options you can modify (**Figure 2.24**). All three options are selected by default, which is probably fine for most users.

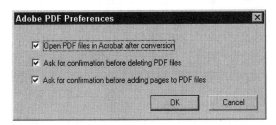

Figure 2.24 Set or modify Adobe PDF preferences in Internet Explorer.

What's Your Conversion Preference?

Consider modifying the two notification preferences if you convert files from the Web on a regular basis (see Figure 2.24). For example, do you need to be prompted before deleting a PDF file or adding pages? If Web conversion is a casual process for you, the confirmation is a good idea. On the other hand, if you work with these activities a fair bit, each time you have to dismiss the dialog, confirm an action, or close Acrobat, you are performing extra steps.

TIP 10: Converting Web Pages through Internet Explorer

TIP 11 Converting Files with Acrobat Distiller

Acrobat Distiller refers both to a printer driver and to the Acrobat Distiller program. Conversions, whether generated by clicking an icon in a program or manually converting a file in Distiller, use the same settings:

1. In Windows, choose Start > Programs > Acrobat Distiller 6.0. As you can see (**Figure 2.25**), the program is listed separately from Acrobat in the computer's program listings.

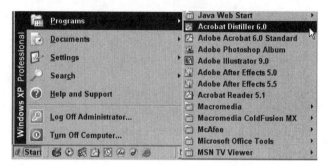

Figure 2.25 Acrobat Distiller is a separate program from Acrobat Standard.

Distiller's interface looks and works like a dialog. It has three menu items. Note that the interface includes the set of prebuilt default settings covered in Tip 8.

2. Choose the Adobe PDF settings you want to use for the conversion process, or create a custom setting.

3. Choose File > Open to open a dialog box in which you can select a file for conversion. Locate the file on your computer and click Open.

Note

You can use either .ps or .prn files in Distiller. The .ps file format uses the PostScript language. Some programs produce .prn files instead of .ps files; other programs generate .prn files if you choose Print to File as a printing option. Both file formats are based on the printer drivers installed on your computer.

4. Distiller processes the file. It displays a progress bar as well as information about the file's processing (**Figure 2.26**).

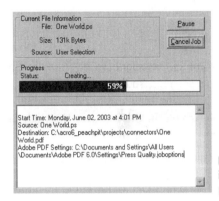

Figure 2.26 Read information about your processed file.

5. Continue converting other files as required or close Distiller. Now you can use the converted PostScript file as you would any other Adobe PDF file.

Note
*Choose File > Preferences to open a small dialog, shown in **Figure 2.27**. If you are working on a Mac, choose Distiller > Preferences. You have choices for several options, such as viewing generated files in Acrobat and managing log files.*

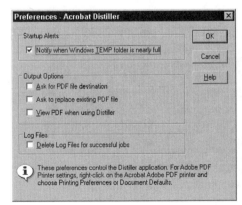

Figure 2.27 Set Distiller preferences, such as viewing PDFs in Acrobat and deleting log files.

Converting with Distiller
Some programs, such as older versions of QuarkXPress, cannot produce a PDF file directly. Instead, you create a PostScript file and then convert it to an Adobe PDF by using Distiller. You can also work with Distiller if you use advanced functions, such as Distiller parameters. Some programs can export a file as a PDF or print a file to the PDF format. If your application cannot generate a PDF file, try saving your file as a PostScript file, which uses the .ps extension; alternatively, you may be able to generate a file using the .prn extension, another format recognized by Distiller.

TIP 11: Converting Files with Acrobat Distiller

TIP 12 Creating Custom Conversion Settings

You can create custom conversion settings for your own work, start from scratch, or modify one of the default options. Many variations on the defaults are available. You can create new job options through the PDFMaker macros and Distiller dialogs. This tip shows the process using Distiller:

1. In Distiller, choose one of the default settings to serve as the basis for your custom settings. You can start from scratch, but modifying the option closest to what you need is a much simpler approach. The example in this tip uses the High Quality default setting as the basis for custom settings.

2. Choose Settings > Edit Adobe PDF Settings.

3. The High Quality – Adobe PDF Settings dialog opens (**Figure 2.28**). The dialog has five tabs.

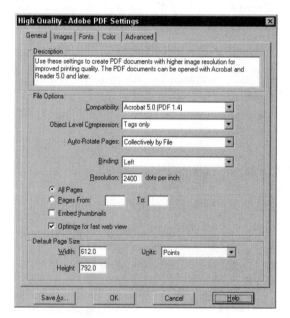

Figure 2.28 Start with one of Distiller's default settings and modify it to suit your needs.

4. On the General tab, you may want to modify these settings:

- Compatibility—The default is Acrobat 5.0 (PDF 1.4). Depending on your users, you can choose an option as far back as Acrobat 3. Older versions of the program have fewer options for settings such as security, font embedding, and color management. For example, Acrobat 6's security settings aren't functional in Acrobat 3.

- Resolution—You can set this option to emulate the resolution of a printer for PostScript files. A higher resolution usually produces higher quality, but larger, files. Resolution determines the number of steps in a gradient or blend. The gradient at the left of **Figure 2.29** is the same as that on the right; the only difference is resolution.

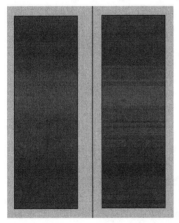

Figure 2.29 Resolution determines the number of steps in a gradient or blend.

Specifying Page Range

The General tab includes an option for selecting a specific range of pages. Don't use this option unless you are sure the custom settings are for onetime use. If you specify a range of pages when you create the job options and then reuse the settings another time, you convert only those pages specified on the General tab. This can lead to time-consuming troubleshooting when you use your custom settings and can't figure out where your pages (those not within the range specified on the General tab) have gone!

- Embed Thumbnails—Thumbnail previews are used for navigation. In earlier versions of Acrobat, you had to specify thumbnail generation. Acrobat 5 and 6 dynamically generate thumbnails. Unless you are planning to use the output with older versions of Acrobat and Acrobat Reader, don't enable this option; it adds to the file size unnecessarily.

(Continued)

TIP 12: Creating Custom Conversion Settings

5. On the Images tab (**Figure 2.30**), you may need to adjust and test setting changes several times when converting files with complex images. Consider these options:

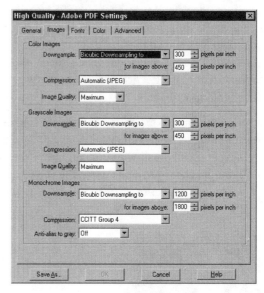

Figure 2.30 Modify and test changes made to the Images tab settings.

• Downsample—In **Figure 2.31**, both examples show the same image; the one on the left is much lower resolution than that on the right; with this type of image in your PDF file, you wouldn't want a great deal of downsampling.

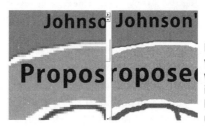

Figure 2.31 Consider how your readers use a document when you're downsampling images. The document on the left will be much harder to use than the one on the right.

- Compression/Image Quality—Select different options depending on the file's color, grayscale, and monochromatic images. You can use different compression settings depending on the type of image (see Tip 6).

- Smooth jagged edges in monochrome images (**Figure 2.32**) by turning on anti-aliasing.

Figure 2.32 The image on the right shows the effect of anti-aliasing.

6. On the Fonts tab (**Figure 2.33**), specify whether you want to embed fonts or subset embedded fonts when the percent of characters used falls below a value you enter. If you are using unusual fonts, or your layout is highly dependent on the fonts, be sure to embed them. Choose subsetting when you want to embed a portion of a font's characters. Don't use a low value if you expect to change any characters in the page.

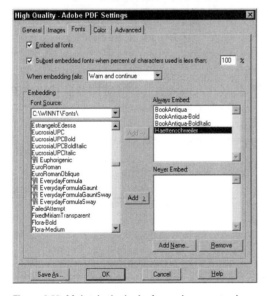

Figure 2.33 Maintain the look of your document using font embedding.

(Continued)

To Embed or Not...

Always embed fonts to save time if you work with a variety of settings but the same suite of files. For example, if you are using a corporate template that requires specific fonts at all times, select the fonts in the Fonts list and click Add to add them to the Always Embed list. This way, when you create files you never have to remember whether or not the fonts are embedded.

TIP 12: Creating Custom Conversion Settings

7. On the Color tab (**Figure 2.34**), choose settings that correspond with files used in your source applications, such as Adobe Photoshop or Illustrator. The options available on this tab depend on the color settings you choose. If you are sending files to a press, you often get settings from the printer.

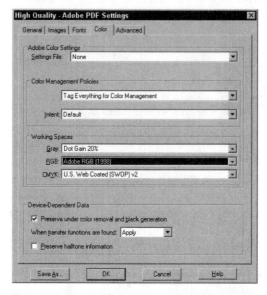

Figure 2.34 Choose from a wide range of color settings.

8. Unless you are familiar with Document Structuring Conventions and the like, you won't have to change many options on the Advanced tab (**Figure 2.35**). The settings on this tab describe how the conversion from PostScript to PDF is performed. Let's look at two default options:

Use RGB for Online Viewing

If you are building files for online use, make sure RGB (not CMYK) is selected. RGB is the native color space for monitors and doesn't require any conversion, making viewing faster.

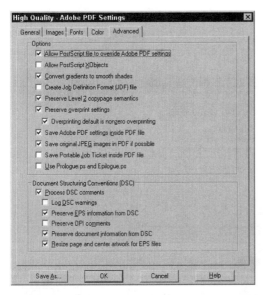

Figure 2.35 Most settings on the Advanced tab work fine using the default options.

- The Convert gradients to smooth shades option converts gradients from a range of programs, including Macromedia FreeHand, QuarkXPress, Adobe Illustrator, and Microsoft PowerPoint. This option produces a smaller PDF file size, and often results in improved output.

- Save original JPEG images in PDF if possible processes JPEG images (which are compressed) without compressing them again, resulting in faster file processing.

(Continued)

Storing Job Options

Conversion settings are stored in a specific folder location. In Windows XP, the files are stored in the Settings folder within the Adobe PDF 6 folder in the system's Shared Documents folder. Because the settings are stored in the same folder, they are available for use by the PDFMaker macro, Acrobat, and Distiller.

TIP 12: Creating Custom Conversion Settings

Sharing Job Options

You can share settings with others. Email the .joboptions file as you would any other type of file. Your recipients add the file to the storage folder. The next time they access the custom settings dialog from a PDFMaker macro, Acrobat, or Distiller, the shared settings are ready to use.

9. Choose Save As to open the Save Adobe PDF Settings As dialog. Name the file and click Save (**Figure 2.36**). The custom conversion settings file is saved with the extension .joboptions.

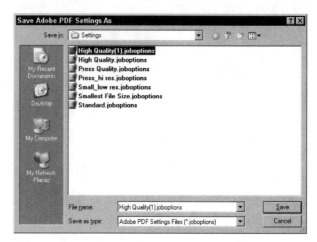

Figure 2.36 Save custom settings as .joboptions files.

TIP 13 Creating a PDF from a File in Acrobat

In Acrobat 6 you can generate PDF files from within the program. You use the Create PDF task button to access several options within Acrobat.

Note

When you open the Create PDF task menu, you'll notice a link to Help at the bottom of the menu. Click the link to open a set of help files outlining how to perform various creation functions.

1. Click the Create PDF task button to display the menu shown in **Figure 2.37**.

Figure 2.37 Acrobat's Create PDF menu offers several ways to convert files.

2. Click the first option, From File. An Open dialog box window opens.

3. Locate the file you want to convert to PDF (**Figure 2.38**) and click Open.

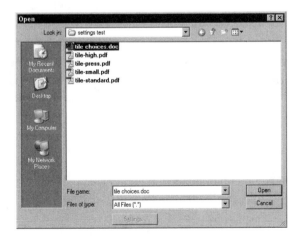

Figure 2.38 Locate the file you want to convert.

(Continued)

TIP 13: Creating a PDF from a File in Acrobat

4. You'll see one of two progress bar windows (depending on the format of the selected file). Acrobat executes a macro that opens the file in the native program and converts it to a PDF.

If the file is in a program that offers PDFMaker (as in the Word file I am using in the example), Acrobat uses the PDFMaker macro with its current settings (**Figure 2.39**).

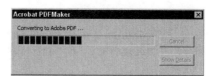

Figure 2.39 If the file's source program has a PDFMaker macro, Acrobat uses it.

If the file is in a program without a PDFMaker macro, Acrobat opens the program and prints the file using the Adobe PDF Converter (**Figure 2.40**).

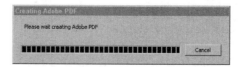

Figure 2.40 The Adobe PDF Converter runs if the file's source program doesn't use a PDFMaker macro.

5. The converted file opens in Acrobat. When converted, the file is named according to the source file's name but isn't yet saved in its PDF format. Choose File > Save to save the file as a PDF.

Note
If you convert files that are governed by the PDFMaker macro—such as Word or PowerPoint files, for example—the last conversion options set in the program are applied to the file.

Where to Convert Documents

Should you convert a document in the source program or in Acrobat? The short answer is: it depends. If you are working in a program and know you will need a PDF version of a file, generate the file then. If you are working in Acrobat and realize you need another file, generate the file from Acrobat.

Even if you are working in Acrobat, if you plan to generate files from PDFMaker macro-governed programs and either can't remember the settings you last left for the PDFMaker macro or know you need to change the settings, you should work through the program instead of Acrobat. That's better than generating a file that is converted using the incorrect settings and then having to redo it.

TIP 14: Creating a PDF from Multiple Files in Acrobat

Working with the Binder feature is a terrific way to organize your work. Rather than trying to remember what files you need and where you stored them, manually converting all the files, and then assembling them one by one in Acrobat, you can work in the Create PDF from Multiple Documents window. This window lets you quickly assemble documents and files (PDF and otherwise), organize them, and visualize the content of the final document before building the file. It's a true timesaver!

1. Click the Create PDF task button to display the menu options.

2. Click From Multiple Files to open the Create PDF from Multiple Documents window (**Figure 2.41**).

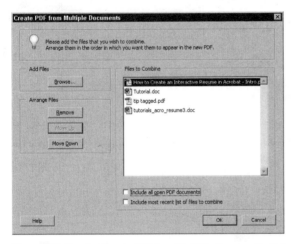

Figure 2.41 Use the Create PDF from Multiple Documents dialog to assemble a group of files.

3. Click Browse to open an Open dialog box.

4. Locate the first file you want to add to the collection and click Add.

5. The browse window closes and Acrobat adds the file. Repeat steps 3 and 4 until you have selected all the files you want in the new collection.

(Continued)

6. Now you should organize the content in the Files to Combine pane. Click a file to activate the buttons on the left side of the window.

7. Move the individual files up or down in the stacking order or delete files until the collection is assembled to your satisfaction (**Figure 2.42**).

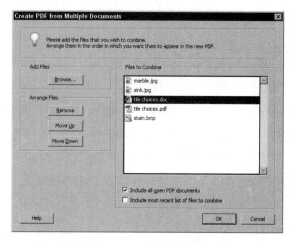

Figure 2.42 Rearrange the order of files using the Arrange Files buttons.

8. Click OK. The window closes, and Acrobat assembles the content. Each file is processed separately, and any files in the list that are not PDFs are converted to PDFs.

Figure 2.43 The selected documents are displayed as thumbnails, then converted to a single PDF document.

Figure 2.43 shows the page thumbnails: the document is page 1, followed by three images, all of which are converted to PDFs and combined into Binder1.pdf.

9. Choose File > Save to save the binder. Your composite file is complete.

Document Source Programs

When converting the content to a finished binder, Acrobat opens the source programs for all non-Acrobat files in the list. This means you cannot add a non-Acrobat file that has been created in Photoshop, for example, if that application isn't on your computer.

TIP 15 Creating a PDF from Web Pages in Acrobat

Although you can easily download a page from a Web site using the Adobe PDF macro that installs in Internet Explorer, you can also download a Web site from within Acrobat and control its content and how it is displayed in the resulting PDF file:

1. Click the Create PDF task button to display the menu in **Figure 2.44**.

Figure 2.44 Click From Web Page to start the conversion process.

2. Click From Web Page to open the Create PDF from Web Page dialog (**Figure 2.45**).

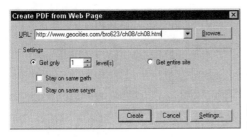

Figure 2.45 Choose a Web site location.

3. You access the file you want to convert in one of three ways, depending on the location and type of file:

   • Type the URL for the file if it's on the Internet.

   • Click the arrow to the right of the URL field to work with Web files that have been opened previously in Acrobat.

   • Click Browse to open the Select File to Open dialog to locate a file that's on a local disk.

4. Click Create to start the conversion process. The Download Status dialog shows you the number of connections active in the downloaded material, as well as the names, sizes, and locations of the files (**Figure 2.46**). *(Continued)*

So Many Pages, So Little Time

In the Create PDF from Web Page dialog, you can specify how many levels of the Web site you want to download. The default level is 1. Don't change this number without careful thought. Level 1 refers to the first set of pages for a Web site, the actual pages that you see if you type the URL in a browser address bar. Additional levels attach more sets of pages. If you choose Get Entire Site, you'll download the entire site, whether that consists of 10 pages or 1000 pages.

Although it is simpler and safer to leave the default level 1 setting, what do you do if you import the page and realize you need additional pages? Luckily, you can easily add more. Choose Advanced > Web Capture > Append Web Page to open the Add to PDF from Web Page dialog, identical to the original Create PDF from Web Page dialog. Select level, and the additional pages are added to those already in the document.

TIP 15: Creating a PDF from Web Pages in Acrobat

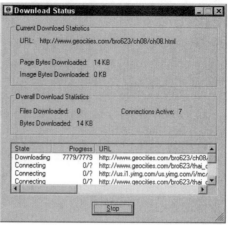

Figure 2.46 You can see the Web site content as it is being converted.

5. When the download is complete, Acrobat displays the new PDF file in the Document pane and adds a document structure to the Bookmarks tab (**Figure 2.47**).

Figure 2.47 The new PDF document automatically opens in Acrobat.

6. Scroll through the document. Note that both a header and footer are added to the page. The header is the Web page's name; the footer contains the URL for the page, the number of pages, and the download date and time (**Figure 2.48**).

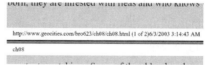

Figure 2.48 Headers and footers are added to the pages by default.

7. Choose File > Save to save your converted Web page.

TIP 16 Modifying Web Page Capture Settings

Acrobat captures Web pages using default settings for both file formats and page layouts. You can configure some formats and modify the page to your requirements. Follow these steps:

1. Click Create PDF and choose From Web Page to open the Create PDF from Web Page dialog. At the bottom right of the dialog, click Settings (**Figure 2.49**).

Figure 2.49 You can customize Web capture settings if you click the Settings button.

2. The Web Page Conversion Settings dialog opens. The General tab offers file type and PDF settings (**Figure 2.50**).

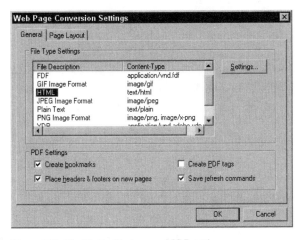

Figure 2.50 Modify the file type and PDF settings.

3. At the bottom of the dialog, you'll see the PDF options used by default, including bookmarks and the header and footer options. Select or deselect the options as desired.

The upper portion of the General tab lists the file formats you can import using the capture process. You can modify both the HTML and the Plain Text file types.

(Continued)

TIP 16: Modifying Web Page Capture Settings

4. Click HTML to select it. This activates the Settings button, which you then click. The HTML Conversion Settings dialog opens (**Figure 2.51**).

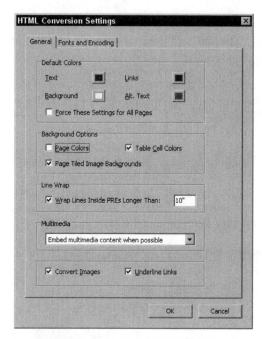

Figure 2.51 You can modify both HTML and Plain Text file types.

5. Set the options for converting HTML files. You can modify such options as color and background. The second tab offers settings for fonts, language, and encoding.

6. Click OK to close the Settings dialog and to return to the Web Page Conversion Settings dialog.

Choose Page Layout Options

The second tab of the Web Page Conversion Settings dialog contains page layout options:

1. Choose standard page layout settings such as the page size, orientation, and margins (**Figure 2.52**).

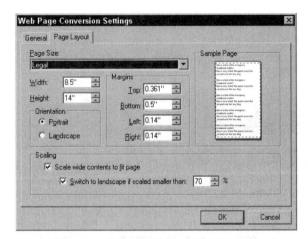

Figure 2.52 You can change the page layout settings using this tab.

2. Click OK again to close the dialog and to return to the Create PDF from Web Page dialog.

3. Click OK to start the conversion. **Figure 2.53** shows the same page as in Figure 2.47, captured using modified settings. In this example, we converted the same Web page using a custom text color and legal-sized page.

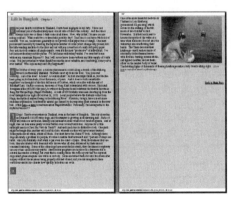

Figure 2.53 This page shows the result of changing settings such as page size and font color.

TIP 16: Modifying Web Page Capture Settings

TIP 17
Creating a PDF from a Scan in Acrobat

Sometimes you don't have an original file document. If you have a printed copy, you can create a PDF version using your scanner.

1. Click the Create PDF task button to display the menu in **Figure 2.54**.

Figure 2.54 Select the option for creating a PDF document from your scanner.

2. Click the fourth option, From Scanner, to open the Create PDF From Scanner dialog (**Figure 2.55**).

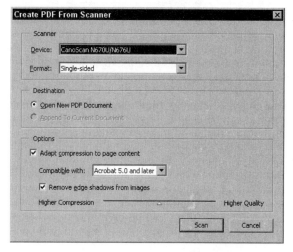

Figure 2.55 Select your scanner and choose conversion settings.

3. Select your scanner from the Device pull-down list, and then choose single- or double-sided scanning from the Format pull-down list.

4. Specify a destination for the scanned page. In Figure 2.55, the only option available is a new document; if other documents are open in Acrobat, you can attach the scanned file.

5. Modify the compression, compatibility, and edge shadow options if necessary.

6. Click Scan. Acrobat opens your scanner's dialog. Your settings will vary depending on your scanner and scanning software. Follow the instructions for choosing scan settings in your scanner, and then perform the scan. When the process is complete, your scanner's dialog closes and your scanned document opens in Acrobat (**Figure 2.56**).

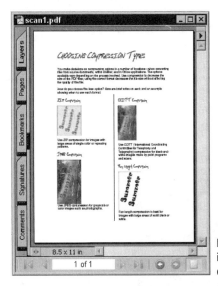

Figure 2.56 When the scan is complete, the document opens in Acrobat.

7. Choose File > Save and save the PDF document.

TIP 17: Creating a PDF from a Scan in Acrobat

Text or an Image of Text?

Many of the files you convert to PDF are composed of text and images. You can manipulate the content on the PDF pages using a variety of tools. PDF files created by scans or from some programs, such as Photoshop, are images only; you can't make any changes to the file's contents. Here's a quick way to tell the difference:

1. Click Select Text on the Basic toolbar. Click an area of text on the document. If you see the flashing vertical bar cursor, you know the page contains text (**Figure 2.57**).

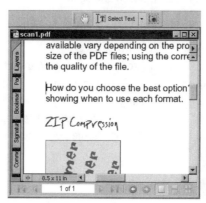

Figure 2.57 If you see the flashing vertical bar cursor, you know the page contains text.

2. If you click a text area on the document and nothing happens, you likely have an image PDF. To make sure, click the pull-down arrow to the right of the Select Text tool and choose Select Image. Then click the page. If the entire page is selected, it is one single image (**Figure 2.58**).

Figure 2.58 Use the Select Image tool to select graphic content on the page. If the whole page is selected, you know that the whole page is an image.

TIP 18 Importing Editable Text from a Scanned Document

A scanned PDF is only an image of a page, and you can't manipulate its content by extracting images or modifying the text. However, you can use the Paper Capture tool to convert the image of the document into actual text. The conversion process is called *optical character recognition* (OCR). Acrobat interprets the image of a character as a letter or number. It is important to evaluate the captured document when the OCR process is complete to make sure Acrobat interpreted the content correctly. It is easy to confuse a bitmap that may be the letter I with the number 1, for example.

To capture the content of a scanned document:

1. Choose Document > Paper Capture > Start Capture (**Figure 2.59**). The Paper Capture dialog opens.

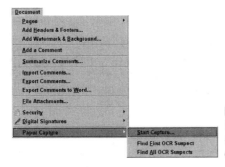

Figure 2.59 Use the Paper Capture tool to convert an image of a document into text.

2. If you are capturing a multipage document, specify whether you want to capture the current page or specific pages in the document (**Figure 2.60**).

Figure 2.60 Specify the page or pages you want to capture.

(Continued)

TIP 18: Importing Editable Text from a Scanned Document

3. Click the Edit button to open the Paper Capture Settings dialog. From the PDF Output Style pull-down list, select Formatted Text & Graphics (**Figure 2.61**). You want to convert all the content to separate elements.

Figure 2.61 Convert the content to separate text and graphics.

4. Next, click OK to return to the Paper Capture dialog. Click OK to start the capture process.

   A progress bar displays on the screen as the document is processed. Be patient. Depending on the size and complexity of the document, the process can take a minute or two. When it is complete, the progress bar closes.

Fixing Incorrect Characters

Converting the bitmap of letters and numbers into actual letters and numbers may result in items that can't be definitively identified. These are called *suspects*. You have the opportunity to check for such characters one by one:

1. Choose Document > Paper Capture > Show All OCR Suspects. All content on the page that needs confirmation is outlined with red boxes (**Figure 2.62**).

Figure 2.62 Suspect words and characters are outlined with red boxes.

2. Choose Document > Paper Capture > Show First OCR Suspect. The Find Element dialog opens, and the suspect content from the page is displayed one item at a time. Often the suspect elements are actual words, and you need to verify them. In **Figure 2.63**, the word *locations*, followed by an em dash, has to be confirmed. If Acrobat's interpretation is incorrect, you select the text and replace it with the correct letters or numbers.

Figure 2.63 Suspect content from the page is displayed one item at a time.

3. Choose Tools > Advanced Editing > TouchUp Text.

4. With the TouchUp Text tool, click at the start of the suspect word and drag to select it.

5. Type to replace the content.

6. Click Accept and Find. The interpretation of the text is accepted as shown, and Acrobat displays the next suspect element.

7. Continue through the document. Click Close to dismiss the dialog.

8. Save the document when you have finished evaluating the Paper Capture results.

The Usual Suspects

Here are some tips for capturing content with a minimum of suspects:

- Evaluate the content of your document. Determine if you can simply scan the document or if you must scan and capture the content.

- If you plan to capture the content, scan using specific resolutions—scan black and white at 200–600 dpi, and scan at 200–400 dpi for color or gray. Otherwise, your conversion won't occur, you'll see a warning message , and you'll have to rescan the document.

- Not all fonts and colors scan well. OCR fonts are available, but any clear font (serif or sans serif) at about 12 points works well. Black text against a white background scans and converts best; colored or decorative fonts are the most difficult.

TIP 18: Importing Editable Text from a Scanned Document

TIP 19 Creating a PDF from a Clipboard Image

Your computer's operating system maintains a storage area called a *clipboard*. Content you select and copy from a document is placed on the clipboard, and you can then paste it into another location or another document. You have two ways of using the clipboard contents in Acrobat—creating a new file or adding the clipboard contents to an existing file.

Creating a New Document

1. In your source program, select and copy the image you want to use for a PDF (**Figure 2.64**).

Figure 2.64 Select and copy the image you want to use for a new document.

2. In Acrobat, click the Create PDF task button and choose From Clipboard Image from the menu (**Figure 2.65**).

Figure 2.65 Once you've pasted the image to the clipboard, choose the From Clipboard Image option.

3. The content of the clipboard is converted to a new PDF file (**Figure 2.66**). Save the file.

Figure 2.66 The clipboard image becomes a new independent PDF document.

Adding Clipboard Content to an Existing File

1. Select and copy the image you want to use in the existing PDF document. The item is pasted to the clipboard.

2. In Acrobat, choose Tools > Advanced Commenting > Attach > Paste Clipboard Image (**Figure 2.67**).

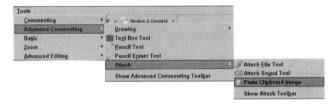

Figure 2.67 You can paste the clipboard's contents as an attachment in another PDF document.

(Continued)

TIP 19: Creating a PDF from a Clipboard Image

3. Move the pointer over the page until the pointer changes to crosshairs. Click the page where you want the image to appear (**Figure 2.68**). The location of the crosshairs will be the center of the image.

ONE OF BROOKE'S FLOWERS.

Figure 2.68 Click the page where you want to paste the image.

4. Acrobat pastes the image to the page. The crosshairs pointer changes to the Hand tool. Click the image on the page to select it.

5. Drag the image to move it, or drag a resize handle to change the size of the image (**Figure 2.69**).

Figure 2.69 Move and resize the pasted image as desired.

6. Save the file with the added image.

CHAPTER THREE

Saving, Exporting, and Printing

Once you have a PDF document open in Acrobat, you can perform a wide range of processes based on the document's structure and content. You can also export documents from Acrobat in a variety of ways.

TIP 20 Finding Information About Your Document

There is a lot more to a document than what you see on the screen or printed page. Use the Document Properties dialog when you want to find or modify information about your documents.

Choose File > Document Properties (or press Ctrl + D/Command + D) to open the Document Properties dialog. The dialog lists six headings in the left pane (**Figure 3.1**); each displays information in the right pane when clicked.

Figure 3.1 Use the Document Properties dialog to find information in these six areas.

The **Advanced** pane displays by default when the dialog opens. Normally, you won't often change this information. The pane shows PDF settings and reading options (**Figure 3.2**).

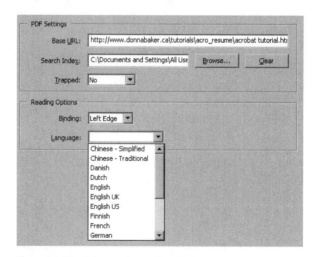

Figure 3.2 The Advanced pane lists PDF settings and reading options.

The **Custom** pane lets you add properties and values that identify the content in the document. This information is often used on an enterprise level to organize large quantities of material. Identifying the same document in different versions is a common custom property; in **Figure 3.3**, the document uses the custom property *version* and the custom value *2.5*. In addition to identifying the content of a document, the custom properties can be used for searching.

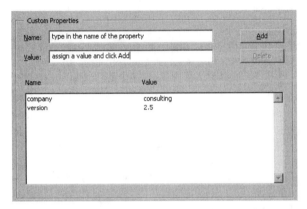

Figure 3.3 The Custom pane lets you add specific properties and values to your document. It's useful when you want to specify a version number, or when you need to distinguish a draft from the final version.

The **Description** pane holds more information about a document (**Figure 3.4**); how much information depends on the source program that created the original document. While you don't have to add a lengthier description to a document, you can use this screen to facilitate searches (you can search by keyword, for example) and to keep better track of material within an office environment. Click to activate a field and add content to any description element.

(Continued)

Feel Free to Make Changes...

You can change information about the document as set by the creator—unless the file has security settings that prevent changes. Converting a file to a PDF document is only the beginning. If your documents are used in document collections, you can add custom keywords and descriptions that can be used for searching, or attach indexes.

If you work with a document, adding navigation options such as bookmarks changes the way the document displays to give your readers the maximum benefit of your efforts. Choose File > Document Properties > Initial View and choose the Bookmarks Panel and Page option from the Show menu.

Once the document is completely finished, then add security.

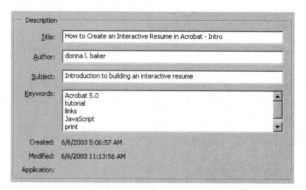

Figure 3.4 The Description pane contains information about a document's content.

The lower area of the Description pane (**Figure 3.5**) lists PDF information about the file, such as the tool used to generate the PDF and where the PDF is stored. This area is a good place to check whether the file is tagged. A tagged PDF includes an XML structure that you can use for a range of purposes, such as Web output, reflow, and delivery to accessibility devices. See Tip 33 in Chapter 4 for more information on tagged PDFs.

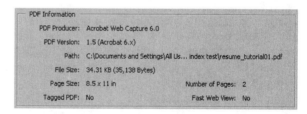

Figure 3.5 Read information on how the PDF file was created.

The **Fonts** pane (**Figure 3.6**) lists the fonts, font types, and encoding information used in the original document. Having this information at hand can be a real timesaver. In situations where you need to expand an original body of work but don't have a template, for example, you can quickly check in the generated PDF and see the fonts in the Fonts pane.

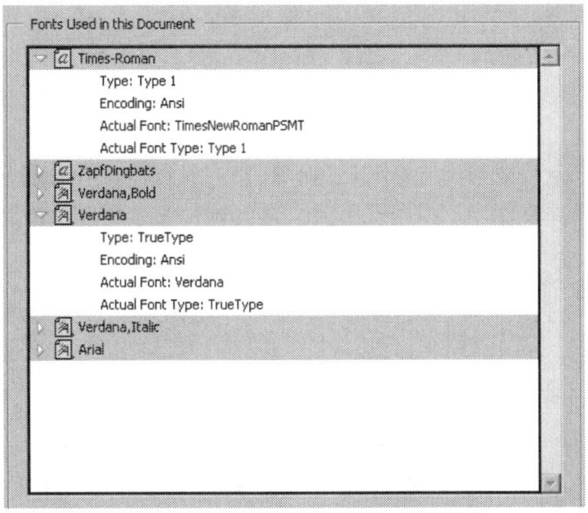

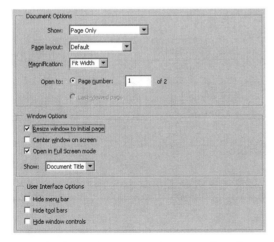

Figure 3.6 Use the Fonts pane as a reference.

Click an arrow to the left of the font name to open a list with more information. For each font, you see the name and font type used in the original document; the drop-down list displays the font, font type, and encoding used to display the document in Acrobat.

Click **Initial View** to display information that defines how the PDF document looks when it is opened (**Figure 3.7**). A range of options related to the document, user interface, and window are available. See Tip 21 for information on controlling these options.

Troubleshooting Text

Check the Fonts list when you aren't satisfied with the way the text in a document looks after conversion. Sometimes fonts are substituted for the originals—the Fonts panel describes what is substituted. If that's the case, embedding the fonts in the original document and regenerating the PDF should take care of the problem. See Tip 28 for more information

Figure 3.7 Choose from these options to configure how a document opens.

(Continued)

TIP 20: Finding Information About Your Document

The **Security** pane describes what level of security, if any, has been added to the document, and lists permissions granted to users of the document. If you are the author of the document, and you can use either the document's password or a security certificate, you can change the security settings. In **Figure 3.8**, you can see that anyone opening this document has the right to do pretty much anything with the contents.

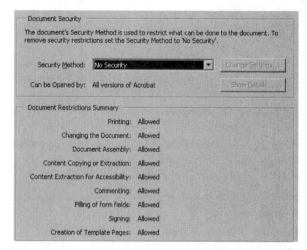

Figure 3.8 No Security gives the reader full rights to alter a document. In this document, readers can do almost anything, from printing to creating templates.

TIP 21 Deciding What Your Reader Sees First

The Initial View pane of the Document Properties dialog lets you modify the Initial View settings. Change the options to control what your readers see when they open your document:

1. Choose File > Document Properties > Initial View to display the document view settings.

2. Choose a Show option based on the document's contents and how the reader uses the document (**Figure 3.9**).

Figure 3.9 Use the Document Options pane to select different ways of displaying your document.

- In a long document, you typically use a bookmark structure as a way to link content in various locations, so provide readers with the Bookmarks Panel and Page view when they open the document (**Figure 3.10**).

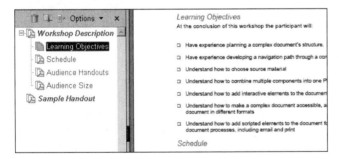

Figure 3.10 Display bookmarks to help readers navigate a long or complex document.

(Continued)

- In an image-based document, such as a slideshow, you can use the Pages Panel and Page view; your reader can easily browse the document using the thumbnail views of the pages (**Figure 3.11**).

Figure 3.11 With image-heavy documents, it's often easier to browse using small page images or thumbnails.

- In **Figure 3.12**, a drawing with several layers displays using the Layers Panel and Pages view.

Figure 3.12 You can set the display to show layers in a document.

3. In addition to a default, there are four ways to display the document's pages. Choose an option from the Page Layout pull-down list (**Figure 3.13**).

Figure 3.13 Choose from several page layout options.

The set of page layout options are the same as those found on the status bar below the Document pane. Unless your document's security settings prohibit it, your readers can choose their own page display using the status bar icons (**Figure 3.14**).

Figure 3.14 Select from the same page display options on the status bar.

4. Select an option from the Magnification pull-down list (**Figure 3.15**).

Figure 3.15 You can choose from numerous magnification presets.

- As with the page layouts, the reader can control magnification from the document using the controls on the status bar (**Figure 3.16**).

Figure 3.16 Use controls on the status bar to specify magnification.

- Choose an option depending on the document's content. With most text documents, Fit Width is a common option. The reader sees the entire width of the document and can scroll through vertically to see the rest.

- Use magnifications carefully. A large image is often best presented at full size, and the reader can zoom in for a closer look. In **Figure 3.17**, the left side shows the Full Page magnification; the right side shows a page at 400 percent. The full page identifies the content clearly, while the magnified view can't be identified at all. Although you may want

(Continued)

Choosing Page Layout Options

Here are some reasons for choosing specific page layouts:

- Choose Single Page if your document is broken into specific content and each topic starts on a new page—for example, technical manuals.

- Choose Continuous if the information covers several pages, with some topics starting on new pages and others using continuous pages. Many business documents fall into this category; you can control how readers move through the document using bookmarks or other types of navigation.

- Choose Facing if the information is laid out in a book format; eBooks are a typical example.

- Choose Continuous-Facing for eBooks or other two-page spreads.

TIP 21: Deciding What Your Reader Sees First

to use a high magnification for impact (the zoomed version does look rather exotic), make sure to use a high-resolution image. The example's image becomes quite pixilated at the magnification shown.

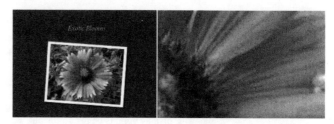

Figure 3.17 Set magnification according to your content. A full page screen is usually easier on the eyes than extreme magnification.

Make Your Content Pop!

Removing access to menus and commands, as in step 6 in the tip, isn't necessarily a bad thing. When screen space is an issue, or if you want your content to jump out at the reader, hiding the menu bar and toolbars helps draw more attention to your document. But be careful when you decide to do this—the next time the document opens you can only use shortcut keys to control the program. Make sure you provide other types of controls from the document, such as links.

5. Choose an option that defines how the window will open (**Figure 3.18**). Again, the purpose of the document determines which option you'll choose.

Figure 3.18 Choose an option that defines how your document will open.

If you are using a full-page layout, pick the Resize option to show your entire page with the document window fitted around it. This produces the most professional-looking layouts.

Note
Choose either the document name or the filename for displaying at the top of the program window. It's a small detail, but contributes to a more polished piece of work. After all, what is more descriptive—"Exotic Blooms" or "ebss050503"? To use a document name, be sure to add the descriptive content on the Description pane of the Document Properties dialog.

6. The final options deal with displaying user controls (**Figure 3.19**). Removing access to menus and commands can make it impossible for your reader to navigate through your document.

Figure 3.19 You can choose to show user controls for your documents, or not.

TIP 22 Saving a PDF as a Text-Based File

Acrobat lets you save a PDF file in several text-based formats. When the document is open in Acrobat, choose File > Save As to open the Save As dialog, and choose from several text-based options: rich text format (RTF), Word document, and plain or accessible text. Choose a format based on how you plan to use the content. For example, if your PDF document uses a lot of text that you'll want to reuse in tables in another program, export as plain text. If you want to work with the document in Word, use RTF or DOC format. (**Figure 3.20** shows the options available when you choose to save as a DOC file.) Choose the accessible or plain text option for output when you don't want any styles or formatting applied to your content.

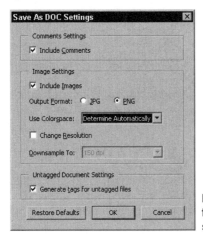

Figure 3.20 You can export a PDF file in several text-based formats, such as Word's DOC format.

Once you choose a format, click Settings to access the options for your desired format. A Save As dialog appears; the options vary depending on the format.

Here are some pointers:

- Include Comments is selected by default; deselect it if you don't need comments in the exported document.

- Don't export the images if you don't need them. They add to file size and processing time.

- If you want to export images and your PDF file contains both color and grayscale images, choose Determine Automatically

(Continued)

Good Reasons for Converting a PDF File

There are two main reasons you'd want to convert a PDF document to other formats:

- The source file is unavailable, and the content needs significant changes. Export in a format you can use for the source application, such as RTF or DOC, to modify a Word file.

- A page needs modification but the original source program isn't available. The New Orleans document example (see Figure 3.21) is a file created originally in Microsoft Publisher and then converted to PDF. If I don't have access to Publisher, I can export the file to a Word-compatible format and modify it.

from the Use Colorspace pull-down list. If you don't absolutely need the images to be in color, it's a good idea to select the Grayscale option.

- The option for generating tags is selected by default. These tags are not maintained in the exported document; they are used only in the conversion process and then discarded. Leave the option selected.

- Be sure to check the content of your output carefully. In **Figure 3.21**, we exported a page from a PDF as a Word document. You can see how text at the upper part of the page looks different than text at the lower part of the page. The reason? The text at the top is considered an image. The two small images, the title, and the accompanying text are included as parts of the right page frame image.

Exported Image Resolution

Image resolution for export defaults to 150 dpi. You can change the resolution depending on the file format chosen; options range from 72 to 300 dpi.

Figure 3.21 Check your document carefully when you export a PDF document to Word format.

TIP 23 Exporting as HTML and XML

What if you have a PDF document and need a Web page in a hurry? Easy. You can export the content and images from Acrobat in HTML or XML format. XML describes data and focuses on what the data is; HTML displays data and focuses on how data looks. If you want to use a PDF document as a Web page, use one of two HTML formats. But if you want your document's contents to be used for data exchange in a corporate environment, choose an XML format.

1. Choose File > Save As and select a file format option from the Save As pull-down list (**Figure 3.22**).

Figure 3.22 You can choose from two HTML formats.

2. Click Settings to open the Settings dialog specific to that format type (**Figure 3.23**).

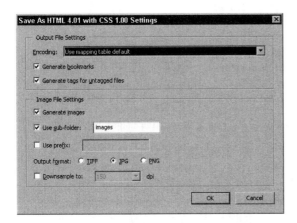

Figure 3.23 Customize settings based on your requirements.

(Continued)

TIP 23: Exporting as HTML and XML

Editing Export Preferences

Do you find you are exporting the same types of files from Acrobat and making the same settings changes? If so, change the preferences. Choose Edit > Preferences (in Mac, Acrobat > Preferences) to open the Preferences dialog. Click Convert from PDF in the left pane. Select the format you want to modify from the list in the right pane. When you select an option, its settings appear in the dialog. Click Edit Settings to open the same settings dialog you use to export an individual file (see Figure 3.23). Adjust the settings as desired and click OK. Click OK again to close the Preferences dialog. Now your file exports use your modified settings, saving you processing time for each file.

3. Choose an encoding format from the pull-down list if you use a specific format, or leave the default (Use mapping table default). Bookmarks and tags are generated automatically.

Note
The tags are generated only for the conversion process and then discarded; they are not integrated into the exported file.

4. Choose options in the Image File Settings pane. Acrobat creates a new subfolder named "images"; you can edit this name to suit your purposes. **Figure 3.24** shows a prefix, "no2002", that Acrobat will attach to image filenames before saving.

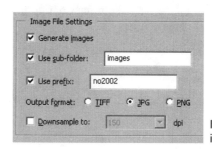

Figure 3.24 Save exported images to a separate folder.

5. Click OK to close the Settings dialog and to return to the Save As dialog.

6. Click OK to convert the file. In the Explorer window, you can see that the file's images are numbered and use the assigned prefix (**Figure 3.25**).

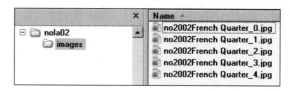

Figure 3.25 Assign a prefix to exported images to keep track of your efforts.

Note
If you are building a large site, you'll find it more efficient over time to write the code by hand or to use an HTML or WYSIWYG editor. Either approach gives you control over the page's structure as well as style sheet design, and lets you attach external style sheets as well.

HTML or XML?

Although their names look similar, HTML and XML function differently and are used for different purposes.

- If you are saving a PDF document for use on a Web site, use an HTML format. Acrobat does a good job of converting a page and creating styles for the page.

- Computer systems and databases contain data in incompatible formats. Converting your document's data to XML reduces the complexity and creates data that can be read by many types of applications. Use an XML format when you want to export a document for data exchange, such as for use in spreadsheets or databases.

TIP 24   Save a PDF as an Image

Often you save a PDF document in a text and image format—as HTML or as a Word document, for example. However, you can also save a PDF document as an image.

1. Choose File > Save As to open the Save As dialog. Select an image export option from the Save As pull-down list (**Figure 3.26**).

Figure 3.26
You can save
a file in one of
several image
formats.

2. Click Settings to open the Settings dialog. The Save As JPEG Settings dialog is shown in **Figure 3.27**. Modify these options according to your requirements.

Figure 3.27 Each image format has customizable settings.

The Spitting Image of a PDF

Why would you want a PDF to be an uneditable image?

Here are some of the reasons why:

- You want to use the content as part of another project or process.

- You want to create thumbnail images of pages for use in other documents.

- You need to protect the content in a page. Exporting as an image with security prevents text and other content changes.

Exporting all the Images in a Document

You can export images along with content when you save a document in an HTML version. You can also export the images alone. Choose Advanced > Export All Images; the Export All Images As dialog opens. Browse for the folder you want to use to store the images, and choose an image format from the pull-down list at the bottom of the dialog. Click Settings to open the Export All Images As dialog. The dialog is similar to that shown in Figure 3.27 with one addition— you can specify the extraction size. The default is set at 1.00 inches, which means that all images in the document that are 1 inch in size and smaller are not exported. If you have a company logo on each page of a large document, for example, setting the extraction size to the logo's size prevents one copy of the image from being exported from each page.

3. Click OK to close the Settings dialog and to return to the Save As dialog.

4. Click OK to convert the file. Acrobat converts each page of your document to an image. The image will be the same size as the document page (**Figure 3.28**).

Figure 3.28 The image is exported at the full-page size.

Note

*An image of a document page makes a very nice link from another document. When you are building a large project incorporating several types of material, you typically link the documents together. You can use text links, but you can also use an image of the linked document, as in **Figure 3.29**. I have a document that is linked to a slideshow. Instead of using text to link, I used a thumbnail-sized image of the first page of the slideshow. Be sure the outcome is worth the effort—don't use an image of an all-text page, for example.*

Figure 3.29 You can use an exported image as a visual link.

When choosing an image file format, consider how you want to use an image. I've exported an image in four different formats—JPEG, JPEG2000, TIF, and PNG—using the default settings.

Figure 3.30 shows the difference in file sizes for the various formats, and it is quite a difference! If you were exporting and reusing a number of images the file size would certainly build up quickly.

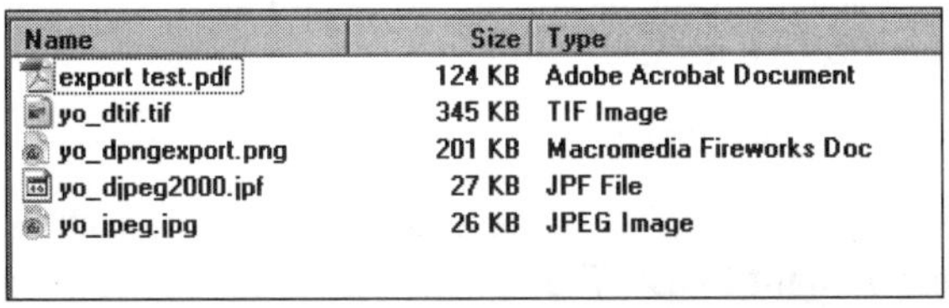

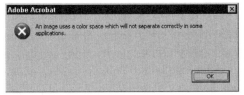

Figure 3.30
Be aware of the file sizes of different formats when exporting images.

For Web purposes, I usually work with the JPEG files, and I use TIF files for printing. Visually, there is a substantial difference in quality between the image types, as you would expect.

Exporting EPS Files

You can export images to applications, such as Adobe Illustrator, that use EPS (Encapsulated PostScript) files. Take care with the settings, however.

If the file is formatted using RGB color space, you won't be able to create an EPS file. Instead, you'll see a message telling you that an image uses a color format that won't separate **(Figure 3.31)**. In this case, you can't export the images as EPS files. The only way to rectify the situation is to use a source image that uses a CMYK color space.

Adobe Acrobat

An image uses a color space which will not separate correctly in some applications.

OK

Figure 3.31
Don't try to export an RGB image to eps format.

TIP 24: Save a PDF as an Image

TIP 25 Choosing Print Settings

Printing from Acrobat can be a bit more complex than clicking the Print button; you can control what you print as well as where and how a document is printed. Acrobat lets you print to a printer or to a file, define a portion of your document for printing, or create a PostScript file. Let's take a look:

1. Select the pages you want to print.

2. Choose File > Print Setup to set general print options, such as the printer you want to use. The options vary according to your printer and printer drivers (**Figure 3.32**). Click OK.

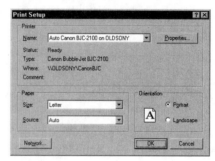

Figure 3.32 Select print characteristics and options in the Print Setup dialog box.

Note
In Windows, click Properties to set driver options; in Mac OS, driver options are set in the Print Center.

Choosing Pages Visually

Using the Pages pane, you can select portions of a document to print. The pages you select may be either grouped or scattered throughout your document:

- To select a group of pages, click the first page thumbnail to select it, hold down the Shift key, and click the last page to select it. Acrobat selects all pages in between as well.

- To select noncontiguous pages, click the first page thumbnail to select it, hold down Ctrl/ Command, and click the other pages you want to print.

3. Choose File > Print to open the Print dialog. Here you can choose specific print characteristics, such as the print range and number of copies. The same settings available in the Print Setup dialog appear at the top of the Print dialog.

4. Choose a printer from the Printer list (**Figure 3.33**); on Mac OS, choose an option from the Presets pop-up menu. Your operating system's printer and printer driver installations, as well as your network configuration, determine the Presets and Printer lists. In Windows, click Print to file to create a PostScript file.

Figure 3.33 Select a printer from the list.

(Continued)

5. Specify a print range and options such as page scaling and the number of copies (**Figure 3.34**).

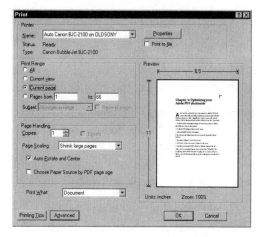

Figure 3.34 Select a range of pages and the number of copies you want to print.

Printing Help

If you run into printing problems, Adobe has a very good technical document that describes print troubleshooting. At the bottom left of the Print dialog, click Printing Tips to load the technical document from Adobe's Web site.

Note

You can quickly change the size of a printed document. Click the Page Scaling pull-down arrow and choose Fit to Paper. Your document is reset at the page size selected in the printer properties.

6. Click the Print What drop-down menu and choose the document only (the default setting), the document and comments, or form fields.

7. Before printing, preview the page in the Preview area of the dialog (**Figure 3.35**).

Figure 3.35 Preview the page layout before printing.

8. Click OK to close the dialog and start the print job.

TIP 26 Print Troubleshooting 101

I am not going to state the obvious, such as telling you to check whether your printer has paper or that it's turned on. However, I will offer some basic troubleshooting tips and hints that you may find handy in times of stress (usually one minute before a deadline!). If you're having trouble printing a PDF:

- Rewrite the file. Choose File > Save As, and resave the file as itself (don't change the name, and click OK when prompted to overwrite the existing file). Although you may choose to give the file a new name, I usually save it as itself so I don't get confused by storing multiple copies of the same document. Each time you save a PDF file, it actually saves a version of itself. When you choose Save As and resave it as a PDF, it overwrites all the stored versions, sometimes clearing a stored problem.

- Print the file as an image. In the bottom left of the Print dialog, you'll see the Advanced button (**Figure 3.36**). In the Advanced Print Setup dialog, select the Print as Image option (**Figure 3.37**). Click OK to close the dialog, and then click OK to try printing again. Sometimes a document won't print because of errors in interpreting the text or font information. If you print as an image, font and text information isn't required.

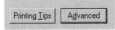

Figure 3.36 Click Advanced to access more printing options.

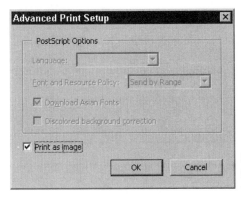

Figure 3.37 You can print any document as an image.

Don't Print Everything

In a pinch, you can try printing the file in sections. You may find the printing problem comes from one object on one page, and that single error prevents the document from printing. Once you isolate the problem, you might have to re-create a page, but that is much simpler than starting over.

- Re-create the PDF file using a different method; for example, if you originally converted the file using the PDFMaker macro, try to use Acrobat Distiller. Sometimes I have had luck converting a file from within Acrobat that didn't work correctly when originally converted from within Word.

- If you are using a PostScript printer, you can set the printer to display printing errors. Check your printer's documentation.

- If you are using a Web file, download it again and try printing once more.

TIP 27 Choosing and Using Fonts

Fonts can be a beautiful thing; there is nothing quite as lovely as a perfectly constructed document. Alas, it isn't always easy to share perfection with others—but you can try! Before converting a document to PDF, make sure your fonts can be used and viewed by others:

1. Create your masterpiece. **Figure 3.38** shows a Word document using two very distinctive fonts.

THIS FONT IS NAMED PRIME MINISTER OF CANADA. I DON'T KNOW WHY, BUT EVERY FONT NEEDS A NAME, DOESN'T IT?

This is another font named Frazzle.

Figure 3.38 This Word document uses two very different fonts.

2. Check the conversion settings. In your document-creation application, choose Adobe PDF > Change Conversion Settings. When the dialog opens, click the Advanced Settings button to open the Adobe PDF Settings dialog.

3. Click the Fonts tab (**Figure 3.39**). Depending on the conversion settings option you are using, you may find the two check boxes at the top of the pane already selected—the default setting for the .joboptions file in use.

Figure 3.39 Some conversion options use embedding and subsetting by default.

(Continued)

Embedding and Subsetting

Embedding means the information about all the characters in the fonts is automatically attached for use after the document is converted to a PDF. *Subsetting* refers to a percentage of the font's information based on the number of characters used in the document.

When you embed a font, the text in the document using that font displays correctly. You can preserve your content precisely using subsetting. Choose a subsetting value up to 100%, which means that all of the characters used are embedded. It's a good idea to subset at 100%—the difference in file size is hardly noticeable.

Subsetting is important for documents sent to a print service or press, since it means that your document contains a collection of the font characters actually used in the document. The collection of characters is given a custom name. If you send the document to a print service or press, the printer's version of the font may or may not be identical to your version. When the document is printed, it uses the information in your document, not that of the printer's version of the font, ensuring precise results.

4. In the lower portion of the window, select the font you want to embed from the list at the left and click Add. The font is added to the Always Embed column at the right (**Figure 3.40**).

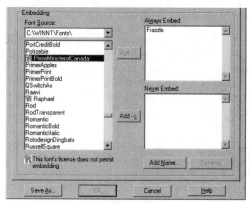

Figure 3.40 Choose which fonts to embed and add them to the list at the top right. Some font licenses prohibit embedding.

Some fonts cannot be embedded. A key to the left of the font's name indicates that the font is locked. If you select that font, Acrobat displays a message below the Font Source column stating that the font's license does not allow embedding. In this case, you have two options: Either you must purchase the font for everyone who uses the document, or you should change to a font that can be embedded.

5. When you have finished, click OK. Before you leave the Adobe PDF Settings dialog, you are prompted to name the .joboptions file.

6. In the source program, convert the document to PDF. In Acrobat, the document looks the same, but is it the same (**Figure 3.41**)? See the next tip...

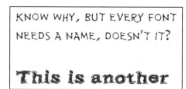

Figure 3.41 Here's the converted document in Acrobat.

TIP 28 Previewing in Acrobat

Before you finish a document that must be visually correct, or a document that is going to an outside printer or press, experiment with it in Acrobat. For documents going to a press, you must check color separations before sending the file.

Previewing Text

A common error is to preview a document only on your computer using the fonts you have installed. You can't evaluate the embedding/subsetting using your computer's fonts—you need to test how other computers display your document.

By default, Acrobat uses the local fonts (those installed on your computer) for displaying documents. **Figure 3.42** shows the fonts installed on my computer for my sample document. In the Advanced menu, deselect the command Use Local Fonts. The results are shown in the lower portion of Figure 3.42.

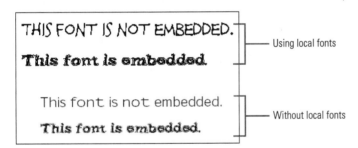

Figure 3.42 Where did the fancy font go?

The difference is clear. The font used for the first row of text, Prime Minister of Canada, is a locked font and can't be embedded. The second font, Frazzle, can and was embedded. As a result, if I shipped a document using these fonts, only one would display correctly.

You can check the Document Properties for confirmation. Choose File > Document Properties > Fonts. The information for the Frazzle font is as you would expect. The dialog states that the font is embedded and also subset.

(Continued)

Substitute Fonts

When you are building PDF documents for distribution, try to use a font that can be embedded whenever possible. If a font can't be embedded, such as the one used in this tip's example, Acrobat substitutes with one of two fonts—Adobe Serif MM for a serif font, or Adobe Sans MM for a missing sans serif font (see Figure 3.43).

The substitute font configures itself to simulate the missing font as closely as possible. In the example, although the font looked different structurally, it still used the same color, size, and spacing.

Look at the first font. Although the name and font type are listed, you see the actual font used, Adobe Sans MM, is a substitute for the original (**Figure 3.43**).

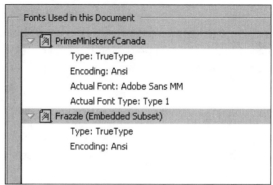

Figure 3.43 The original font is replaced by a substitute font.

Previewing Images

Documents going to a printer for a full-color printing use color separation plates. The image is composed of four layers: cyan, magenta, yellow, and black. Collectively, the color space is referred to as CMYK.

All colors in a color print are composed of varying amounts of these four colors of ink. *Overprint* colors are two unscreened inks printed on top of each other. For example, when magenta ink is printed over yellow ink, the resulting overprint is the bright orange color of the flower shown in **Figure 3.44**. If overprinting isn't turned on, only the magenta ink prints.

Cyan (C) Magenta (M)

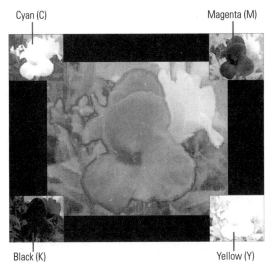

Black (K) Yellow (Y)

Figure 3.44 A bright orange flower is printed using four colors of ink.

In the figure, the large flower is a bold orange color. The proportions and depths of the colors in each channel are shown in the four corner images.

Note

I created the figure in Photoshop to show you the color separations; in Acrobat you see only the central image.

To preview your images:

1. In Acrobat, choose Advanced > Overprint Preview to estimate the overprint color. Use this command for a quick check of your document before sending it to the printer to make sure all colors are present. If they are not, open your source document or Distiller and check the settings.

2. In the Settings dialog, select the Advanced tab. Check that the Preserve Overprint Settings option is selected (**Figure 3.45**). If it isn't, select it, save the settings, and reconvert the document.

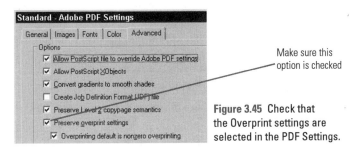

Make sure this option is checked

Figure 3.45 Check that the Overprint settings are selected in the PDF Settings.

TIP 28: Previewing in Acrobat

CHAPTER FOUR

Making Documents Accessible

Acrobat 6 offers a range of options, configurations, and settings that allow users who are visually or motion-impaired to work with PDF documents. Acrobat provides these features:

- Mouse-free navigation using both keyboard navigation and auto-scroll functions

- Speech capabilities for translating text to spoken words

- Visibility modifications that allow readers to use screen-enhancing software and tools, as well as configure the program to make content easier to view

- Program capabilities that you can use to make a document more accessible

Understanding how accessibility functions work is only the first part of the equation. The second part is figuring out how you can modify documents before converting them to PDFs to make them easy to use, and knowing what you can do once you get a document into Acrobat.

TIP
29 # Navigating with the Keyboard

For the user, the important issue is getting around a document, so the most basic accessibility feature is keyboard navigation. Appendix C contains an extensive set of keyboard shortcuts.

Common shortcuts for moving around the program appear in **Table 4.1**. Some shortcuts have more than one option; I have listed the most common or the one I prefer. Check the Acrobat Help menu for the complete list of optional key combinations.

Setting Up Keyboard Access on a Mac

Those of you using Mac OS 10.1.2 and later have more keyboard access capabilities than in earlier versions of Acrobat. The improved access is based on system-level preferences. Follow these steps to set it up:

1. Choose Apple > System Preferences > Keyboard. The Keyboard Preferences dialog opens.

2. Select the Full Keyboard Access tab, and enable the options Turn on Full Keyboard Access and Any Control.

3. Choose System Preferences > Quit System Preferences.

Table 4.1 **Common Shortcuts for Moving Through a Document**

To do this...	In Windows, press...	In Mac OS, press...
Go to the previous screen	Page Up	Page Up
Go to the next screen	Page Down	Page Down
Go to the first page	Shift+Ctrl+Page Up	Shift+Command+Page Up
Go to the last page	Shift+Ctrl+Page Down	Shift+Command+Page Down
Scroll up	Up arrow	Up arrow
Scroll down	Down arrow	Down arrow
Zoom in	Ctrl+plus sign	Command+plus sign
Zoom out	Ctrl+minus sign	Command+minus sign
Temporarily select the Zoom tool and zoom in	Ctrl + spacebar + click	Command + spacebar + click

Automatic Scrolling

You can automatically scroll through a document. Scrolling is useful if you're scanning for a particular piece of information, such as an image or table. Choose View > Automatic Scroll, or press Ctrl/Command+Shift+H. The document starts scrolling from the position currently in the Document pane and stops when you reach the end of the document.

Use the keyboard shortcut to pause the scroll as well. If you're using the mouse, click the page; as long as you're pressing down the mouse button, the page stops. Release the mouse button to start scrolling again.

Here are a couple of tips for working with Automatic Scroll:

- The Automatic Scroll feature uses the continuous page layout option (**Figure 4.1**). You don't have to change the layout yourself. It is done automatically when you select the command or press the keyboard shortcut.

Figure 4.1 The Automatic Scroll feature uses the Continuous page layout option.

- Be sure to click the Hand tool before starting. If you don't and you are using the mouse, each time you click the page Acrobat not only pauses the scroll but also applies the tool selected. In **Figure 4.2**, you can see the effect of having a commenting tool active when scrolling.

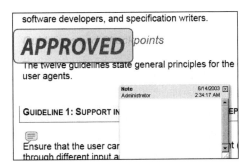

Figure 4.2 If you use Automatic Scroll with a commenting tool activated, you'll end up with comment boxes all over your pages.

You can control the scroll characteristics as well:

- Press the down arrow key to increase the speed or the up arrow key to decrease it. You can also use the number keys to change speed: 0 is the slowest and 9 is the fastest.

- Reverse the direction of the scroll. Press the minus key (-) on the keyboard or number pad.

- Use the left arrow key to return to the previous page and the right arrow key to jump to the next page.

- Press Esc to stop the scrolling.

Working with Web Browsers

If you're working with a Mac in a Web browser, the keyboard commands are mapped to the Web browser. When you make Acrobat the active application, the keyboard commands shift as well.

In Windows, Acrobat can be controlled within Microsoft Internet Explorer. Again, the active area is the Web browser, so keyboard shortcuts are those used for navigation and selection in the browser. Make Acrobat the active area by pressing the Tab key. Make the browser active again by pressing Ctrl+Tab.

TIP 29: Navigating with the Keyboard

30 Setting Document Color

Before distributing a document that will be used by vision-impaired users, you should test the settings using the methods described in this tip to see how your document looks. You may be surprised.

Making Text More Visible

You can check your document using custom color and text visibility options. I'm going to improve the visibility of the document shown in **Figure 4.3**.

Creating Multipurpose Doc

Description of Workshop:
Adobe Acrobat is a widely used tool for
sample project, you'll learn how to deve
production. You'll learn how to plan the
options. You'll learn tips for choosing so
You'll learn to integrate documents in A
modifying content in your PDF docume
through your document, and how to add
You'll see how to create a multi-purpos
in print, and as a presentation. You'll se
Acrobat. You'll learn how to make a doc
in different formats.

Learning Objectives
At the conclusion of this workshop the

☐ Have experience planning a complex d
☐ Have experience developing a navigati

Figure 4.3 Although the colors used in this document may look fine, I can improve the visibility of the pages.

1. Choose Edit > Preferences > Accessibility to display the Accessibility preferences dialog.

2. In the Document Colors Options section check the Replace Document Colors checkbox to activate the accompanying options. **Figure 4.4** shows the default selections: black text on a bright yellow background.

Figure 4.4 Choose custom colors for text and pages.

3. Click Custom Color to select colors for your document. To choose a page color, click the color swatch and select an option from the standard palette (**Figure 4.5**).

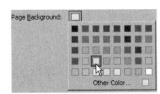

Figure 4.5 Pick a standard color from the color swatch palette.

4. Click Other Color to open the Color Picker shown in **Figure 4.6**. Choose the desired color, and click OK.

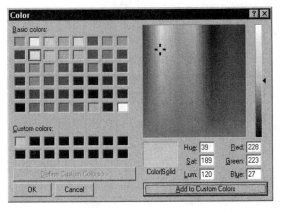

Figure 4.6 Choose a custom color from the Color Picker.

5. The final two options in Preferences are Change only the color of black text and Change the color of line art. Leave the first option selected (the default) and enable the second option as well.

(Continued)

Colors to Avoid

If you know that vision-impaired users will be viewing your documents, be careful with the colors you choose. One of the biggest problems is light-colored backgrounds. While a pale background behind a title looks attractive on a white background, if you use a high-contrast color scheme, for example, the text becomes virtually illegible. The light background and the light text used for high-contrast schemes are similar in color, thus making the text hard to read.

TIP 30: Setting Document Color

6. Click OK to close the dialog and to apply the changes.

Now all the text and the colored elements (such as bullets) are changed to black (**Figure 4.7**).

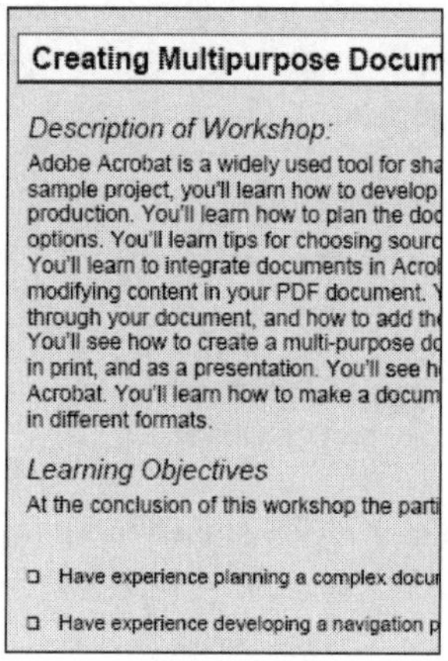

Creating Multipurpose Docum

Description of Workshop:

Adobe Acrobat is a widely used tool for sha
sample project, you'll learn how to develop
production. You'll learn how to plan the doc
options. You'll learn tips for choosing sourc
You'll learn to integrate documents in Acrot
modifying content in your PDF document. Y
through your document, and how to add the
You'll see how to create a multi-purpose do
in print, and as a presentation. You'll see h
Acrobat. You'll learn how to make a docum
in different formats.

Learning Objectives

At the conclusion of this workshop the parti

❑   Have experience planning a complex docu

❑   Have experience developing a navigation p

Figure 4.7 Change color for all the text and line art on the page to make them more visible.

Making Form Fields More Visible

When designing a form, a form designer's goals are typically ease of input and a pleasing appearance. However, it can be difficult to visualize form fields, as you can see in **Figure 4.8**; the form field is not colored, nor is it set apart from the field's label or the table outline. The only way to know it is an active field is to move the pointer over the areas until you see the pointer change to an I-beam cursor.

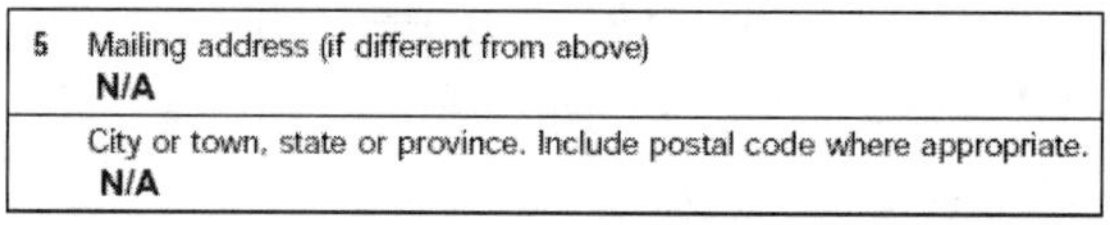

5	Mailing address (if different from above) **N/A**
	City or town, state or province. Include postal code where appropriate. **N/A**

Figure 4.8 Form fields that have no visible borders or background color can be hard to see on a document.

You can test form fields for visibility by modifying certain preferences:

1. Choose Edit > Preferences > Forms.

2. The Forms preferences include settings for the background color. Click the option Show background and hover color for form fields. Then, click the color swatch to choose a custom color (**Figure 4.9**). Click OK to close the Preferences dialog.

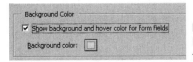

Figure 4.9 You can choose a background color to highlight form fields.

The form fields are now identified with the background color. When you move the pointer over a field, Acrobat places a black outline around the field (**Figure 4.10**).

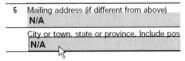

Figure 4.10 Setting the background color preference makes a selected form field stand out.

Using both custom document colors and form field color settings produces a different page appearance than before (**Figure 4.11**). Here, the background of the page is yellow and the form fields' lavender color is overlaid on the yellow, resulting in a darker color. When the field is clicked, the darker color disappears and the edges of the field are outlined.

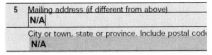

Figure 4.11 Form field background color overlays a custom page color.

TIP 30: Setting Document Color

TIP 31 Reading a Document Aloud

You can have Acrobat read a document aloud. This is a terrific feature when your goal is to make your documents more accessible, because the reader simulates some features of a full-blown screen-reader program. But be warned: a document that appears to be a simple, well-planned page isn't always simple for a reader.

To set reading preferences:

1. Choose Edit > Preferences > Reading.

2. In the Read Out Loud Options section, choose a voice, pitch, and volume (**Figure 4.12**). In Windows I prefer to listen to "Michelle," but you can also choose from "Michael" and "Microsoft Sam." On a Mac, you have a choice of numerous voices (**Figure 4.13**).

Figure 4.12 Make your selections in the Read Out Loud Options section. Windows users can choose from one of three voices: Michelle, Michael, and Microsoft Sam.

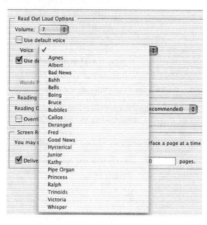

Figure 4.13 Mac users can choose from a large variety of voices, some of which aren't even human.

3. Click OK to close the Preferences dialog and to apply the voice settings.

Note
You have to return to the preferences to make adjustments. Unfortunately, you can't modify the settings and listen to the outcome of your adjustments at the same time.

4. Choose View > Read Out Loud. Choose Read This Page Only or Read To End of Document (**Figure 4.14**). The reading starts.

Read This Page Only	Shift+Ctrl+V
Read To End of Document	Shift+Ctrl+B
Pause	Shift+Ctrl+C
Stop	Shift+Ctrl+E

Figure 4.14 Choose an option for reading the page.

5. You can pause/resume or stop the reading using the menu commands or shortcut keys:

- Ctrl+Shift+C to pause/resume

- Ctrl+Shift+E to stop

Read or Listen?

Aside from testing the accessibility potential of a document, is there any reason to use the Read Out Loud feature? Actually, yes. I have had Acrobat read books to me as I work (now that's multitasking!) However, it can be difficult to listen to the words and not to the delivery. The words of the damsel in distress in *Dracula* sound pretty funny when Microsoft Sam reads them. Like most things in life, using the feature to read books is an acquired taste.

TIP 31: Reading a Document Aloud

How Should I Read That?

The page may read exactly as you would read it yourself, or it may do a peculiar thing—rather than reading down a column and then starting the next column, the reader reads from left to right across the page (**Figure 4.15**) If you're following along as the reader reads aloud, you clearly understand what is happening. However, if you're depending on the reader to tell you what is in the document, the message is quite garbled.

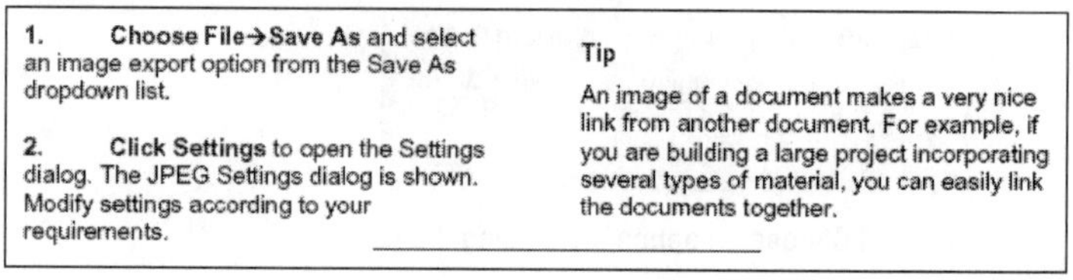

1. **Choose File→Save As** and select an image export option from the Save As dropdown list. 2. **Click Settings** to open the Settings dialog. The JPEG Settings dialog is shown. Modify settings according to your requirements.	Tip An image of a document makes a very nice link from another document. For example, if you are building a large project incorporating several types of material, you can easily link the documents together.

Figure 4.15 In an untagged document, text in columns is read from left to right across the page, even across multiple columns.

You can solve the problem by *tagging* the document—which is the subject of the next tip.

TIP 32 Adding Tags to a Document

Some program features used to enhance accessible use (covered in Tips 35 and 34, respectively) such as articles and reflow, don't work properly or predictably unless a document is *tagged*, which means it has a logically defined structure. Tags are invisible and are a part of the document's information. They define relationships among elements in the document, including tables, lists, images, and text. Tagging can be done in the source document (if you're using Microsoft Word, Excel, or PowerPoint) or in Acrobat.

To tag a document in Word:

1. In Word, choose Adobe PDF > Change Conversion Settings. The Change Conversion Settings dialog opens to the Settings tab.

2. In the Application Settings section, select the option Enable accessibility and reflow with Tagged PDF (**Figure 4.16**). Then click OK.

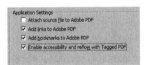

Figure 4.16 The PDFMaker macro includes a setting that adds document tags on conversion.

3. Click Convert to Adobe PDF or choose Adobe PDF > Convert to Adobe PDF. Word creates your PDF file.

4. Open the document in Acrobat. Choose View > Read Out Loud. The reading path through the document follows the direction shown in **Figure 4.17**—that is, the page is read down the first column, back to the top of the second column, and down the second column.

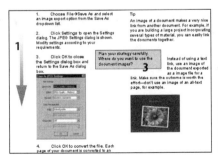

Figure 4.17 A tagged document reads page content in the correct order.

Should You Tag a Document?

The short answer is yes. I generally tag a document that is going to be used for anything other than simple conversion and storage of content. If I plan to combine PDF content from different sources, I tag everything I can. Tagging doesn't add much to the file's size, and it can make working with and repurposing content a lot simpler down the road.

Using Alternate Reading Orders

The Accessibility Quick Check suggests that you try other reading orders by modifying choices in the Reading Order options in the Reading preferences dialog. The default setting is to allow the program to infer the reading order. Sometimes this works; sometimes it doesn't. Often reading errors occur, as in the example used in this tip. You can also choose to read from left to right and from top to bottom, or to use the reading order from the raw text stream. These options can make a difference in some circumstances.

Many programs you use to create documents don't offer tagging options. You can easily add tags from within Acrobat.

1. First, check for preexisting tags by choosing Advanced > Accessibility > Quick Check. The Accessibility Quick Check looks for a document structure (tags), used for defining the reading order. An untagged document displays the results shown in **Figure 4.18**.

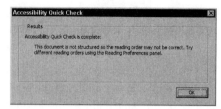

Figure 4.18 Check the accessibility status of your document.

2. To tag the document, choose Advanced > Accessibility > Make Accessible. Acrobat processes the document and adds tags.

   Note
   You don't see tags. They are a part of the document structure and invisible to you.

3. Check the document again by selecting Advanced > Accessibility > Quick Check. The new message states there are no accessibility problems with the document, meaning it is tagged (**Figure 4.19**).

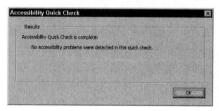

Figure 4.19 Check the accessibility status again after running the Make Accessible command.

4. Choose File > Save to save the document with its tagged structure.

TIP 33 Planning Documents for PDF Accessibility

When a screen reader reads a document aloud, it describes objects such as blank lines and borders on images as well as the text, which can make it difficult for your user to glean meaningful information from your document.

Let's look at an example. The document in **Figure 4.20** contains one chart and one table. It looks simple, doesn't it? From a visual perspective, it is simple, yet in terms of tag structures, charts and tables are complex.

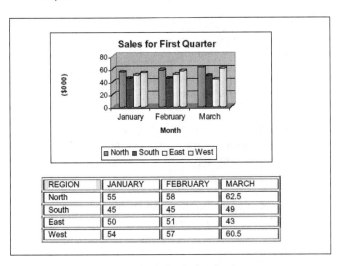

Figure 4.20 Tables and charts look simple, but they're complex page structures, which can make it hazardous for screen readers to try to make sense of them.

You cannot see the structural tags in Acrobat 6 Standard. However, you can see how the document is tagged by saving it as XML (Extensible Markup Language), which is a language created to structure, store, and send information. Once you see how a document is structured, you can understand the importance of planning accessible documents.

(Continued)

With the document in Figure 4.20 active, I choose File > Save As and select XML from the pull-down list. Opening the XML page in a browser reveals quite a surprise (**Figure 4.21**). The figure shows a portion of the list of graphic object tags in the document. Each element of the chart, such as lines and bars, is a separate object. A screen reader identifies each of these objects individually.

```
- <Figure>
    <GraphicData src="images/table_img_0.jpg" />
    <GraphicData src="images/table_img_1.jpg" />
    <GraphicData src="images/table_img_2.jpg" />
    <GraphicData src="images/table_img_3.jpg" />
    <GraphicData src="images/table_img_4.jpg" />
    <GraphicData src="images/table_img_5.jpg" />
    <GraphicData src="images/table_img_6.jpg" />
    <GraphicData src="images/table_img_7.jpg" />
    <GraphicData src="images/table_img_8.jpg" />
    <GraphicData src="images/table_img_9.jpg" />
    <GraphicData src="images/table_img_10.jpg" />
    <GraphicData src="images/table_img_11.jpg" />
    <GraphicData src="images/table_img_12.jpg" />
    <GraphicData src="images/table_img_13.jpg" />
    <GraphicData src="images/table_img_14.jpg" />
    <GraphicData src="images/table_img_15.jpg" />
    <GraphicData src="images/table_img_16.jpg" />
    <GraphicData src="images/table_img_17.jpg" />
    <GraphicData src="images/table_img_18.jpg" />
    <GraphicData src="images/table_img_19.jpg" />
    <GraphicData src="images/table_img_20.jpg" />
    <GraphicData src="images/table_img_21.jpg" />
    <GraphicData src="images/table_img_22.jpg" />
```

Figure 4.21 You can export a tagged document as XML to view its structure. Pretty formidable!

The chart in the example is made up of 105 separate JPEG images. Not only will listening to the screen reader describe 105 images put your user to sleep, the value of the chart is minimal. Here are some solutions:

- Group objects wherever possible. In Word, you can place the chart into a text box; the page looks the same once it's converted to PDF. Exporting as XML shows a different scenario, as you can see in **Figure 4.22**. This time, the chart's content is arranged in a table. The tags are simpler, but the chart is still difficult for the screen reader to read and the user to understand.

```
- <Frame>
  - <Table>
    - <TBody>
      - <TR>
        - <TD>
            <Normal>REGION</Normal>
          </TD>
        + <TD>
        + <TD>
        + <TD>
        </TR>
      - <TR>
        - <TD>
            <Normal>North</Normal>
          </TD>
        + <TD>
        + <TD>
        ⊞ <TD>
        </TR>
      - <TR>
        - <TD>
            <Normal>South</Normal>
```

Figure 4.22 With the chart or table placed in a text box, it's easier for a screen reader to read and understand.

- Convert the chart into an image using a screen-capture utility, and then place the image on the page. You'll see no difference in the document in Acrobat, but there is a significant difference when you see the tags—one tag instead of more than 100 tags (**Figure 4.23**).

```
- <Shape Alt="">
    <ImageData src="images/pix instead_img_0.jpg" />
  </Shape>
```

Figure 4.23 Converting the chart to a single image makes it much less complex.

- Configure the document pages correctly. Don't add blank lines to make a space, for example (**Figure 4.24**). As you can see, each is listed in the XML page, and each is read by the screen reader (**Figure 4.25**). Instead of inserting blank lines, use and modify styles to achieve the layout you require.

Figure 4.24 The series of blank returns at the far right of the image can cause problems for screen readers.

```
- <Sect xml:lang="EN-GB">
    <Normal />
    <Normal />
    <Normal />
    <Normal />
    <Normal />
    <Normal />
    <Normal />
    <Normal />
    <Normal />
    <Normal />
    <Normal />
```

Figure 4.25 Blank lines are described in an XML page and identified by a screen reader. Use styles instead of repeated returns to make large spaces in your document's layout.

Add a Text Tag to Describe Your Chart

If you add a chart or an image of a chart to a text box, you can add a text tag for the screen reader to use to describe the object. Select the text box or image in the Word document, and choose Format > Text Box (or Image) > Web. Type a text description of the chart. When the file is converted to XML, you can see the description the screen reader uses for the object.

TIP 33: Planning Documents for PDF Accessibility

TIP 34 Reflowing a Page

Readers using assistive devices or very small screens like those on personal digital assistants (PDAs) often experience a problem called *reflow*. When you zoom in closely to a page, what happens? You see a few words and maybe an image (**Figure 4.26**). Not only do you have to scroll back and forth to see the entire line, but also it's difficult or impossible to understand where you are in the document at any given time.

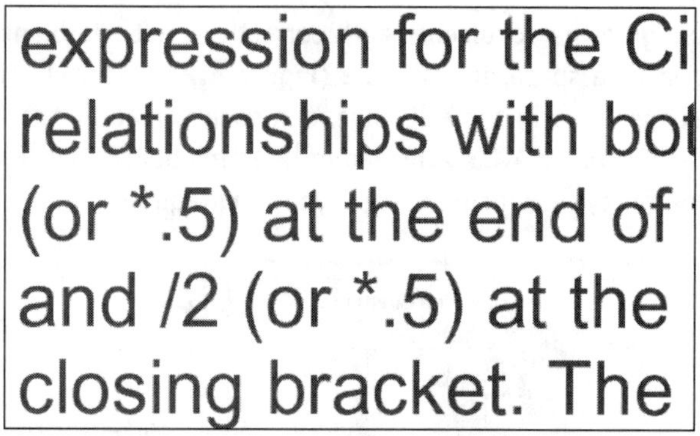

The Way Reflow Works

Reflow is not a permanent format. Each time you reset the magnification with a Zoom tool, the reflow is turned off. It's adjustable, based on the viewer's settings and device. Reflow adjusts itself to whatever magnification the viewer uses, and it also resizes itself to whatever document page size the viewer uses if viewing a document in Acrobat.

> # expression for the Ci
> # relationships with bot
> # (or *.5) at the end of
> # and /2 (or *.5) at the
> # closing bracket. The

Figure 4.26 You can zoom into a page at a very high magnification, but then it is difficult to determine where you are on a page.

If the document is tagged, you have more viewing options available. You can control how the page reflows to make viewing the content simpler. Use the Zoom tools or shortcut keys to zoom in to the size you want to view. At the bottom of **Figure 4.27** the size of the document is shown as 1.69 x 19.64 inches. As you zoom in and out of the Document pane, the size of the document changes. Choose View > Reflow. The text automatically wraps itself to the next lines, and you don't need to use the horizontal scroll bar to read the text.

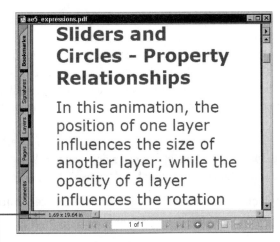

Figure 4.27 Choosing Reflow Page wraps the content of pages automatically, no matter what size they are.

Document Size

The process is fairly reliable. However, with a complex document such as one using numerous columns, images, and text boxes, the page isn't necessarily presented in the optimal reading order. For example, a person reading the entire page may read a sentence, refer to the image, and then return to the next sentence. In a reflow view, the document is read as presented—that is, in the order the content appears on the page (**Figure 4.28**). The content can be controlled using *articles*, which we discuss in the next tip.

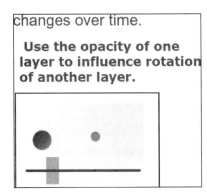

Figure 4.28 A document is read from top to bottom regardless of the layout or how you would ordinarily read a page when seen in a reflow view.

TIP 34: Reflowing a Page

35 Organizing with Articles

Articles are areas on a page that you define to give you control over how the viewer reads your page. They're especially useful for viewing complex documents, such as magazine articles, that contain the story in several columns on different pages of a document. They let you design a document both for visual appearance (as in a multicolumned, multipage layout) and for ease of reading using magnified views.

Adding articles to a document is much simpler than reformatting and providing optional versions of the same document. Follow these steps to control a reading path through a document using articles:

1. Choose Tools > Advanced Editing > Show Advanced Editing Toolbar to open the toolbar shown in **Figure 4.29**.

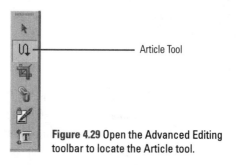

Article Tool

Figure 4.29 Open the Advanced Editing toolbar to locate the Article tool.

2. Click the Article tool to select it. The pointer changes to crosshairs.

3. In your PDF document, click and drag a rectangle marquee to draw the first article. Release the mouse, and Acrobat draws the first article box in your document. The article box is numbered 1-1 (**Figure 4.30**). The Article tool doesn't select text or images, it merely draws a shape on the page. Anything within the margins of the article box become part of the article.

Article Number

Using Expressions and Parent-Child Relationships in After Effects

Figure 4.30 Articles are defined by boxes and automatically numbered.

4. Continue adding article boxes (**Figure 4.31**). As you draw boxes around pieces of text or images, Acrobat numbers the articles consecutively. The sequence of boxes using the same article number is called an *article thread*.

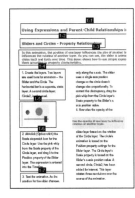

Figure 4.31 Draw a series of boxes with the Article tool to identify consecutive areas on the document.

5. Press Esc (or Return) or select another tool to stop the article drawing. The Article Properties dialog opens (**Figure 4.32**).

Figure 4.32 Name the article thread and add other information if desired.

6. Enter information about the article in the dialog. You must name the article, but the other information is optional.

7. Click OK and save the document.

The key is understanding how one reads a page and then simulating that as closely as possible for all your viewers.

The Shape of Article Boxes

When you select an article box, you see handles at the sides of the box. Drag the handles to resize the box. You can also drag the entire article box to another location on the page. The content on the page and the article box aren't one and the same.

Reading Articles

Adding articles to a complex document, such as one using multiple pages and columns, determines a path through the document to make it easier to read when using magnified views. You view articles in a different way than you would using a reflow view (covered in Tip 34). When you have finished adding a set of articles to a document, use the Hand tool or keystrokes to test the articles. Click anywhere on the page to start reading an article.

The pointer changes to the follow-article pointer 🖑. Scroll through the page using the mouse wheel or by dragging the Hand tool down the page. To navigate through the article:

- Press Return to go to the next page in the article.

- Shift-click or Shift-Return in the article to return to the previous page.

- Ctrl/Option-click in the article to go to the beginning.

When you reach the end of the article, the pointer changes to the end-article pointer 🖑. Press Return or click to return to the view displayed before you started reading the article.

You can also use the Articles pane to read articles in a document. Choose View > Navigation Tabs > Articles to open the Articles pane, and click the article you want to read (**Figure 4.33**). Double-click the article's title or icon to start reading at the beginning of the article. Acrobat displays that article in the Document pane.

Articles or Bookmarks?

In some types of documents, such as those with multiple columns, it's simpler to navigate through the document using a set of articles (assuming they are given descriptive names) than to use bookmarks, as the content is displayed sequentially regardless of where it actually is placed in the document.

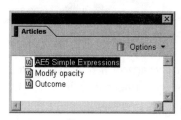

Figure 4.33 Use the Articles pane to select different article threads.

Note
You can't use the Articles pane in a Web browser; you must use it from within Acrobat on either a computer or handheld device.

CHAPTER FIVE

Touching Up a PDF Document

Acrobat is not an editing program. Although you can convert documents originally produced by page-layout, image-manipulation, word-processing, and spreadsheet programs, Acrobat isn't meant to do extensive editing of content.

Instead, Acrobat offers effective tools for managing various aspects of your document. You can readily recombine content from a number of sources, as discussed in the tips in Chapter 2. Using Acrobat as a controlling mechanism, you combine documents and add pages from other documents and other sources.

Once the material is in Acrobat, you have a lot of choices for organizing and reworking page arrangements. You can combine a variety of documents and then apply page numbers, backgrounds, and watermarks. Acrobat also lets you touch up content and work with images, tables, and text. You can even modify text attributes, such as font sizing and spacing.

The key question to ask yourself as you work on a project is whether your efforts are simple touchups or actually full-blown edits. Replacing content in Acrobat is easy, and you may find it quicker to return to the source program to make any significant edits, and then convert and replace the content in your Acrobat document.

Deleting Pages from a Document

Sometimes when you combine content from several documents, you have pages of information you don't need. You can easily delete a single page or a group of pages.

1. Open your document and click the Pages tab at the left of the screen to display the Pages pane. The pages are shown in small images, called *thumbnails* (**Figure 5.1**).

Figure 5.1 Content appears as small thumbnail images in the Pages pane.

The first page is displayed in the Document pane. In the Pages pane, you can see that the first thumbnail is highlighted and that a red box surrounds some of the page contents (**Figure 5.2**). This means that page 1 is showing in the Document pane, and the visible portion of the page is outlined with the red box.

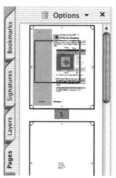

Figure 5.2 A box in the thumbnail indicates what content is displayed in the Document pane.

2. Let's remove the third page from the document. Use the scroll bars in the Pages pane to move page 3 into view and click the page to select it (**Figure 5.3**). The thumbnail is highlighted; the page displays in the Document pane.

A Quicker Way To Delete

If you're deleting only one page, not a range, there's a faster method. Instead of choosing the menu item and then following through the dialogs, you can select the page in the Pages pane and press Delete on the keyboard. You'll see the confirmation dialog; click OK, and the page is gone.

Figure 5.3 Select a page thumbnail to display the page in the Document pane.

3. From the Options menu in the Pages pane, select Delete Pages (**Figure 5.4**). The Delete Pages dialog opens.

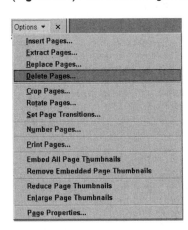

Figure 5.4 Use the Options menu in the Pages pane to access common page commands.

(Continued)

TIP 36: Deleting Pages from a Document

4. The Delete Pages dialog has two options. Choosing the Selected option deletes the pages you have selected. If you prefer, you can click the From option and enter the range of page numbers you want to delete. In this example, I selected page 3 in step 2; the Selected option is active in the Delete Pages dialog (**Figure 5.5**), so simply click OK.

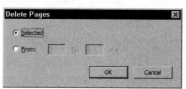

Figure 5.5 Select an option for deleting a page or pages.

5. A confirmation dialog opens; click OK to confirm the page deletion (**Figure 5.6**). The dialog closes, and Acrobat deletes the page from your document.

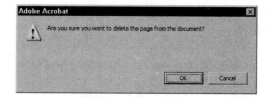

Figure 5.6 This warning dialog asks you to confirm page deletions.

TIP 37 Inserting Pages

Although you can combine several documents into a single PDF file called a *binder*, you don't have to combine complete documents. You can quickly add particular pages to a document using the Pages pane.

1. In the Pages pane, click the page *before* the location where you want to insert additional pages. For this example, we want the first of our new pages to follow page 3, so click page 3's thumbnail picture.

2. In the Pages pane, choose Options > Insert Pages. The Select File To Insert dialog opens (**Figure 5.7**). Locate the file you want to use and click Select. The dialog closes, and the Insert Pages dialog opens.

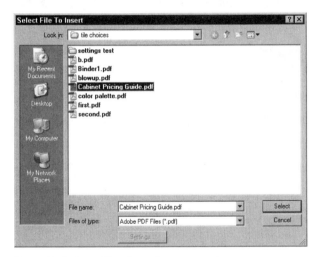

Figure 5.7 Select a file to insert into an open document.

Note

If you choose a PDF document, the pages are added immediately. If you choose another type of file, the document is converted to PDF before the process continues.

(Continued)

3. Specify the location where you want to add the document. The default is After; because we selected page 3 before opening the dialog, the Page radio button is automatically selected and 3 appears in the text box (**Figure 5.8**). The page will be inserted after page 3.

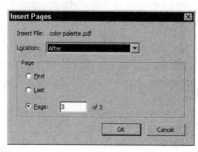

Figure 5.8 If you select the page thumbnail, the Page option is already enabled when you open the dialog.

4. Click OK to close the Insert Pages dialog. Acrobat adds the page to your document; as the Pages pane in **Figure 5.9** shows, we now have four pages.

Figure 5.9 The new document page is added at the location you specify, in this case, at the end.

Insert Pages in Front

Sometimes you need to insert a new page *before* an existing page in your document. For example, you may need to add a cover page to a catalog or marketing brochure. In the Insert Pages dialog box, simply click the Location pull-down list and choose Before, then click OK to close the dialog. Acrobat adds the page to your document precisely where you want it.

TIP 38
Building Documents Using the Pages Pane

Here's a real timesaving process that's terrific for visual people. Rather than combining document content through dialogs, you can do it visually using the Pages pane.

Start with two documents, one to which you want to add pages (the *recipient*) and the other from which you're taking pages (the *donor*).

1. With both documents open, choose Window > Tile > Horizontally. The two document windows display in a stack on the screen (**Figure 5.10**).

2. Click the Pages tab on each document to open it and generate thumbnails. Drag the right margin of the Pages pane to the right to display the largest possible number of page thumbnails.

Note
You can drag the Pages pane to fill the entire screen, but in a very large document you still won't see all the thumbnails in the document.

Figure 5.10 Stack the two documents on top of each other. In these documents, the Pages panes are enlarged to show several thumbnails.

(Continued)

3. Select the page thumbnails from the donor document (**Figure 5.11**).

Figure 5.11 You can select multiple page thumbnails.

4. Drag the thumbnails from the donor document's Pages pane to the recipient document's Pages pane. You see a heavy black line at the position of the pointer (**Figure 5.12**).

Figure 5.12 When you drag thumbnail images from one document to another, you see a heavy black line between the thumbnails at your pointer's position.

5. When you're in the right spot, release the mouse. Acrobat adds the page thumbnails to the Pages pane and the pages themselves to the document (**Figure 5.13**). The original donor document is unaffected.

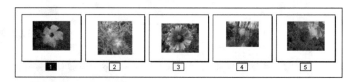

Figure 5.13 The page thumbnails are added to the Pages pane and the pages are added to the document.

6. Organize and arrange the pages as desired. Save the file, and then close the donor document.

TIP 39 Extracting Content

Suppose you have a multipage document and you want to remove a part of it for another purpose, such as combining it with other information for another document. In this tip, I'll explain how to separate, or *extract*, a portion of a document.

1. Let's extract several nonconsecutive pages from the same document. First, we'll group them together. In the Pages pane's thumbnails view, click page 5 to select it, and then drag it up to the current page 2 position. A solid line appears above page 4. As the page is moved, a solid line shows where it will relocate if you release the mouse.

2. Now the three pages we want to work with are in consecutive order and can be selected as a group. Click page 2 to select it, and then Shift+click page 4 to select all three pages (**Figure 5.14**).

Figure 5.14 A selected thumbnail and its page number are framed in black; as you drag the thumbnail, a solid black line indicates where the page is moved if you release the mouse.

3. Choose Options > Extract Pages from the Pages pane menu. The Extract Pages dialog opens. Because we selected the pages in the Pages pane, the page numbers (2–4) already appear in the dialog (**Figure 5.15**).

Figure 5.15 Preselected page thumbnails are listed in the Extract Pages dialog when it opens.

(Continued)

Deleting Pages for Good

If you're sure that you want to permanently separate content from one document into two (or more) documents, click the Delete Pages After Extracting option in the Extract Pages dialog. Be warned, however: If you choose this option, the extracted pages will be permanently removed from your original document.

Extracting from a Large Document

This tip shows a quick and simple method for reorganizing the pages in a short document to make extraction a one-step process. For large documents, that isn't always a good idea. It is too easy to get confused, extract pages you don't need to or forget those you do, costing you time in the long run. In a large document, it is simpler to extract groups of pages and then recombine them into one new document.

To the default *"Pages from"* names that Acrobat gives to extracted pages, I append a number for each separate group, such as "Pages from xx.pdf 1" and "Pages from xx.pdf 2". Later, when I combine the extracted material into a single document, it's simple to arrange them numerically, and I don't have to spend time trying to figure out which extracted pages go where.

4. Click OK to close the dialog. Acrobat extracts the pages and creates a new document. As **Figure 5.16** shows, the document filename includes the "Pages from" prefix.

Figure 5.16 The new document is named according to its source.

Note

When working on complicated projects I leave the default "Pages from" names. It helps to organize content, the location of some documents, and where they originated.

5. Save the new file and close it. Acrobat returns you to the original document.

6. In step 1 you moved pages to make selecting pages for extraction a one-step process. Before finishing, you should restore the order of the document. Choose File > Revert to open the dialog shown in **Figure 5.17**. Click Revert to return to where you started before the extraction, with the pages in their original order.

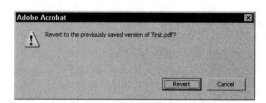

Figure 5.17 Use the Revert command to restore your document to its last-saved status.

TIP 40 Replacing Pages

Say you edit a page in a source program, whether it's changing text, adjusting margins or some other non-Acrobat work. After you convert it to PDF, you want to put it back into the Acrobat document. Should you insert it or replace it? What's the difference? It depends on what else is on the page.

For example, you may have a page with a large number of comments or links on it. If you merely inserted an edited version of the page and deleted the one you want to remove, you'd lose all your comments and links. When you use the Replace command, Acrobat replaces the underlying page and the overlying content, including comments and links, isn't affected.

In our sample document, let's modify the layout of the final section on page 1 (**Figure 5.18**).

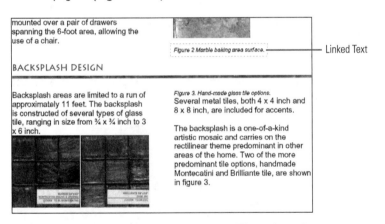

Figure 5.18 The third section of this page needs a different layout but we don't want to disturb the linked text.

1. Make your changes in the source program and convert the page to a new PDF.

2. Open the document in which you want to replace the page.

3. In the Pages pane, choose Options > Replace Pages.

(Continued)

Sometimes you have a choice of whether to replace or insert pages; other times, you should most likely just replace. Whichever your choice, you can easily access the command in the Options menu of the Pages pane.

Choose to either insert or replace when:

- You are in the early stages of a document and haven't added backgrounds, headers and footers, or interactive elements such as links.

- Your document is simple, containing no overlying elements.

- You want to rebuild the whole document, and the existing links, bookmarks, or actions will be replaced.

Replace a page when:

- Your document has a lot of overlying structures such as links, bookmarks, or hyperlinks that you want to preserve.

- You want to make changes to a page that are more than the Acrobat editing tools can handle. Revise the original, make a PDF, and replace the corrected page(s).

4. In the resulting browser dialog, locate the new PDF file and click Select (**Figure 5.19**). The dialog closes, and the Replace Pages dialog opens.

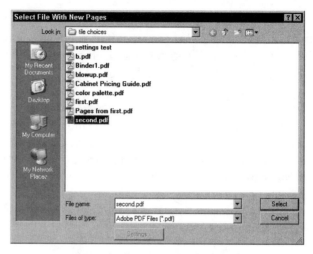

Figure 5.19 Choose a document that will replace the content in your open document.

5. Specify the page numbers in both the Original and Replacement sections of the dialog (**Figure 5.20**). Click OK.

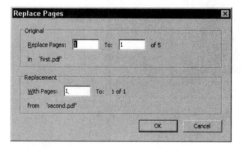

Figure 5.20 Specify the page numbers in both documents.

6. Click OK in the confirmation dialog (**Figure 5.21**). The dialog closes and Acrobat replaces the original page with the new one.

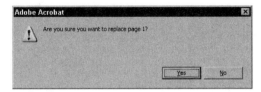

Figure 5.21 Confirm the page replacement.

You can see that the content in the lower section of the page is changed and that the link is still visible around the "Figure 2. Marble baking area surface" text (**Figure 5.22**).

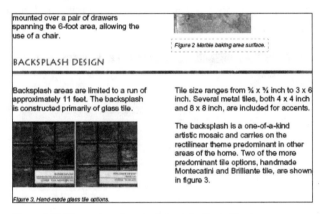

Figure 5.22 The replaced content doesn't affect objects such as links.

TIP
41 Cropping and Rotating Pages

Acrobat lets you import a document in one layout and then customize its appearance. However, if you combine several documents from different sources, you may find discrepancies in the page sizes or orientations. A neat feature in Acrobat is the ability to crop and rotate pages to get them looking just so.

Cropping Pages

Let's say two pages in our sample document need cropping.

1. Click the page you want to crop in the Pages pane.

2. Choose Options > Crop Pages. If you're working from the Document pane, choose Document > Pages > Crop. The Crop Pages dialog opens (**Figure 5.23**).

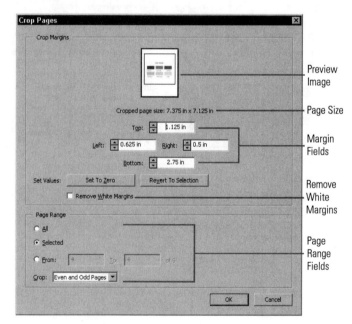

Figure 5.23 You can crop on all four sides in the Crop Pages dialog.

3. The page appears as a thumbnail at the top of the Crop Pages dialog. Adjust the crop settings using the four margin fields. As you change the values, the cropping outline in the preview image changes to reflect the new values. You can type values in the fields, or use the arrows to adjust the settings.

4. Click OK to close the dialog, and Acrobat resizes the page. You can see the effects of the cropping in the Document pane, as well as in the Pages pane's thumbnail (**Figure 5.24**).

Figure 5.24 You can see the cropped page in the Pages pane.

5. Save the document to preserve the cropping.

Lose Those Margins

In the Crop Pages dialog, click Remove White Margins to crop the page to the content. Then click the option again to deselect it. The values in the crop directions remain, and you can make final adjustments. If your page's content is quite small compared to the page's size, using this option is much quicker than clicking, and clicking, and clicking...

Rotating Pages

I want to rotate page 3 of my document. The page is an image of a slab of concrete that I'd like to be vertical instead of horizontal.

1. Select the page in the Pages pane. Choose Options > Rotate or Document > Pages > Rotate to open the Rotate Pages dialog.

2. Choose a direction from the Direction pull-down list (**Figure 5.25**).

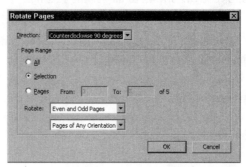

Figure 5.25 Choose a direction for rotating the page.

3. Select a Page Range option. Because in step 1 you selected the page in the Pages pane, the Selection option is automatically active.

Note

You can choose pages within a selection according to orientation and position. Click the pull-down list and choose either odd or even pages; click the lower pull-down list to specify portrait or landscape orientation.

4. Click OK, and Acrobat rotates the page (**Figure 5.26**).

Figure 5.26 The page is rotated; the text is now vertical.

TIP 42 Configuring the Pages Pane

The default layout of the Pages pane displays a single column of small thumbnail pictures of the pages. The default is fine for most kinds of work when you have a document consisting of several pages. However, when working with a very large document, you might want to make the thumbnails smaller and increase the number of thumbnail columns to see more at once. If you have to be able to see the content of the thumbnails, you'll want to increase their size.

• To increase or decrease the size of thumbnails, choose Options > Enlarge (or Reduce) Page Thumbnails.

Use a thumbnail size that is meaningful. In **Figure 5.27**, the thumbnails are set to the smallest size available—so small that they are of limited reference value. Conversely, you can enlarge thumbnails to the size of the Document pane, but that pretty much defeats the purpose.

See More Pages

Decrease the size of the thumbnails when working with large documents. This gives you a better overview of the content and can reveal problems like irregular page sizes.

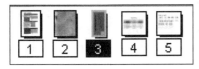

Figure 5.27 You can change the size of page thumbnails in the Pages pane. These thumbnails are too small to see content, but you can look at various page sizes.

• Resize the Pages pane. Move the pointer over the right margin of the panel. When it changes to a double-ended arrow and vertical bars, click and drag to the left or right to adjust the size of the panel (**Figure 5.28**).

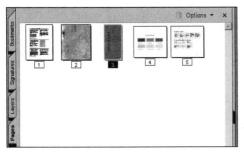

Figure 5.28 Resize the Pages pane horizontally.

(Continued)

TIP 42: Configuring the Pages Pane

Managing Thumbnails

You can choose to embed or unembed thumbnails. Which is best?

Embedded thumbnails add to a file's size. On the other hand, if you embed the thumbnails when you're working with large documents, opening, closing, resizing, and scrolling through the Pages pane is much speedier. Embed thumbnails from the Pages pane by choosing Options > Embed All Page Thumbnails; unembed by choosing Options > Remove Embedded Page Thumbnails.

Be careful when using embedded thumbnails. Although they give you an instant view of the pages, changes you make to your pages are not updated in embedded thumbnails. To display the thumbnails with your changes, you have to unembed the old ones first and then re-embed the edited ones.

- Use thumbnail views to control what you view in the Document pane. Click a thumbnail view and do one of the following:

  - Position the pointer over the lower-right corner of the red page-view box until the pointer changes to a double arrow. Drag the corner to reduce or expand the page view in the Document pane (**Figure 5.29**).

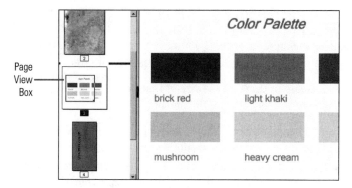

Figure 5.29 Resize or shift the page-view box to show a different portion of the page in the Document pane.

  - Move the pointer over the red page-view box until the pointer changes to a hand. Drag the page-view box around on the thumbnail to see a different portion of the page in the Document pane.

TIP 43 Adding Page Numbers to a Document

When you combine pages for a project you end up with one document. Page numbers are shown on the status bar below the document in the Document pane and are numbered in logical order—that is, the first page is page 1, and so on. Depending on the size and purpose of the document, you often have to renumber pages, or even number pages in sequences.

My example document has five pages, currently numbered 1 through 5. I want to change the numbering:

- Page 1 remains page 1 (nothing to change here!)
- Page 2 becomes page 1-a
- Page 3 becomes page 1-b
- Page 4 becomes page 2
- Page 5 becomes page 3

Here's how to add and modify page numbers.

1. In the Pages pane, click page 2 to select it. Choose Options > Number Pages to open the Page Numbering dialog.

The Selected option is already active because I selected the page in the Pages pane (**Figure 5.30**).

Figure 5.30 Selected page thumbnails are identified in the dialog.

(Continued)

2. Leave the Begin new section option selected in the Numbering section of the dialog. Then click the Style pull-down list to choose a page format. As shown in **Figure 5.31**, our example uses lowercase letters for the page renumbering.

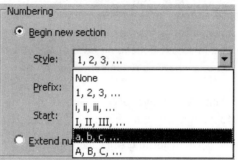

Figure 5.31 You can choose among several page-numbering formats.

3. Enter a value in the Prefix field, as well as punctuation if desired. Then enter the starting letter in the Start field (**Figure 5.32**). Click OK to close the dialog.

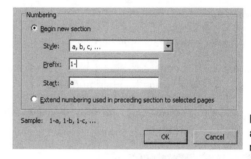

Figure 5.32 You can add a prefix to page numbers.

Acrobat modifies the page numbers; as **Figure 5.33** shows, we now have pages 1-a and 1-b. The last two pages are renumbered pages 2 and 3.

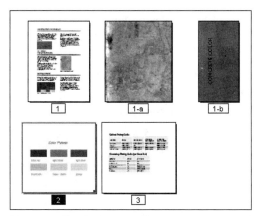

Figure 5.33 Numbering is applied to pages automatically; the other page numbers change accordingly.

4. In the status bar, the page numbers reflect both the page count as well as the numbering you added (**Figure 5.34**).

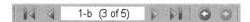

Figure 5.34 The status bar displays both the logical numbering as well as the custom numbers.

Numbering Nuggets

- Whenever possible, remove visible page numbers from source material before converting it to a PDF. Using Acrobat-based page numbering is easier when the pages contain no numbers to conflict with the numbers displayed on the status bar or in the Pages pane.

- Consider the document's use. Many documents need simple page numbering. However, if you are assembling a technical manual, you will likely use prefixes identifying content based on chapters, systems, and so on.

- If you are building a book structure, consider how the book will look when printed. Books use front matter like a table of contents and other introductory material that is numbered differently from chapter content.

TIP 44 Adding Headers and Footers

Along with assigning page numbers to documents, you can add precise headers and footers to the pages. When adding them in Acrobat, you should avoid using source documents with visible headers and footers to prevent confusion. I'm going to add some footer information, including custom text, to a document.

1. From the main program menu, choose Document > Add Headers & Footers. The Add Headers & Footers dialog opens (**Figure 5.35**). Click the Footer tab to open the appropriate dialog. Headers and footers use individual tabs in the dialog; each contains the same options.

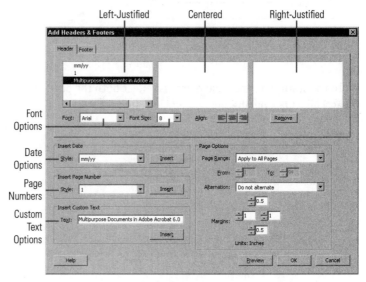

Figure 5.35 The dialog gives you a lot of options for adding custom headers and footers to your document.

At the top of the dialog are three boxes, which will hold the content that you want to be left-justified, centered, or right-justified on the document page. All the content is added initially to the left-justified box; you can move it to the location where you want it placed.

2. Choose the font and font size from the dropdown lists below the header/footer content boxes.

Note
You have to preview the page to see font effects.

3. Make entries in the Insert fields as desired. For this example, you want to use a date, page numbering, and custom text (**Figure 5.36**):

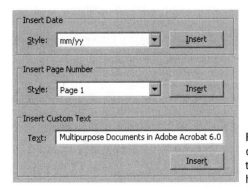

Figure 5.36 Select content to insert and type content for the header or footer.

- To insert the date, click the Style pull-down list under Insert Date, choose a format, and click Insert.

- To insert page numbers, click the Style pull-down list under Insert Page Number, choose a format, and click Insert.

- To add custom text, type your text in the field under Insert Custom Text and click Insert.

4. When the items are added to the Footer box, click each item and then click the alignment icon to move it to its respective location (**Figure 5.37**).

Figure 5.37 Move content to its respective page locations.

(Continued)

Fun with Headers and Footers

Well, maybe not fun, but experimenting with headers and footers can be interesting and useful for guiding readers through your document. This book, for example, displays either the chapter or tip title in the footer, depending on the page number. Short of setting up this style in a page-layout program, how can you add a touch like this to your long documents?

In the dialog, enter the footer information for the right-hand, odd numbered pages into the right-aligned field. Choose Odd Pages Only from the Alternation listing in the Page Options area of the dialog. Click OK to apply.

For the left-hand pages, reopen the dialog and repeat with the even-numbered page information. This time, choose Even Pages Only from the Alternation listing, and enter the text in the left-aligned field.

TIP 44: Adding Headers and Footers

5. The final layout shows the correct blocks of text in the correct areas. To remove text, select it in the text boxes and click Remove (**Figure 5.38**).

Remove Button

Figure 5.38 Select an item to delete and click Remove.

6. In the Page Options section, make selections as required for your document. For our sample document:

- Choose Apply to Page Range from the Page Range pull-down list. The other option is Apply to All Pages.

- Define the page range in the From and To fields.

- Set the margins for the layout. To use a nonstandard value, type the number in the field, as shown in the bottom-most field (**Figure 5.39**).

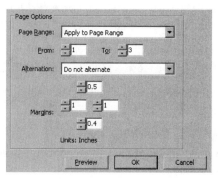

Figure 5.39 Define locations for the footer by setting margins.

Note
The top margin applies to headers; the bottom margin applies to footers.

7. Click Preview to see the layout of the footer elements in a pop-up Preview window. You can see the selected font and font size in the preview as well **(Figure 5.40)**. Click OK to close the Preview window.

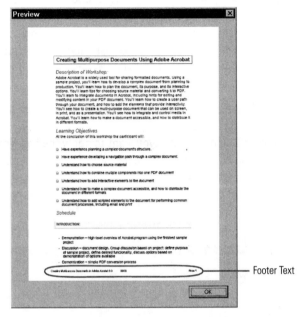

Footer Text

Figure 5.40 Preview the page before closing the dialog.

8. Click OK to close the dialog and apply the footer. The content and numbering are applied to the page in the area specified.

Modifying Headers and Footers

To modify headers or footers after you've applied them to the document, choose Document > Add Headers & Footers, then make your changes. If you've already saved the document and you want to delete the header or footer, open the dialog and click OK without inserting anything in the boxes. The header or footer will disappear. You can also edit the information using the TouchUp Text tool (covered in Tip 47).

Using Watermarks and Backgrounds

Acrobat lets you add watermarks or backgrounds to a document once the components are assembled to create a cohesive product. Watermarks overlay the page content; backgrounds are, to state the obvious, applied to the background of the page behind the content. In this tip, we show you how to apply and configure a background.

Note
Before you start, create the background content and save it as a PDF file.

1. Open the document to which you want to apply the background or watermark. Our sample document has five pages, each containing one large image.

2. Choose Document > Add Watermark & Background to open the dialog shown in **Figure 5.41**.

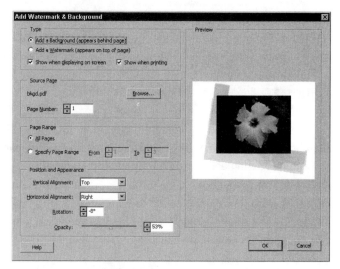

Figure 5.41 You can apply both backgrounds and watermarks to documents using the same dialog.

3. Choose watermark or background in the Type area, and then specify where you want the background to display (it can be shown on screen and in print) (**Figure 5.42**).

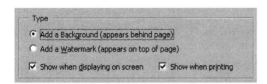

Figure 5.42 I want this background to display both on screen and in print.

4. Click Browse to select a source document to use for the background. If the document has more than one page, select the page you want to use.

5. Select the range of pages you want to receive the background (**Figure 5.43**).

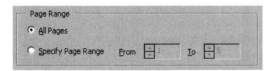

Figure 5.43 You can apply the background to a specified range of pages.

Note

If you want to apply the background to pages that are scattered throughout a document, arrange them in the Pages pane in a continuous sequence before opening the Watermark & Background dialog. Or you can reapply the command several times to apply the background throughout the document.

6. Modify the position and appearance of the background content as desired. Then set the horizontal and vertical alignments and rotation. Adjust the opacity by using the slider (**Figure 5.44**).

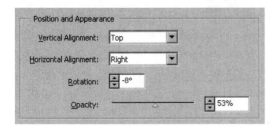

Figure 5.44 You can adjust the background's location on the page.

(Continued)

TIP 45: Using Watermarks and Backgrounds

Some Background on Backgrounds

Once the file is saved with the background, you can't remove it, so if you aren't sure about the background, or want to use the document both with and without a background or watermark, save the file with another name.

There is a tricky workaround for the permanent background. Create a PDF from a blank source document, such as a single-page, blank Microsoft Word document. Then open the PDF file with the undesired background. Choose Document > Watermark & Background to open the dialog. Click Browse, locate the blank background, and select it. The blank page replaces the background.

7. Check your adjustments in the Preview area (**Figure 5.45**). When you are satisfied with the results, click OK to close the dialog.

Figure 5.45 Preview the page before closing the dialog.

Note

If you have one page in particular that you aren't sure about, move that page to the start of the document. In the Watermark & Background dialog, the first page is shown in the preview area.

8. Acrobat applies the background to the pages selected, as you can see in the page thumbnails view of the document (**Figure 5.46**).

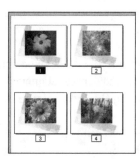

Figure 5.46 The background is applied to the document according to your settings. You'll see it displayed in the Pages pane.

TIP 46 Reusing Page Elements

Love that illustration, or want to quote a block of text from an Acrobat document? If the security settings for a document allow changes, you can reuse most of its components (such as text or images) in a PDF file. If you didn't create the document and can't get a copy of the source document, you can work from within Acrobat. Sometimes you'll want to combine pieces from several PDFs into a single document, in which case it's much more efficient to work with the PDF files rather than the source material.

Acrobat provides three Select tools, all located on a submenu off the Basic toolbar (**Figure 5.47**). Rather than reopening the submenu and changing tools, you can display the toolbar. Click the pull-down arrow next to the visible Select tool and choose Show Selection Toolbar. When I am starting to assemble a project, I prefer to keep the toolbar open (**Figure 5.48**).

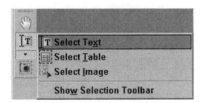

Figure 5.47 The Select Text tool is one of three Select tools on the Basic toolbar.

Figure 5.48 The Selection toolbar can be moved or docked like any other toolbar.

Editing Text

Although sometimes it's simpler to modify a source document than edit text on the PDF document, that isn't always the case. For small or simple text changes, you can work in Acrobat. Acrobat offers three different tools to work with text.

Use the Select Text tool [IT] to select text for copying and pasting into another document. On the Advanced Editing toolbar, use the TouchUp Text tool [IT] to modify and edit text, or to add new text to a page. You can also use the Text Box tool [TE] on the Advanced Commenting toolbar, discussed in the next chapter.

Reusing Text

Use the Select Text tool to identify text in a document for use in other documents or to attach actions:

1. On the Basic toolbar, click the pull-down arrow next to the visible Select tool to open a submenu. Click the Select Text tool to activate it.

2. Click within the document text with the tool. Acrobat outlines the paragraph with a black bounding box (**Figure 5.49**).

Figure 5.49 Use the Select Text tool to identify a block of text on a document page.

3. You can select only one paragraph at a time. Click at the start of the paragraph and drag down to select the text (**Figure 5.50**).

Figure 5.50 Click and drag with the tool to select a paragraph or portion of a paragraph.

Note
If you want to select all the text in a document, select a word or paragraph with the Select Text tool, then right-click (Control-click on a Mac) and choose Select All Text from the shortcut menu.

4. Choose Edit > Copy, or Ctrl+C/Command+C. Open the document you want to add the text to and paste it in place.

Note
The Select Text tool is also great for selecting precise words and phrases to use for bookmarks and links, discussed in Chapter 7.

Reusing Images

You can reuse individual images from a document. Begin by clicking the Select Image tool ▒ Select Image ▾ on the Selection toolbar. Then, to select an image:

1. Click the image you want to copy. The "negative" of the image appears on the page (**Figure 5.51**).

Figure 5.51 When you select an image, you'll see a negative of it on the screen.

If you want to select a portion of the image, click and drag a marquee around the area (**Figure 5.52**).

Figure 5.52 Drag a marquee to select a portion of an image.

Note

*Be careful how you select an image when it overlays a background. In **Figure 5.53**, although it appears that the flower image is selected, in reality only the background is selected.*

Figure 5.53 You can also select an image background applied to a document. Make sure you're selecting the right thing.

(Continued)

TIP 46: Reusing Page Elements

Drag and Drop Shot

You don't have to mess around with copying and pasting when you're moving images. Open the recipient document next to the document with the image. Arrange the windows on the screen. Then, select the image in the PDF document and drag it to the other document.

2. Once you have the image or image segment copied, you can reuse it. Use the old standby Edit > Copy and choose Edit > Paste in the document where you want to use the image.

3. You can also save the image as a file. Select the image in the document, and then right-click to open the shortcut menu. Choose Save Image As, name the image, and specify the save location.

Reusing Both Text and Images

What if you want to reuse some of the content on a page that contains both text and graphics? You can copy and paste each element separately, or you can use the snazzy new Snapshot tool.

1. Select the Snapshot tool 📷 on the Basic toolbar.

2. Select the content from the page:

- Click anywhere on the document to capture the visible content on the Document pane.

- Drag a marquee around a portion of the page.

- Drag a marquee around a portion of an image (**Figure 5.54**).

Figure 5.54 Using the Snapshot tool, you can drag a marquee to select a portion of the image.

3. An information dialog appears telling you that the content has been copied to the clipboard (**Figure 5.55**). Click OK.

Figure 5.55 Your captured content is copied to the clipboard.

4. Paste the clipboard content wherever you need it.

Snapshot? Maybe Not

If you need to modify or index the text you're copying, don't use the Snapshot tool; use the Select Text tool instead. Content copied with the Snapshot tool creates a graphic, uneditable image of whatever it captures, whether it's images or text.

TIP 47 Editing Text in a PDF

Here's a common scenario: You publish a catalog, which is updated once a year, but you want to keep the date on the pages current. Do you have to regenerate the PDF file from the source application every time you want to modify the date? Here's another example: You send marketing material to certain people, and you have a couple of spots on the document where you want to use the client's name. Do you have to make separate PDF files for each client?

No and no. You can easily touch up text in Acrobat using the TouchUp Text tool, hidden in the Advanced Editing toolbar. Save some time by opening the toolbar instead of just choosing the tool. Choose Tools > Advanced Editing > Show Advanced Editing Toolbar. Drag the toolbar to the toolbar area or to the side of the program window to dock it (**Figure 5.56**).

TouchUp Text tool ————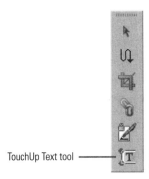

Figure 5.56 Open the Advanced Editing toolbar to find the TouchUp Text tool.

Touching Up Text

You can easily make small edits to lines of text in a document:

1. Select the TouchUp Text tool [T] on the Advanced Editing toolbar.

2. Click within the text you want to edit. A bounding box outlines the text you can select (**Figure 5.57**).

(Continued)

Consider the Source

Sometimes the touch-up results aren't what you expect. It isn't Acrobat's fault; it's related to what you used in the source program. For example, many Word documents contain bold or italic text—or so it appears. In reality this is probably just a bold or italic text *appearance*. Unless you are using a bold or italic font (Arial Bold or Arial Italic, for example) when you try to touch up text in Acrobat you won't have an exact match for the replacement font as Acrobat doesn't simulate a bold or italic appearance.

The solution is simple. Before converting a document to PDF, check the fonts you are using. If the fonts and font faces you use are embedded and subset, you can safely make changes to the text in Acrobat.

A 6-foot baking area is planned with a counter height of 32 inches. This baking area's surface is a red and gold veined marble, shown in Figure 2.

To accommodate the family's needs, the baking area does not have lower cabinets. Instead, the surface is mounted over a pair of drawers spanning the 6-foot area, allowing the use of a chair.

Figure 2 Marble baking area surface.

BACKSPLASH DESIGN

Figure 5.57 Selected text is identified by a bounding box; it can include images and other content.

3. Drag the I-beam pointer to select all or part of the line of text, or position the I-beam pointer where you want to start typing (**Figure 5.58**).

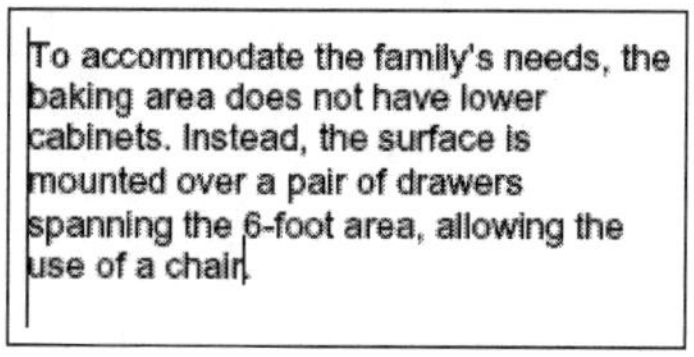

To accommodate the family's needs, the baking area does not have lower cabinets. Instead, the surface is mounted over a pair of drawers spanning the 6-foot area, allowing the use of a chair.

Figure 5.58 Position the I-beam pointer where you want to start typing.

Note

Edit > Select All will select all the text in the bounding box. Click outside the highlighted area to deselect the text.

4. Type the replacement text or add new text at the position of the I-beam pointer (**Figure 5.59**).

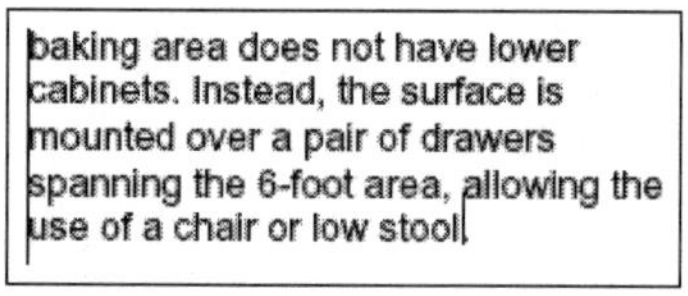

baking area does not have lower cabinets. Instead, the surface is mounted over a pair of drawers spanning the 6-foot area, allowing the use of a chair or low stool.

Figure 5.59 Type text on a row selected with the TouchUp Text tool.

Note

In order for you to edit text in a document, the font must be embedded or available on your system; that's covered in Tip 12 and also in Tip 28.

Adding New Text

You can also add new text to a document using the TouchUp Text tool:

1. Ctrl-click/Option-click within the document where you want to add the text. The New Text Font dialog box opens with the default options—Arial text and horizontal writing mode.

2. Select the font and writing mode (horizontal or vertical), and click OK (**Figure 5.60**).

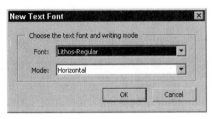

Figure 5.60 Select the desired font and writing mode for your inserted text.

3. The default text "New Text" displays on the page. Select it, and then type the new text (**Figure 5.61**).

Figure 5.61 Your text will appear just as you specified.

4. Click outside the new line of text to finish the process. The text is unselected and the new line of text is complete.

What Goes Up...

If you select a vertical writing mode (available in the dialog shown in Figure 5.60) and the font doesn't write vertically, you'll see an error message informing you that the requested font with the requested writing mode doesn't exist in your system.

If you see this message, click OK to dismiss the dialog. You must either use the font horizontally or use another font that will write in a vertical mode.

TIP 48 Modifying Text Attributes

You can modify properties of new text as well as text already in the document, including:

- Font and font size
- Fill and stroke options
- Font embedding and subsetting
- Spacing between words and characters
- Baseline adjustments

Here's how to do it:

1. With the TouchUp Text tool, click the row of text or select the words or characters you want to edit.

2. Right-click/Control-click the text to open the shortcut menu and choose Properties (**Figure 5.62**) to open the TouchUp Properties dialog.

Figure 5.62
Right-click the text to open a shortcut menu.

3. Click the Font pull-down list and choose a font if necessary. The fonts used in the document appear first; other fonts on your system are listed below a blank space (**Figure 5.63**).

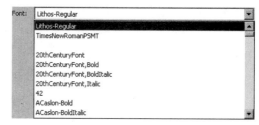

Figure 5.63
Choose a font from the TouchUp Properties dialog.

4. Adjust other text attributes as desired and as the font's attributes allow (**Figure 5.64**).

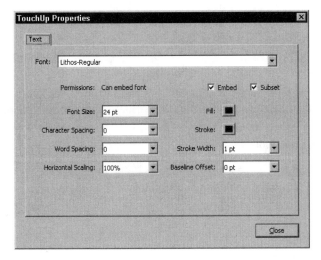

Figure 5.64 Modify other attributes as desired.

5. Click Close to dismiss the dialog and apply the settings.

TIP 49 Reusing Table Information

Tables are not generally considered exciting. They are, however, a very necessary part of business. Up to now, it's been difficult to deal with tables in PDFs, but Acrobat's new Select Table tool is a real timesaver.

Suppose you have a PDF document containing tables, and you need to use the table information but don't have the original source file. Or suppose you want to cut a table out of a PDF document to use as a separate PDF file. Prior to Acrobat 6, the only way to reuse table data was to export the content from the PDF as a rich text format (RTF) file, and then reassemble and restructure the table in Microsoft Word or Excel. Now you can do it quickly and accurately using the Select Table tool.

1. Choose the Select Table tool from the Basic toolbar or from the Selection Tools toolbar if it is open.

2. Drag a marquee around the table you want to export (**Figure 5.65**).

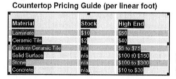

Figure 5.65 Select the table for exporting.

3. Right-click the table to open the shortcut menu (**Figure 5.66**). Choose one of three ways to use the table content:

Figure 5.66 Select an export option from the shortcut menu.

- Choose Copy Selected Table to copy it to the clipboard. Open the document you want to paste the table into, and choose Edit > Paste.

- Choose Save Selected Table As. Name the table, and choose a format from the pull-down list (**Figure 5.67**). Then click Save.

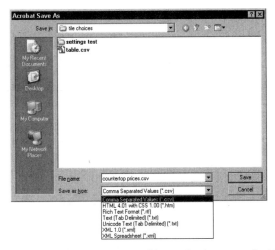

Figure 5.67 Choose a name and format for the exported table.

- Choose Open Table in Spreadsheet. Your spreadsheet application, such as Excel, opens and displays the imported table in a new worksheet (**Figure 5.68**).

	A	B	C
1	Material	Stock	High End
2	Laminate	$10	$50
3	Ceramic Tile	$2	$40
4	Custom Ceramic Tile	n/a	$5 to $75
5	Solid Surface	n/a	$100 t0 $1
6	Stone	n/a	$100 to $3
7	Concrete	n/a	$10 to $30

Figure 5.68 An exported table is converted to an active Excel worksheet.

In both Word and Excel, the tables taken from the PDF document are editable and ready to use.

Note

Spreadsheet programs are designed using a structure called comma-separated values (CSV). When you choose Comma Separated Values from the type list in the Save As dialog, Acrobat pastes the content from a cell location in the Acrobat table to the equivalent location in the spreadsheet.

How to Handle Tables

How you work with a table in a PDF document depends on what you want to do with it.

- If you need part of a table, drag a box around only the portion of the table you want. This method saves time when you paste the table into a receiving document.

- If you aren't sure where you need to use the table save two copies, as both RTF and CSV. That way you have a visual table if you need it in a program such as Word, and a CSV-compliant copy if you need to use it in a spreadsheet. It only takes a few seconds to save the copies in two formats, and can save time later if you have to export in another format.

TIP 49: Reusing Table Information

CHAPTER SIX

Commenting and Sharing Documents

One of Acrobat's strongest features (among a collection of strong features!) is the ability to communicate with others using a single document. In the old days, you could share a document with others, but it wasn't as easy.

Here's a scenario: you're writing a draft of a procedure that requires input from several people. Once you finish the draft, you start it on its route, either as a single or multiple copies, depending on your standard practice. Eventually you receive your original document back from your reviewers, laboriously interpret the comments and notes scribbled in the margins and backs of pages, and generate a second draft. The second draft is circulated; repeat endlessly.

You don't have to do that anymore. Acrobat 6 lets you add a wide variety of comments and then share the comments with your workgroup. Unlike manual paper-based commenting, Acrobat's tools include many types of text comment and edit tools; you can even attach other documents and sound files to a document.

The reviewing feature, new to Acrobat 6, allows you to distribute content by email or online, and then collect and collate the comments. If you created the original document in Microsoft Word XP, you can even import the comments directly into that program for revision. If you are working in Windows, you can set up a review cycle using a Web browser—much faster than interoffice mail!

These tips will show you how to work with the comment tools easily and efficiently, how to use a review cycle, and how to manage comments.

Using the Comment Tools

Acrobat 6 has two commenting toolbars: Commenting and Advanced Commenting. Within these toolbars you'll find pull-down menus and subtoolbars for tool groups, such as drawing tools.

To open the Commenting toolbar, click the Review & Comment taskbar button (**Figure 6.1**). Click the pull-down arrow on the task button to open a list of options, which includes the Commenting toolbar (**Figure 6.2**).

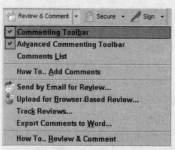

Figure 6.1 Open the Commenting toolbar from the Review & Comment taskbar.

Figure 6.2 The Commenting toolbar consists of several commands and pull-down menus.

The best way to understand how to use the toolbar is to examine its contents. **Table 6.1** breaks the Commenting toolbar down into sections and explains what each item is used for, as well as what the pull-down menus contain.

Toolbar icon	Contains...
Note Tool	The Note tool, which lets you add notes to the document
Text Edits	The Text Edit tools let you indicate text edits on a document.
Stamp	The Stamp tool allows you to add a variety of stamps to a document. You can also use dynamic stamps and create custom stamps.
Highlight	An electronic version of a traditional highlighter, as well as tools that lets you cross out and underline text.
Show	The Show tools, which let you access comments sorted in various ways, view the Comments list, and view the content of comments.

TIP 50   Adding a Note Comment

Of all the comment tools, you'll probably use the note comment most frequently. Here's how it works:

1. Select the Note tool ![Note Tool] on the Commenting toolbar.

2. Click within the document where you want to place the note, or drag to create a custom-sized window. A pop-up window opens (**Figure 6.3**).

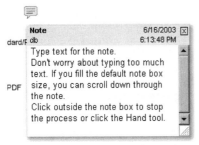

Figure 6.3 A box for typing notes opens automatically over the document.

3. Type the text for your note. If you enter more text than fits in the pop-up window, the text scrolls.

4. To tidy up the page, click the close box in the pop-up window. You can still read the content of your note; just move the pointer over the note's icon on the page and Acrobat displays its contents in a gray tool-tip box (**Figure 6.4**).

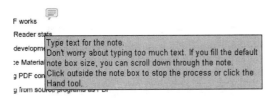

Figure 6.4 Move the pointer over the note icon to display the note's text.

Note
Once a note is added, double-click its icon to open the text box. To delete a note, click the note icon with the Hand tool to select it. Then press Delete on the keyboard.

Working with Note Text

Want to quote some text in your comment, but don't want to type it into the pop-up window? You can use the Select Text tool from the Selection toolbar to copy and paste text from a PDF document into the note. Select, copy, replace, and edit text in the text box as with any other text.

Setting Note Comment Properties

Once the note is added to your document, you can change its appearance and characteristics:

1. Right-click/Control-click the note icon to open the shortcut menu shown in **Figure 6.5**. Choose Properties to open the Note Properties dialog.

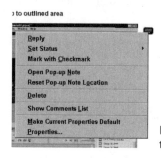

Figure 6.5 Right-click a note icon to open a shortcut menu.

2. On the Appearance tab, choose an icon and a color for the note, as well as an opacity setting for the note box (**Figure 6.6**).

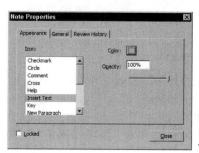

Figure 6.6 Choose the icon style and color on the Appearance tab.

3. Click the General tab and specify the comment author name. You can add a subject for the comment as well (**Figure 6.7**).

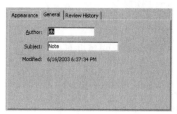

Figure 6.7 Customize the author name and add a subject for the note.

Lock Your Notes

Sometimes you need your comment to stay in place, and don't want to take the risk that another reviewer will go in and change it. Click the Lock option at the lower left of the Note Properties dialog to prevent the comment from being modified or deleted (see Figure 6.6).

4. Click the Review History tab to see the status of the comment. In **Figure 6.8**, you can see that the comment has been accepted by another user.

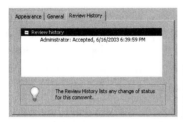

Figure 6.8 During a review, a comment may be changed several times. Check out the story in the Review History panel.

5. Click Close to close the Note Properties dialog and apply the changes.

Using the Properties Bar to Modify Notes

If you're working with a number of notes using various icons, colors, text, and so on, you may find it easier to use the Properties bar than the dialog. Working with the Properties bar is a timesaver because it switches the options available to you depending on what you click. Click the note icon, and the Note Properties options display in the toolbar (**Figure 6.9**).

Figure 6.9 Click the note icon to display the Note Properties options.

The bar switches from the note options to the text options if you click within the note's text area or select some text in the note (**Figure 6.10**).

Figure 6.10 Click or select the text within the note to display the Text Properties.

To access the Properties bar choose View > Toolbars > Properties Bar (Ctrl+E/Command+E). Or right-click/Control-click anywhere on the toolbar area at the top of the program window. The list of toolbars appears; choose Properties Bar.

The Subject at Hand

It isn't necessary to add a subject for comments, but it's a good practice to develop. If you are working in a large review process involving dozens or hundreds of comments, subjects can be useful for scanning lists of comments. The author of a comment is listed next to the comment type in the Comments list; if you add a subject, it appears below the author's name.

TIP 50: Adding a Note Comment

TIP 51 Setting Commenting Preferences

After you work with comments for a while, you should evaluate how you use them and how you modify them. If you find you make the same modifications repeatedly, it's a good idea to modify the preferences. Begin by choosing Edit > Preferences > Commenting to display the Commenting Preferences dialog (**Figure 6.11**).

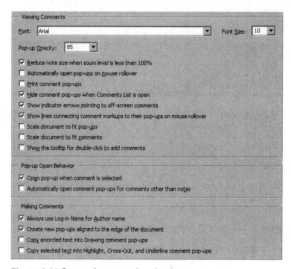

Figure 6.11 Set preferences for viewing comments.

The top section of the pane includes options for specifying how comments are viewed. Arial font at 10 points is the default for comments. If you want, click the pull-down list and choose another font, type a different point size, and choose the opacity percentage for the pop-up box.

The remaining options selected by default are shown in Figure 6.11. If you tend to work with several comments on each page of a document during a review, leave the defaults. In particular:

Hide comment pop-ups when the Comments list is displayed. When you click the Comments tab in the Navigation pane to open the Comments list, the pop-ups in the document collapse, giving you more space on the screen for viewing both the comments and your document.

Show lines connecting comment markups to their pop-ups on mouse rollover, as shown in **Figure 6.12**.

Figure 6.12 Use connecting lines to pair text and the comment icon.

The default setting for the Pop-up Open Behavior section of the Commenting Preferences dialog is to open a pop-up window when the comment is selected (**Figure 6.13**). Leave the setting selected if you are working on documents from the Document pane. If you are working with comments from the Comments list, discussed in Tip 56, you can deselect this option to omit screen clutter.

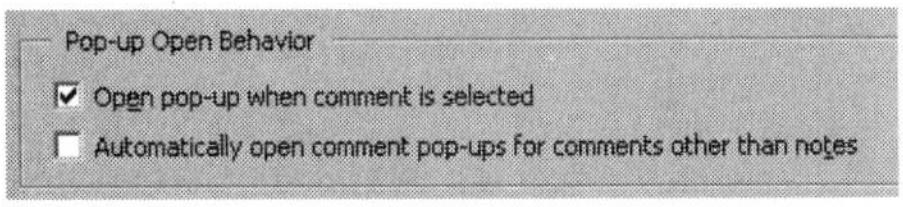

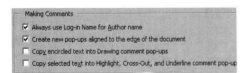

Figure 6.13 Choose to view pop-ups or keep them closed to reduce screen clutter.

In the Making Comments section, the first option (Always use Log-in Name for Author name) is selected by default (**Figure 6.14**). If the only name you work with is the log-in name for your computer, then leave the option selected. If you use another name, or use different names depending on the work or workgroup you are involved with, deselect it.

Figure 6.14 Comments use default properties for displaying on the document page.

If you are the type of person who uses drawing comments (described in Tip 61) to scribble on a document, check the option Copy encircled text into Drawing comment pop-ups. This way, as you scribble you can add text from the document to the comment's text pop-up without having to select another tool.

Personal Preferences

Sometimes it's a good idea to modify Commenting preferences, either your own, or those of a larger group.

- Color-code members of a work-group who use commenting regularly. Each person uses a different color for their comments. That way you can see at a glance who added comments. In an office environment, consider color-coding departments. Many documents and processes require input from a variety of departments; if each has its own color for commenting, it is easier to see where a document is in the commenting and reviewing cycle.

- Increase the font size if you are working with someone who reads comments on the page. I work on projects with another person who likes to read the comments as is (without opening the Comments list). If I use a large font size, he can clearly see my comments on the page.

- In a graphics layout review (a catalog, for example) decrease the opacity of the comments. That way, other members in the group can read the comments in place on the page and still see the graphics content underneath.

TIP 51: Setting Commenting Preferences

Working with Text Edit Comments

The text edit tools, new in Acrobat 6, let you edit a PDF document the same way you would with a printed page and a red pencil, but much more efficiently. Instead of having to print a document, add comments and edits by hand, and then deliver the document to someone who will make the changes, you can do it all from within Acrobat.

You'll find the text edit tools 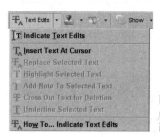 on the Commenting toolbar. Click the Text Edits pull-down arrow to display the list of tools (**Figure 6.15**). You have two options for activating the tools. Which option you choose depends on what you need to work with in the document:

Figure 6.15 The text edit options are unavailable until you select some text in the document.

- Clicking Indicate Text Edits activates the Text Select tool. Use this option if you need to strike through, underline, or highlight text.

- Click Insert Text at Cursor if you want to add a comment or additional text.

Editing text in a document is a two-step process. First you select the text in the document, and then you select a Commenting tool:

1. Click Text Edits in the toolbar and choose Indicate Text Edits from the Text Edits pull-down menu on the Commenting toolbar. In the document, drag to select some text (**Figure 6.16**).

Figure 6.16 Select text on the page to activate the Text Edit tools.

2. Click Text Edits again. All the edit tools are now active (**Figure 6.17**). Choose a tool from the list—for our example, I choose the Replace Selected Text tool.

Figure 6.17 Choose a Text Edit tool option from the list.

Acrobat automatically draws a line through the text we selected and a caret appears next to it. In addition, an Inserted Text pop-up window opens.

3. Modify the text. As you can see in **Figure 6.18**, the new text appears in the window.

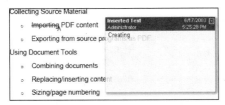

Figure 6.18 Text Edit comments are similar to those done manually on paper.

Adding new text to a document is a slightly different process.

1. Click the Text Edits tool's pull-down arrow on the Commenting toolbar to display the menu.

2. Click Insert Text at Cursor. By default, Acrobat places the pointer before the first character of text on the page.

3. Click on the page where you want to add the new text and a caret appears at the pointer's position. Start typing; the text you type is added to a comment box, as shown in **Figure 6.19**.

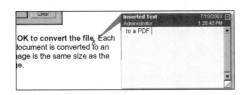

Figure 6.19 You can add text as a comment using the Insert Text at Cursor command.

Adding Comments to Your Edits

Need to explain why you deleted a specific paragraph in a document, or just want to leave a note to verify that your changes are correct? Acrobat makes it easy. Once you've added an edit with any of the text edit tools, you can also add a comment. Simply double-click the edit to open a note box, then type your comment.

TIP 52: Working with Text Edit Comments

TIP 53 — Exporting Comments to a Word Document (Windows)

If you're working with a tagged PDF that was originally built in Word XP, you can export the PDF directly from Acrobat back into Word and make the corrections there. Rather than having to work with both the PDF document and the original Word document open side by side, while making corrections manually, you can have your reviewers' comments exported directly from the PDF document back into the original Word document and have the changes made automatically.

If you intend to export the comments for processing, make sure the document is tagged before you convert it to PDF. If you don't tag the document, instead of a smooth comment-exporting process you'll see the message shown in **Figure 6.20**. (See Tip 33 for information on tagging a document.) The export process works only in Word XP in Windows, and it doesn't work through a Web browser.

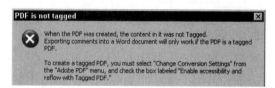

Figure 6.20 You must use a tagged PDF document to use the automatic comment conversion process.

You can import comments only once; if you are working on several versions of a document, save copies and number them sequentially. That way, each time you send comments for a round of reviews you have a copy of the document that can accept comments.

To export comments to a Word document:

1. Click the Review & Comment task button's pull-down arrow to display its menu (**Figure 6.21**). Choose Export Comments to Word.

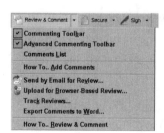

Figure 6.21 Choose Export Comments to Word from the Review & Comment menu.

Will the Real Highlighting Tool Please Stand Up?

If you are planning to export the comments to a Word XP source document, don't use the Highlighting tool available on the Commenting toolbar. The Commenting Highlighting tool merely adds highlights to the PDF document. The Text Edits menu's Highlighting tool transfers the highlight with the document content when you export to Word.

2. Microsoft Word opens, and a dialog describes the process (**Figure 6.22**). Once you are familiar with the process, click Don't Show Again at the bottom left of the dialog. Then click Yes to close the dialog and start the import process.

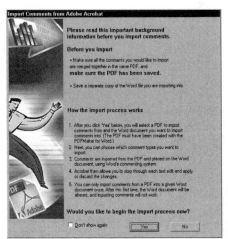

Figure 6.22 This window explains the comments export and import processes.

3. The Import Comments from Adobe Acrobat dialog opens (**Figure 6.23**). The name of the PDF file from which you are exporting appears in the top field. Click Browse and locate the source Word document used to generate the PDF.

Figure 6.23 Specify the file that contains the comments, and then specify the file in which you want to insert them.

(Continued)

TIP 53: Exporting Comments to a Word Document (Windows)

4. Choose from the various comment-import options. Read the sidebar "Choosing Which Comments to Export" on page 158 for more information.

5. Click the Turn Track Changes On Before Importing Comments option if you are involved in an editing or review process and are using several versions of the document.

6. Click Continue. Acrobat processes the comments and adds them to the Word document.

7. Acrobat displays the Successful Import dialog once it processes the comments (**Figure 6.24**). The dialog summarizes the activity and describes how text edits can be integrated. Click Integrate Text Edits to start the process.

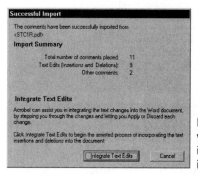

Figure 6.24 Acrobat tells you when it has finished integrating the comments into the document.

8. The Adobe Acrobat Comments dialog opens, displaying the number of comments available for converting. The dialog identifies the first comment in the document and displays the replacement text (**Figure 6.25**). Click Apply to make the edit. The text is modified in the Word document (using colored or underlined text if changes are being tracked).

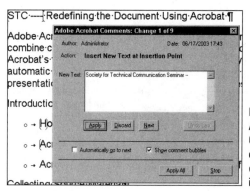

Figure 6.25 The Adobe Acrobat Comments dialog displays the first comment you can integrate.

9. Click Next in the Adobe Acrobat Comments dialog to continue with the next edit; repeat until you've finished all the edits.

Note

You can also click Apply All. A confirmation dialog opens asking if you want to apply all the converted comments. Click OK. The dialog closes, and the comments are applied to the Word document.

10. You'll see the Text Integration Summary dialog when all the comments are processed (**Figure 6.26**). Click Done.

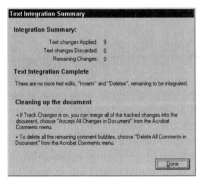

Figure 6.26 The Text Integration Summary dialog appears when all comments are processed.

11. Check the document. You'll see that the edits are applied and that basic note comments are attached to the document as well (**Figure 6.27**). Save the corrected Word document.

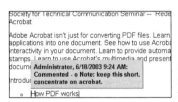

Figure 6.27 Both text changes and comments are applied to the document.

What happens next with the Word document depends on its purpose. If you originally created the PDF to circulate it and collect comments, you're finished, and can print or email the document. If you need a second review, create another PDF document and start over.

TIP 53: Exporting Comments to a Word Document (Windows)

Choosing Which Comments to Export

When exporting comments from a PDF to be integrated in a Word XP document, you can choose certain groups of comments to export. Decide how much you want to edit the Word document, and then in the Import Comments from Adobe Acrobat dialog (see Figure 6.23), choose a type of export accordingly. You don't want to import all the comments into the document if your intention is to simply correct the content of the document. For example, you might not want to deal with comments that address responsibility for actions, office politics, and so on. By the same token, you might not want to make corrections without having supporting comments from the person who suggested the changes.

- If you have set up a personal commenting system using checkmarks, you can select the option All Comments with Checkmarks under Choose Comment Types to Import. You'll import only those comments marked with checkmarks. (Read more about checkmarks in Tip 56.)

- If you are editing the document's content using the Text Edits tools, select the Text Edits Only: Insertions and Deletions option. That way, only the comments pertaining to the document's content and structure are transferred. This option is especially useful for large reviews where you're dealing with many comments, not all of which actually apply to modifying the document.

- Often you develop commenting systems, particularly in large organizations. Acrobat lets you design a custom set of comment-conversion options. Choose Custom Set and then filter the comments you want to export to Word. The filter can be based on the author, status, or checkmark. (Learn more about filtering in Tip 56.)

TIP 54 Using the Stamp Tools

The Stamp tools are like the old-fashioned ink stamps you apply to a document (such as Draft, Approved, or Confidential). Unlike ink stamps, some of the Acrobat stamps are dynamic in that they automatically add the time or date when you apply the stamp to the document. You can also create custom stamps.

1. On the Commenting toolbar, click the Stamp tool's ![icon] pull-down arrow to open the menu shown in **Figure 6.28**. The upper three commands on the menu have submenus containing the Stamp choices (the figure shows the Standard Business options).

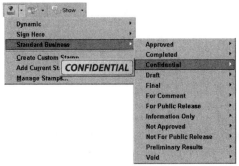

Figure 6.28 Choose from a wide range of stamps.

A Few of My Favorite Stamps

If you use a stamp and then choose Add Current Stamp to Favorites, that stamp will appear at the top of the Stamp tool submenu, so you can quickly use it again without having to navigate the system of submenus. You can easily change to a different favorite when the whim strikes you.

2. Move the pointer over a stamp name to view a thumbnail of the stamp's appearance.

3. Click a stamp to select it. The pointer changes to resemble the comment's icon. Click the document where you want to apply the stamp (**Figure 6.29**).

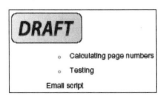

Figure 6.29 Click the document to apply the stamp.

(Continued)

TIP 54: Using the Stamp Tools

As you can see in Figure 6.28, the Stamp tool's pull-down menu also offers Dynamic and Sign Here stamps. The Dynamic stamps, shown as a collection in **Figure 6.30**, include the username as well as the date and time the stamp was applied. The Sign Here stamps, shown as a group in **Figure 6.31**, are specific formats used for common communications.

Figure 6.30 Dynamic stamps include the username as well as date and time information.

Figure 6.31 To indicate when a signature is needed, use the Sign Here stamp collection rather than adding note comments.

For some people, stamps are the perfect way to comment on a document. If you add similar types of comments repeatedly, consider constructing your own custom stamp. For example, you may be an intermediate reviewer and have your work forwarded to a supervisor for final review. There's no stamp that explains that process, but you can create one using the method described below. Use a custom stamp along with a Dynamic stamp if you need a date and time stamp (**Figure 6.32**).

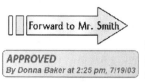

Figure 6.32 Use a Dynamic stamp in conjunction with your own custom stamp to cover all your bases.

Creating and Managing Custom Stamps

You can easily add a custom stamp to Acrobat:

1. Click the Stamp tool's pull-down menu and choose Create Custom Stamp. The Create Stamp dialog opens (**Figure 6.33**).

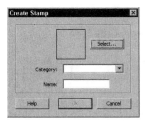

Figure 6.33 Create custom stamps to use for your projects.

2. Click Select to find the file you want to use for the stamp. You can use a range of graphic formats, as well as PDF and Word files. The Select dialog opens and displays the chosen file (**Figure 6.34**). Click OK to close the dialog and return to the Create Stamp dialog.

Figure 6.34 Select a file to use for the stamp.

3. Click the Category field and type a name for the new stamp category; then type a name for the stamp (**Figure 6.35**). Click OK.

Figure 6.35 Name the new stamp.

(Continued)

Use a Custom Stamp When...

There are some circumstances where it makes sense to take a few minutes to build a custom stamp:

- You write the same comment repeatedly. You may be a department head who needs to add a date and time stamp to a document when you are finished reviewing, but also needs department information. Build a stamp that asks for the information; you can now use a dynamic date/time stamp, and your new custom stamp.

- Your work includes different roles. For example, you may be a writer but also a supervisor, or a departmental representative in a review cycle. You can make separate identification stamps defining what your role is for the particular review.

TIP 54: Using the Stamp Tools

4. To use your new stamp, first click the Stamp tool's pull-down arrow. Your custom stamp category now appears along with any other custom stamps you have added to your system. You can click the stamp name to display a thumbnail of the stamp (**Figure 6.36**).

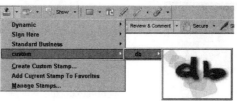

Figure 6.36 Choose your custom stamp from the pull-down menus.

5. Click the stamp, and then click the document page to apply the stamp (**Figure 6.37**).

Figure 6.37 Apply your custom stamp to the document.

You can also remove a custom stamp from Acrobat:

1. Open the Stamp tool's pull-down menu and choose Manage Stamps to open the Manage Stamps dialog.

2. Select the stamp you want to remove (**Figure 6.38**) and click Delete. Click Close to dismiss the dialog.

Figure 6.38 You can add and delete stamps using the Manage Stamps dialog.

TIP 55 Working With the Comments List

Each comment added to a document is stored in the Comments list, which is one of the five panes displayed in the program by default. If you have closed the pane, choose View > Navigation Tabs > Comments. Click the Comments tab at the left margin of the program window to open it. Unlike the other panels that open to the left of the Document pane, the Comments list is displayed horizontally below the document (**Figure 6.39**).

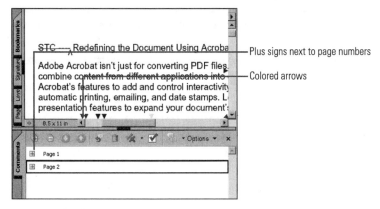

Figure 6.39 The Comments list appears horizontally below the document. Both the document pages have been commented on.

As you can see in Figure 6.39, both Page 1 and Page 2 appear in the Comments list, meaning that our two-page sample document contains comments on both pages. The plus sign (+) to the left of a page number indicates that the page contains comments.

Finding Comments in a Document

Comments are organized in levels within the Comments list. Here are some tips for viewing comments:

- Click each page's plus icon (+) to open the page and display the comments (**Figure 6.40**). Once the page is open, you can see the list of comments. You also see an additional plus sign to the left of the comment; click it to open the comment and read details such as the author and the time the comment was added.

(Continued)

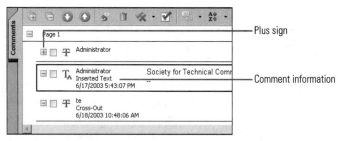

Figure 6.40 Click the plus sign (+) to reveal the comment's information.

- Look at the portion of the Document pane displayed above the Comments list (see Figure 6.39). Notice the colored arrows along the bottom and right edges of the visible area? This indicates that there are comments both below and to the right of the area shown in the Document pane—which is a pretty neat feature.

- Instead of scrolling through the document in the Document pane looking at comments, you can work through the Comments list. Click a comment in the list, and as long as it's visible in the Document pane, it appears highlighted in the document (**Figure 6.41**).

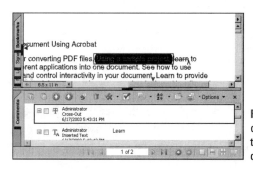

Figure 6.41 Click a comment in the list to highlight it in the document.

- Position the comment in the Document pane and highlight it as well using the directional arrows on the Comments toolbar. The downward-pointing arrow moves the view to the next comment in the list; the upward-pointing arrow goes to the previous comment.

Managing Comments

Working on a long document can involve dozens or even hundreds of comments. That's a lot of information to keep track of. Here are a few tips for identifying comments you have worked with:

- Sometimes you need to reply to a comment for future reference. You can include another comment of your own, but then you add to the overall number of comments, and sometimes the response is lost in a large collection. Instead of adding more comments, *reply* to comments. First, click the comment to select it in the Comments list. Then click the Reply button  on the toolbar. A copy of the comment is added to the list, nested within the original comment (**Figure 6.42**). Type the reply in the text field. Acrobat places the Reply icon before your text. After you deselect the reply, the row stays a pale gray color to distinguish replies from comments.

Figure 6.42 Comment replies are nested within the comment.

- You can click a comment row to display a text field, which is used to add a note to an existing comment. It isn't the same as adding a reply because it originates with the person creating the original comment. Sometimes you need to add information to a comment, such as explaining why you want to make a change in the document. Such notes appear in a tool tip when the pointer moves over the comment (**Figure 6.43**).

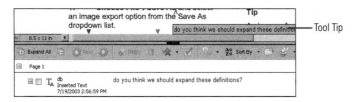

Figure 6.43 You can add information, which will appear in a tool tip when the pointer is moved over the comment.

(Continued)

TIP 55: Working With the Comments List

Check It Off

Checkmarks can help you organize your work. Here's some ways to use them:

- If you are responsible for a certain number of corrections, changes, or actions, after a review is completed, quickly go through the list and checkmark all your tasks.

- If you have a list of changes from a number of people, checkmark those from one reviewer, complete the tasks and delete the checkmarks, and then continue with the next reviewer, and so on.

- Sometimes you don't want your work "officially" included in a review cycle. As you analyze a project to determine your work-load, checkmark comments that you want to respond to privately.

- If you need clarification on comments, checkmark them as you make your first pass through the document.

- Delete comments you don't want to maintain. Simply click the Delete icon ▣ on the Comments list toolbar.

- Add a checkmark to the comment. Click the Checkmark tool ☑ or right-click the comment in the Comments list or on the document and choose Mark with Checkmark from the shortcut menu (**Figure 6.44**). Checkmarks aren't shared with other people as part of a review; you use them to organize your own work. For example, add checkmarks as you finish a correction.

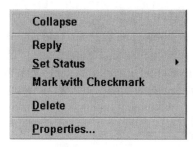

Figure 6.44 Use checkmarks to organize your work.

TIP 56 Organizing Comments in the Comments List

There are a number of ways you can organize the comments in your document. By default, comments are listed as they appear in the document from start to end. Here are a few tips:

- If you are working on a large document, or if you want to check what you have added to a document, filter the comments. Click the Filter icon  to open a pull-down menu. For example, click Show by Reviewer (**Figure 6.45**) to open a submenu of the reviewers in the document. Click a name to select it. For our example, choose *te*.

Figure 6.45 You can sort comments by reviewers' names.

In the Comments list, you see that only comments written by te are showing (**Figure 6.46**). For reference, the message "Comments are hidden because a filter is active in the Show menu" appears below the Comments list toolbar. This way, you can check whether you have addressed all the comments in the document (if you are te) or whether a certain reviewer has seen and commented on the document.

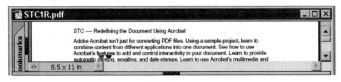

Figure 6.46 Filtering hides all comments except those fitting the criteria you choose.

(Continued)

Sorting It Out

A good time to use the Sort function is when you're managing the review process for a document. You can sort by Author, for example, and quickly determine which reviewers have added comments. On the other hand, in a review that requires several rounds of commenting, sorting by Author isn't of much value because all members of the review are bound to have added comments at some time. In that case, you should sort the comments by Date.

Note

Filtering does not apply to the comment replies. If you have added a series of comments and replied to other comments as well, sorting the comments by author displays only your original comments.

- You can sort comments as well as filter them. The difference is that a filter hides all but certain comments, whereas a sort organizes the entire collection of comments in a specific way. Click Sort By [icon] to open a pull-down menu and choose an option from the list (**Figure 6.47**).

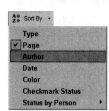

Figure 6.47 Use sorting to arrange the comments in the Comments list.

- In the Comments list, sorting according to the Checkmark Status reduces the list to two categories: Marked and Unmarked. The categories are closed initially; in **Figure 6.48** we've expanded the Marked category to show you its contents. Note that the list is organized according to the time the comments were added within the marked category.

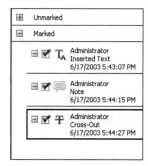

Figure 6.48 Open the sorted categories to see the comments.

- You can search for comment content directly from the Comments list. Searching comments is particularly useful when you are working on a big review with numerous people. Click Search [icon] to open the Search window (**Figure 6.49**) at the right of the screen. Next, type the search term and specify whether the results should be whole words and whether they require specific capitalization. Then click Search.

Figure 6.49 Search for comments based on their content.

Once Acrobat processes the search, it displays the results in the Search pane, and the comments containing the search terms are framed in the Comments list (**Figure 6.50**). Move the pointer over the search result in the list to see the page number where the search result is located.

The comment is highlighted   The comment is framed   The search result

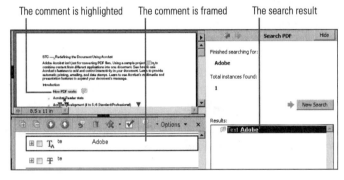

Figure 6.50 Use the search results to find specific comments in your document.

TIP 56: Organizing Comments in the Comments List

TIP 57 Starting a Review Process

In Acrobat 5 you could share comments with others, then incorporate all the comments into the original PDF document. The process in Acrobat 6 is simpler, and is managed through wizards and prompts. In order for the review to work automatically, all participants must be using Acrobat 6 Standard or Professional. The process involves several steps:

1. Someone initiates the review, sending out copies of the PDF file and any initial comments he or she may have added.

2. The recipient opens the document and adds comments.

3. Comments are returned to the initiator.

4. The recipient's comments are integrated into the original document.

Send Out a Document

Let's say you have a document that you want to share with a colleague for commenting. Follow these steps to set up an email review from within Acrobat:

1. Choose File > Send by Email for Review to open the Send by E-mail for Review dialog.

2. If this is your first email review and you haven't defined an email address in the preferences, type your address in the dialog and click OK (**Figure 6.51**).

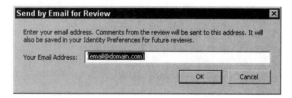

Figure 6.51 You must define an email address before starting a review.

Reviews from Office

You can start a document review directly from a Microsoft Office program. Choose Adobe PDF > Convert to Adobe PDF and Send for Review, or click the Convert to Adobe PDF and Send for Review icon.

Commenting and Sharing Documents

3. The invitation dialog, called Send by Email for Review: [file-name], opens (**Figure 6.52**). The dialog includes instructions to follow for starting the review, as well as information that the recipient will read in the email. Click To and enter the email address for the recipient (you can also fill in the cc and bcc fields if you want). Then click Send.

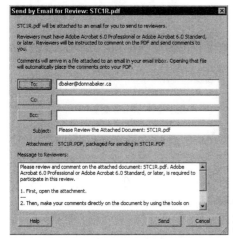

Figure 6.52 Follow the instructions in this dialog to set up the review.

4. An Outgoing Message Notification information dialog opens explaining what happens next (**Figure 6.53**). Depending on your security settings, the email may be sent automatically, or you may need to move through dialogs approving the mail process. Click OK to dismiss the dialog.

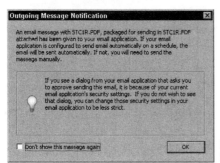

Figure 6.53 You're notified before the email is sent.

When the Mail Doesn't Work

The Send by Email for Review dialog uses a specific filter on the email name you enter. If your email address doesn't use a three-letter suffix—for example, *com, net,* or *edu*—the address is rejected. Here's what you do instead:

In the Identity panel of the Preferences dialog box, type your email address in the email address field, then click OK. Now when you choose File > Send by Email for Review you go directly to the Send by Email for Review: [filename] dialog using your email address.

TIP 57: Starting a Review Process

Respond to a Document

That's it for the first part. You've added comments to a document, assigned a recipient, and emailed it. Next it lands in the recipient's email inbox. In this example, I'm also the recipient (cue the spooky movie soundtrack).

1. Open the email message (**Figure 6.54**). Read the instructions. You can see that the PDF document is attached to the email.

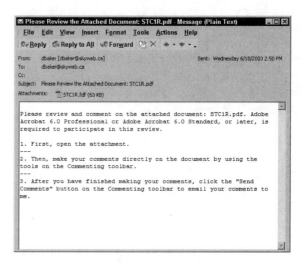

Figure 6.54 The recipient receives the email and attachment, as well as instructions for participating in the review.

2. Double-click the email attachment to open it in Acrobat.

3. Make comments and review the comments sent from the initiator (**Figure 6.55**).

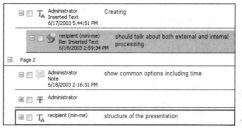

Figure 6.55 Review and add comments to the document.

4. When you have finished, choose File > Send Comments to Review Initiator. The comments are emailed back to the initiator.

Once the comments return to you (the initiator), they are integrated into the PDF one last time as soon as you double-click the email attachment to open the document in Acrobat. You can then review the contents of the Comments list and finish the document's processing.

It's a good idea to save a copy of the document prior to incorporating reviewers' comments. Edit the document using the copy to preserve the layout and structure. This way, imported comments are in the correct locations on the document. Acrobat reminds you about document versions. If you open a copy of a document that is part of an active review, a message window appears asking if you want to open the copy or incorporate any changes into the document being tracked (**Figure 6.56**). A handy feature!

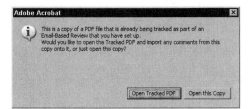

Figure 6.56 If you open a copy of a document that is part of an active review, a message window asks if you want to open the copy or open the version being tracked.

TIP 58 Tracking a Review

It's simple to keep track of a simple two-person document review cycle. But many business and professional processes require several participants and several rounds of reviewing—tracking a beast like that isn't so easy. Use the Review Tracker to keep tabs on the process:

1. Click the pull-down arrow on the Review & Comment task button and choose Track Reviews (**Figure 6.57**). The Review Tracker opens at the right side of the program window.

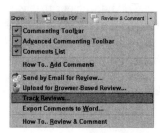

Figure 6.57 Choose Track Reviews to get a handle on review cycles.

2. If you have active browser-based and email reviews, the two headings are listed. In our example, we are using only an email review. Click the plus sign indicator at the left of the name to open the list of reviews (**Figure 6.58**), where you can do the following:

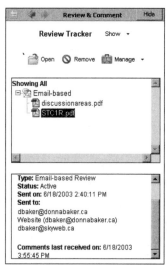

Figure 6.58 Look at the list of correct reviews in the Review Tracker.

- Click a document in the list and click Show to open it in the Document pane.

Note

When you click a document in the review list, information about the status of the review appears at the bottom of the Review Tracker.

- Click Remove to remove a selected document from the Review Tracker (this option has no effect on the file itself).

- You can sort the documents on the list. This is a good idea if you are involved in several reviews. Click Show to open a list of sort options (**Figure 6.59**). Choose options to sort according to the status of a review.

Figure 6.59 If you're involved in numerous reviews, you can sort the reviews to keep track of all your projects and their status.

- You can also manage the list. Select a review from the list, and then click Manage to open a set of options that allow you to send reminders and emails and invite others to participate in the review (**Figure 6.60**).

Figure 6.60 You can send reminders, emails, and invite others to participate by using the Manage options in the Review Tracker.

Taming the Wily Review Process

If you're the person starting a review, all comments are returned to you. To maintain control of the review process, you, as the initiator, should control invitations to the review. That way, the comments always return to you and can be incorporated into the original document.

TIP 58: Tracking a Review

TIP 59 Setting Comment Status and Creating Summaries

Once a document has been through a review cycle or two, it's time to take care of some last-minute issues. These include defining a status for the comments, creating summaries, and printing comments and comment summaries for reference or archiving.

On the Comments list toolbar, click Status to display a list of options (**Figure 6.61**). Unlike the checkmark (which is used only on your copy of the document), you can set a status for a comment that can be shared with other reviewers. **Figure 6.62** shows the various status options for a list of comments.

Figure 6.61 Set a status for your comments that can be shared with other reviewers.

Figure 6.62 You can assign a status to comments that displays with the other comment information.

When you're collecting feedback from reviewers, or when a project is coming to a close, creating a comment summary is a good idea—that way, all the comments are organized and collated in one handy place for easy reference. On the Comments list toolbar, click Options to open a pull-down menu (**Figure 6.63**).

Figure 6.63 Choose one of several options for managing a document's comments.

What's Your Status?

Once you assign status to comments, you can sort or filter the comments on the basis of the status. For example, if you've rejected a number of comments, just hide them from view rather than dwelling on them. Or you can choose to show only Completed comments to keep track of your accomplishments.

Choose Summarize Comments to open the dialog shown in **Figure 6.64**. Choose layout options (see the sidebar "Choosing a Comment Summary Layout"), a sort option, and a font size. Click OK to generate the summary.

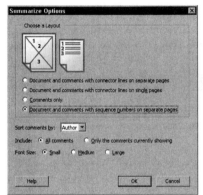

Figure 6.64 Define the options for a comment summary.

Acrobat opens the summary as a PDF file named Summary of Comments [filename] and lists all the comments information sorted according to the option you chose (**Figure 6.65**). Save this file for reference.

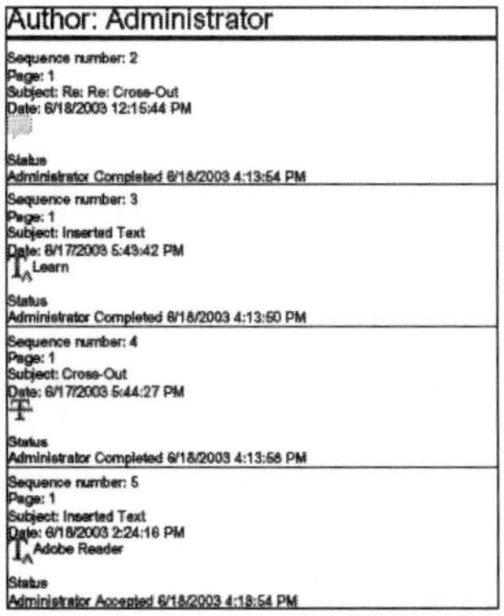

Figure 6.65 The summary appears in a new PDF file.

Finally, you can print the comments and comment summaries. Click the Print 🖨 pull-down arrow and choose an option from the resulting menu. You can print the comments summary or configure the comments using the same dialog and processes available from the Options pull-down menu.

TIP 59: Setting Comment Status and Creating Summaries

Choosing a Comment Summary Layout

You can generate a Summary of Comments in one of several ways using the Summarize Options dialog. Choose an option depending on the characteristics of the document and its comments, how you like to work, and what you intend to do with the summary:

- Choosing the Document and comments with connector lines on separate pages option is a good idea if you have very lengthy comments. This summary type is complicated when you're using a printed paper copy because you have to follow the lines across pages.

- In a short document or one with short comments, use the Document and comments with connector lines on single pages option.

- If you have finished a project and want a paper copy for archiving, or you want to work on a document away from your computer (does that really happen?), use Documents and comments with sequence numbers on separate pages.

Using a Browser-Based Review (Windows)

You can coordinate document review with a browser and Web server if you are using Windows. When you start the review, Acrobat adds two buttons to the Commenting toolbar—Send Comments and Receive Comments—that you can use for browser-based reviewing.

Follow these steps:

1. Choose Edit > Preferences > Reviewing. Choose a server from the pull-down list (**Figure 6.66**). Click OK to close the dialog.

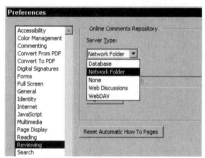

Figure 6.66 Choose a server type for reviewing online.

2. Open the document and choose Review & Comment > Upload for Browser-Based Review (**Figure 6.67**). In the resulting dialog, specify a server folder and click Upload (**Figure 6.68**).

Figure 6.67 Use the Upload for Browser-Based Review command to start the process.

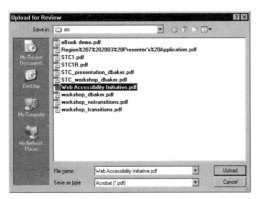

Figure 6.68 Specify a server folder to use for the review and click Upload.

If a PDF file is already on your server, open the document in a Web browser, and then choose Review & Comment > Invite Others to Review this Document.

3. In the Start Browser-Based Review dialog, specify the email addresses of reviewers, and then click Send (**Figure 6.69**). The recipient follows the instructions, similar to those used for an email review, except that the PDF file opens in a browser window. When the recipient has finished reviewing the document, he or she uses the Send and Receive Comments tools on the browser-based Commenting toolbar (**Figure 6.70**).

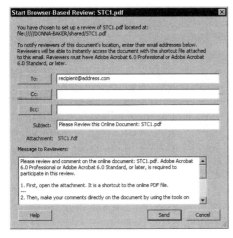

Figure 6.69 Invite participants to a browser-based review the same way you invite participants to an email review.

(Continued)

TIP 60: Using a Browser-Based Review (Windows)

Figure 6.70 Send and Receive Comments commands are added to the Commenting toolbar for browser-based reviews.

4. In Acrobat, the browser-based review is added to the Review Tracker. Click the file to read information on the review process. In our example, since we set up the review locally, the review process is termed "offline" (**Figure 6.71**).

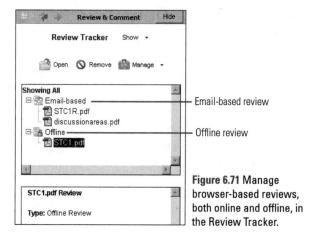

Figure 6.71 Manage browser-based reviews, both online and offline, in the Review Tracker.

Note

A document can be reviewed offline. Click Save and Work Offline *on the browser Commenting toolbar. A Save dialog opens; save the document. When the document is ready to send, click Go Back Online* *on the Commenting toolbar to reconnect to the server. Then click Send and Receive Comments* *to send the comments back to the initiator.*

TIP 61 Using Advanced Commenting Tools

You can use the Advanced Commenting tools for specific types of tasks, such as drawing or attaching other files or sound clips. Choose Tools > Advanced Commenting > Show Advanced Commenting Toolbar. The toolbar contains several tools, and there are also pull-down arrows, indicating submenus.

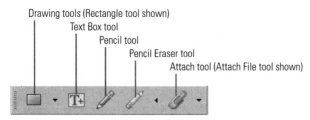

Figure 6.72 The Advanced Commenting toolbar is used for specific types of comments.

In **Figure 6.72**, you can see the Drawing tool group at the left; at the far right is the Attach tool group. I'll come back to those shortly. The Text Box tool 🔲 is similar to the Note tool on the Commenting toolbar with one exception: the text box doesn't close, which makes the Text Box tool especially useful for adding captions or callouts to images (**Figure 6.73**).

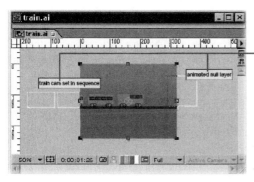

Figure 6.73 Use the Text Box tool to add captions to images.

(Continued)

TIP 61: Using Advanced Commenting Tools

You can use the Pencil tool and the Pencil Eraser tool  in tandem. The Pencil draws a freehand line (**Figure 6.74**); the Pencil Eraser removes segments of the line. Fortunately, you don't have to follow a drawn line precisely to remove it with the eraser. Click the arrow to the right of the Pencil Eraser tool to close the eraser and display only the Pencil. Personally, I like showing both, because I never figured out how to use a pencil without an eraser.

Figure 6.74 Draw freehand using the Pencil tool.

The drawing tool you used most recently displays at the far left of the Advanced Commenting toolbar. Click the pull-down arrow to open the list of available tools, or click Show Drawing Toolbar (**Figure 6.75**) on the Advanced Commenting toolbar. The Drawing toolbar opens as a separate toolbar (**Figure 6.76**). The drawing tools are terrific for those people who can't make a point without scribbling all over a page.

Figure 6.75 Choose a drawing tool from the Advanced Editing toolbar or open the Drawing toolbar separately.

Figure 6.76 The Drawing toolbar contains five basic drawing tools.

Draw Your Own Conclusions

I use the drawing tools for one very useful purpose—as electronic whiteout. Suppose you find an error in text or an image at the last minute, and you don't have time to rebuild the PDF document. No problem. Click a tool on the Drawing toolbar and draw an area that will cover the offending content. Right-click/Control-click the shape and choose Properties from the menu. In the Properties dialog, set the Fill color and Line color to match the document's background and click OK. The correction is made.

The final set of tools is used to attach other elements to a document. On the Advanced Commenting toolbar, click the pull-down arrow next to the Attach File tool to open a list of available tool options. Click Show Attach Toolbar to display the toolbar separately (**Figure 6.77**).

Figure 6.77 Attach different objects to a document using the Attach tools.

You can use the Attach File tool to attach a file to the PDF document. I use this feature when building a large document that has a lot of accessory material that is not necessarily of interest to everyone reading the document but that should be available. For example, spreadsheets may show financial data, and information used to generate the numbers in the tables can be attached. Select the tool and click the page where you want the icon to display. A small dialog opens to let you locate the file you want to attach. Select the file and click OK. **Figure 6.78** shows the paper clip icon placed on the page. The comment's information in the Comments list includes the name of the file.

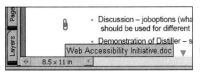

Figure 6.78 Use the Attach File tool to attach a file to your open document.

Note
If you email a document containing Attach File comments, the attached files are emailed as well.

Click Sound to attach a sound to a document. A recorder dialog opens (**Figure 6.79**). You can either record the sound directly (if you have the appropriate hardware) or click Browse to locate a prerecorded file. Acrobat plays WAV and AIFF files.

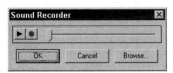

Figure 6.79 Use the Sound Recorder dialog to record sound or attach a sound file.

(Continued)

A Talking PDF?

Two areas where the use of sound comments is really starting to take off are medicine and government/law. For example, one hospital in Tennessee uses PDF forms and documents to record patient information. Patient care staff add data to forms (such as medication administration) using handheld devices. Notes are dictated to the file using sound comments. The sound comments are then exported from the PDF and interpreted by a voice recognition program that types the content, which is then added back to the patient material.

TIP 61: Using Advanced Commenting Tools

Using the Snapshot Tool

Use this tool to add content to or move content around a page. I use it to move content regularly. Sometimes when I'm converting a Word document containing a large number of images, an image or its label is displaced and appears on the page following its proper location. No problem. I use the Snapshot tool to snap the image and make a new PDF document containing the single image. I add the new document to the original and delete the page with the error. It takes some getting used to, but once you figure out how to use the Snapshot tool in combination with Insert, Delete, and Replace Page commands, you can manipulate a document quite extensively.

Finally, you can attach the contents of the Clipboard to a document. To activate the Paste Clipboard Image tool, you must first capture a portion of the page with the Snapshot tool (located on the Basic toolbar). As soon as content is available on the Clipboard, the tool is active. Click the tool, and then click the document page where you want the content pasted (**Figure 6.80**). Interestingly, as you can see in the figure, image pasted from the clipboard is considered a form of a stamp tool. If you are searching for pasted content in the Comments list, look for the Stamp icon.

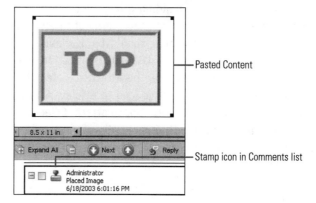

Figure 6.80 Paste the contents of the clipboard to a document as a stamp comment.

CHAPTER SEVEN

Navigating and Searching a Document

Bookmarks—text links arranged in a list in the Bookmarks pane—are one of the most powerful ways to use Acrobat to create user-centric documents. If you are planning to have your documents used electronically (that is, read using Adobe Reader or Acrobat), use bookmarks as a table of contents for your document. That way, you let your reader see at a glance what is in your document by viewing the Bookmarks pane. Simply clicking a bookmark takes the reader to the bookmarked location in the document. Bookmarks provide orientation for your readers, and they are invaluable for large and complex documents. For any type of document using headings, from a resume to a user's manual, bookmarks add a professional touch.

Acrobat lets you create bookmarks in a variety of ways. Typically, you add them when you're converting a document using the PDF-Maker macro in a source program. But you can also add bookmarks to any document from within Acrobat itself. And you can configure, modify, and customize your bookmarks in Acrobat as well.

Bookmarks are a useful way to move through a document, but certainly not the only way. In Acrobat 6.0, you can work with layered documents for the first time, and move through a document by displaying a selected layer. And although searching is not a "formal" navigation process—there are no buttons or links to click—you can navigate by using search terms.

These tips will reveal the best ways to navigate your Acrobat documents.

TIP 62 Creating Bookmarks from a Source Document

The PDFMaker macro lets you assign bookmarks in Office XP programs. If the source document is constructed properly using styles or headings, you can easily create bookmarks by using the macro. However, if you aren't that well versed in the source document's program, you may find the process of converting headings or styles to bookmarks a bit confusing—and your results will be less than optimal.

Let me begin with a sample document made from one of this chapter's tips (with apologies to my editor and publisher for the mess I made of the text).

Figure 7.1 shows the first page of the test document in Acrobat. I created the document in Word XP and laid it out using sections; the content is defined with headings.

Figure 7.1 Organize your source document if you need to convert the document with bookmarks.

If I wanted to simply print the document, it would be fine as is. However, I want to use the document interactively and employ bookmarks as a means of navigation. **Figure 7.2** shows a short set of bookmarks in a nested arrangement with subheadings. As you can see, this arrangement makes it easy for my reader to see what's in the document and then click bookmarks to display the linked content in the Document pane.

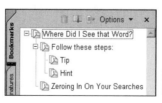

Figure 7.2 Use a simple set of bookmarks for clarity.

In **Figure 7.3**, on the other hand, I've created far too many bookmarks for such a short document. They are too long, their organization doesn't make sense—and I even have a blank bookmark. Why all this chaos? Because I chose every available option in the PDFMaker macro, applied headings and styles indiscriminately in the document, and even used some heading styles to add blank space in the document.

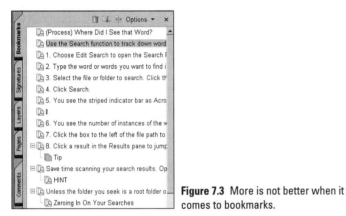

Figure 7.3 More is not better when it comes to bookmarks.

Yes, I created both these examples using the same document—but let's see what changing a few settings and organizing the content differently will do.

To convert a document resulting in logical bookmarks, keep these points in mind:

- Choose the option that is most convenient for your purposes. If you have a corporate template, for example, you can't arbitrarily assign headings to use for bookmarks; in many cases you have specific styles for your corporate template instead of generic headings. In that case, use the Styles conversion option.

- If you aren't constrained by policy or other business-related issues, and you aren't an advanced user of Office applications, use the Word Headings conversion option. It is simple to attach a Heading1 style to major document headings, a Heading2 style to subheadings, a Heading3 to lower-level headings, and so on.

What Are Little Bookmarks Made Of?

Decide when you're designing the source document how you want to convert it. The PDFMaker macro lets you convert Word headings or Word styles to bookmarks, or both. You may want to use both styles and headings depending on the structure of your document. For example, if you use the default headings in the document and create a style for a specific type of information (such as a sidebar), you may want to convert both the headings and your custom style to bookmarks.

TIP 62: Creating Bookmarks from a Source Document

- In the document, don't use headings or styles for any text but the text you intend to use for bookmarks. Anything on the page that uses the heading or style is converted to a bookmark regardless of whether it contains any text. You will run into problems if you use headings to create blank space on your page. Assigning a heading to a blank line adds extra space (**Figure 7.4**). But that line becomes the dreaded blank bookmark in your table of contents.

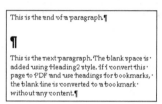

Figure 7.4 Many people use heading styles to add blank space in a document. This is a bookmarking no-no.

Follow these steps to configure your document for conversion (we're using a Word document for our example):

1. When your source document is complete, choose Adobe PDF > Change Conversion Settings. The Change Conversion Settings dialog opens.

2. Click the Bookmarks tab. **Figure 7.5** shows the default settings.

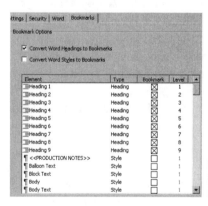

Figure 7.5 Define the bookmark structure in the PDFMaker macro.

No More Blank Spaces

Document designers: Break your users of their habit of applying a heading style to create a blank space by creating a custom style for your templates that includes blank space before and after the paragraph.

3. Choose the settings you need:

- To use the headings as bookmarks, leave the default selections and click OK to close the dialog.

- To use styles as bookmarks, deselect the Convert Word Headings to Bookmarks option and click Convert Word Styles to Bookmarks. Scroll through the list and click the styles you don't want to use for conversion, leaving selected only the styles you do want to use.

Note

Don't simply click the Word styles conversion option. Unless you deselect the headings option, you get both types of content converted to bookmarks. Remember Figure 7.3? It isn't a pretty sight.

4. Click OK to close the dialog.

Note

You can convert the document using either styles or headings, and then wait until you get the document into Acrobat to choose the specific options you want to use for bookmarks. However you must use a tagged PDF. See Tip 67 for more information.

5. Click Adobe PDF > Convert to Adobe PDF or click Convert to PDF 🗋 on the Adobe PDF toolbar. The document is converted to a PDF document with your chosen bookmarks nestled inside it.

Once you convert the document, you have to change some settings in Acrobat so that your readers see your bookmarks when they view the document. Open the document in Acrobat and follow these steps:

1. In Acrobat, click the Bookmarks tab on the Navigation pane to open the Bookmarks pane. You can resize the pane by dragging the bar dividing the Navigation and Document panes.

2. Click File > Document Properties > Initial View to set options on how the document will look when it opens.

(Continued)

3. Click the Show drop-down list in the Document Options section at the top of the dialog. Then choose Bookmarks Panel and Page (**Figure 7.6**). Click OK to close the dialog.

Figure 7.6
Set a document to open with both the document and its bookmarks displayed.

4. Choose File > Save to save the PDF document. The next time the document is opened, it will display page 1 of the document complete with bookmarks.

TIP 63 Adding Bookmarks in Acrobat

You can create, configure, and customize bookmarks from within Acrobat. Acrobat lets you add new bookmarks to a document using one of two methods: you can either add blank bookmarks and fill them in manually, or you can use selected text from the document to create your bookmarks. The approach you use depends on how many bookmarks you have to add—if you want only four bookmarks you can easily type in the text, but if you want 54, that's another story. For either method, start with the document and the Bookmarks pane open in Acrobat.

To add blank bookmarks:

1. Click Create New Bookmark  on the Bookmarks pane toolbar to add a blank bookmark to the Bookmarks pane (**Figure 7.7**).

Figure 7.7 A new bookmark is named *Untitled*.

2. Click the selected *Untitled* text in the new bookmark and type your bookmark's text.

To create a bookmark using your document's text:

1. Click Select Text 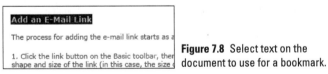 on the Basic toolbar.

2. Click and drag to select the text that you want to use for the bookmark label (**Figure 7.8**).

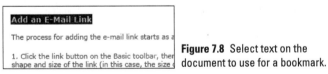

Figure 7.8 Select text on the document to use for a bookmark.

3. Click Create New Bookmark 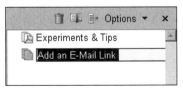 on the Bookmarks pane toolbar to add a bookmark using the selected text (**Figure 7.9**).

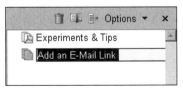

Figure 7.9 Convert the selected text to a bookmark label.

Bookmarks in a Hurry

Speed up the bookmarking process. Click the existing bookmark in the list above where you want the new bookmark added, and click the Create New Bookmark icon. The new bookmark magically appears below the selected bookmark.

TIP 63: Adding Bookmarks in Acrobat

TIP 64 Setting a Bookmark's Destination

Creating a bookmark in Acrobat requires two simple steps:

- Add and name the bookmark.

- Set the view, referred to as the *destination*.

When you add a bookmark in either a source program or in Acrobat, the bookmark is usable as soon as it's deselected. Once you click the bookmark, the destination appears in the Document pane. The problem is that the Document pane displays only the part of the document visible when you created the bookmark. Sometimes that isn't always the ideal view (**Figure 7.10**).

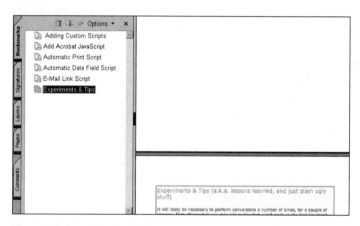

Figure 7.10 A new bookmark displays the part of the document that was visible when you created the bookmark. It's not always what you want to display.

To reset the document view, follow these steps:

1. Click the bookmark in the Bookmarks pane. The original view appears in the Document pane.

2. Position the document page in the window, and set the magnification using any of the various Zoom tools or shortcut keys.

3. Right-click/Control-click the bookmark to display the shortcut menu and select Set Destination (**Figure 7.11**).

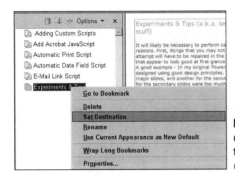

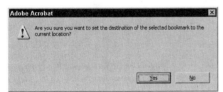

Figure 7.11 Set the destination using the shortcut menu command.

4. In the resulting confirmation dialog (**Figure 7.12**), click Yes to set the destination and to dismiss the dialog.

Figure 7.12 Confirm the bookmark's destination.

Note
Be sure to click the bookmark's name in the Bookmarks pane to activate it before setting the destination view. If you position the document in the desired location and set the magnification, as soon as you click the bookmark you want to change it jumps to the original view—which means you have to start all over again.

Bookmarking an Image
You don't have to stick with boring old text to define a bookmark location—you can use an image as a bookmark location instead. Click Select Image in the Select options on the Basic toolbar. Then, click an image or draw a marquee around a portion of an image on your document. Right-click/Control-click the image and choose Add Bookmark. A new bookmark named Untitled appears at the bottom of the list (or below a selected bookmark).

TIP 64: Setting a Bookmark's Destination

TIP 65 Organizing a Bookmark Hierarchy

Bookmarks form an interactive table of contents that lets your readers quickly see an outline of the contents of your document. For your readers' convenience, it makes sense to organize your list of bookmarks into a logical hierarchy. That is, the main headings expand to display lower-level headings, which in turn expand to display another heading level. From a technical standpoint, there's no limit to the number of levels you can use—but from a functional perspective, you probably shouldn't use more than three levels; more than that makes your list confusing (**Figure 7.13**). The more nested levels you have, the more screen space is required to display them, which decreases the size of the Document pane and ultimately reduces the value of using bookmarks at all. What good is an interactive table of contents if the entire screen is filled with the table and you can't see the contents?

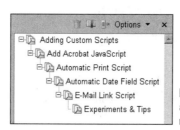

Figure 7.13 Bookmarks can be nested in an infinite number of levels, but the content may be difficult to see and work with.

Everything in Its Place

Before you start organizing the contents of your bookmark list into a hierarchy, make sure the heading levels are in the right order. Depending on how methodical you were when you created the bookmarks, they might not accurately reflect the order of the contents. To fix the sequence, first select the bookmark you want to move. Drag it up or down in the list to position it in its proper place. You'll see a small, red, downward-facing arrow below each title as you drag the bookmark up or down the list. The red arrow indicates where Acrobat will drop the bookmark. When you have the bookmark in the right location, just release the mouse.

Nesting Bookmarks

You can create *parent* and *child* relationships between entries in your document's Bookmarks list. If you have a complex document with dozens of headings, create several main headings and then nest child headings for each main heading. That way, your readers can scan the main headings, and when they see a topic of interest, they can click the heading to open the nested list displaying the child bookmarks. Nesting bookmarks decreases clutter and makes it easier for your reader to see what's in the document.

1. Click the bookmark to select it. Drag up or down with the pointer positioned over the bookmark's icon. You'll see a horizontal red line below the icon (**Figure 7.14**).

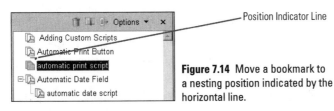

Position Indicator Line

Figure 7.14 Move a bookmark to a nesting position indicated by the horizontal line.

Note

If you select and drag the bookmark label, you'll just move the bookmark in the list, not change its hierarchy. Make sure you're moving the icon.

2. When you see the horizontal bar below the bookmark you want to use as a parent, release the mouse. The bookmark moves into a nested position below the parent bookmark (**Figure 7.15**). A level indicator—either a minus or plus sign within a small box—appears to the left of the parent bookmark.

Figure 7.15 The child bookmark settles in beneath its parent.

3. Click to expand and collapse the bookmark. When you move the parent bookmark, Acrobat includes any children bookmarks in the move.

Note

Not only do child bookmarks move if you move the parent bookmark, but if you delete a parent bookmark, all levels of bookmarks nested within it are deleted as well.

4. If you want to move a bookmark out of a nested position, drag the bookmark icon to a position below the parent bookmark. When you release the mouse, Acrobat moves the bookmark up the hierarchy.

Using Arrow Keys to Navigate Bookmarks

Use the arrow keys on the keyboard to move through a long list of bookmarks:

- The up arrow key moves up the list.
- The down arrow key moves down the list. (Yes, these first two are pretty obvious.)
- The left arrow key moves up a hierarchy to the parent.
- The right arrow key moves down a hierarchy to the innermost-nested child bookmark.

TIP 65: Organizing a Bookmark Hierarchy

TIP 66 Modifying Bookmark Appearances

We naturally see bold and colored text as more important than regular black text. Use that natural tendency to make it easier for your reader to understand how your document is organized. This is a great strategy to use in combination with a hierarchical listing. For example, use bold, italicized text for the first-level bookmark; bold text for the second level; and regular black text for the third level.

Coordinating a bookmark list with the document's color scheme gives it a professional look, especially when you set the document's initial view to open displaying both the document and bookmarks.

Figure 7.16 shows the "before" look in our sample project. The bookmark hierarchy is in place, but it is difficult to see what's really important in the list—all the bookmarks use the same weight and color of font and are differentiated only on the basis of their indentation.

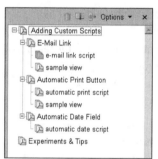

Figure 7.16 A document's bookmarks nested appropriately display the content in a hierarchy, but it's difficult to get a sense of more or less important headings.

Contrast that with the "after "look in **Figure 7.17**. The bookmarks have the same structure as before, but you can easily see that the first and last bookmarks are the most dominant in appearance and that the sample view headings are the least dominant. The third-level bookmarks in italics are bookmarked images in the document.

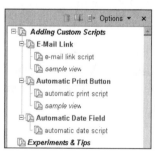

Figure 7.17 The modified set of bookmarks clearly shows the most dominant headings and makes the document's content easier to see at a glance.

Here are some tips on manipulating the appearance of bookmarks, including some shortcuts and timesaving methods:

- Before you start modifying, open the Bookmarks list and click a top-level bookmark. From the Options menu choose Expand Current Bookmark from the Bookmarks pane menu so that all lower-level bookmarks are visible.

- How you manipulate the bookmarks depends on the content and how you like to work. I prefer to use right-click or shortcut keys when practical. I also like to group items and work with them simultaneously. Open and close levels as needed to keep track of what you are doing.

- Another method that works well is to define an appearance for your bookmarks when you start. Add the first bookmark and then configure it using the Bookmarks Properties toolbar (**Figure 7.18**). Right-click/Control-click the bookmark and choose Use Current Appearance as New Default.

Figure 7.18 Use the Bookmarks Properties toolbar to save time as you work with bookmarks instead of opening the Properties dialog for each bookmark.

Note

The Bookmark Properties toolbar also has a button named More. That button leads to an Actions dialog containing options that let you extend the functionality of bookmarks. See Tip 69 for information on how to use the Set Layer Visibility action. Because the bookmarking and linking actions are the same, I've covered the other actions in Chapter 8.

- Sometimes your bookmarks are quite lengthy. Although you should try to keep the titles short, sometimes that isn't possible. Acrobat 6 lets you set bookmarks to wrap depending on the width of the Bookmarks pane. Right-click/Control-click a long bookmark and choose Wrap Long Bookmarks from the shortcut menu. Regardless of the width of the Bookmarks pane, your reader can always read the bookmarks without scrolling (**Figure 7.19**).

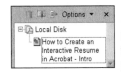

Figure 7.19 You can wrap bookmarks to view the content regardless of the Bookmarks pane's width.

(Continued)

TIP 66: Modifying Bookmark Appearances

Belly Up to the Toolbar

All of the tools used for modifying bookmarks are in the Bookmark Properties toolbar; it's a good idea to open that toolbar to make configuring quicker (see Figure 7.18). Use the shortcut Ctrl+E/Command+E. When you click a bookmark in the list, the Properties bar is activated. Move the toolbar into a convenient location on the screen. I usually leave it floating in the Bookmarks pane (or dock it at the left of the window if the Bookmarks list is lengthy).

- You can resize the text in the Bookmarks tab. Click the Options menu and choose Text Size > Large (**Figure 7.20**). The bookmarks' text increases in size, making the content easier to read (**Figure 7.21**). Changing size has no effect on the other text characteristics, such as italic, that you set in the Bookmark Properties toolbar.

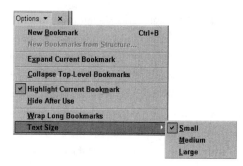

Figure 7.20 Choose an alternate text size.

Figure 7.21 This larger size makes for easier reading.

- When you have finished modifying the bookmarks, close the levels of bookmarks according to how you want them displayed when the document is opened. Be sure to save the file.

- Test the final document. Close and reopen the file and check the bookmark hierarchy. In **Figure 7.22**, our sample document shows the first- and second-level bookmarks, and displays the top of page one of the document—which is exactly the effect I wanted.

Figure 7.22 Test the bookmarks and the destination views.

Develop a Bookmarking Workflow

This is my method of creating a set of bookmarks easily, consistently, and accurately:

- Build the bookmark title list.
- Organize and arrange the hierarchy structure in the Bookmarks pane.
- Test and set destinations for the list.
- Modify the appearance of your bookmarks.
- Test the Bookmarks list.
- Set the document properties to include the bookmarks in the initial view.
- Save the document.

TIP 67 Using Tagged Bookmarks

In the Bookmarks pane, one of two icons appears before the name of a bookmark. They may be prefaced by the bookmark icon 🔖, or in a converted and tagged document you see another icon 📄. Although you can configure both types of bookmarks' appearance in the same way, functionally they are different.

Acrobat lets you add and delete bookmarks at will without affecting the content of your document. However, if you use tagged bookmarks you can modify the content of the document as well as provide navigation in the document. You can export a document from either Adobe InDesign or Microsoft Word XP as a tagged document. Don't bother to export styles or headings as bookmarks—you will build the bookmarks from the document tags rather than using styles or headings. Refer to the tips in Chapter 4 for more information on tagging documents.

Adding Tagged Bookmarks

So your first step is to open the PDF in Acrobat. Then:

1. Open the Bookmarks pane. Choose Options > New Bookmarks from Structure to open the Structure Elements dialog.

2. Scroll through the list in the Structure Elements dialog and select the tags you want to convert to bookmarks. The tags are based on the styles or headings used in the original Word XP document.

3. Ctrl-click to select specific tags (**Figure 7.23**). Choose tags according to the levels of headings you want in your Bookmarks list. In our sample, I want to convert the Head1 tags as well as the Code tags to a set of bookmarks. You might also want to convert other heading tags depending on the length and complexity of the document and how many bookmarks you need.

(Continued)

When Creating Bookmarks from Styles…

If you are converting a document from Word XP and plan to build the bookmarks from the styles, it is much faster to *select* the specific styles in Acrobat than it is to *deselect* the unwanted styles in the PDFMaker macro in Word. Refer to Tip 62 in this chapter for more on converting a Word document that defines bookmarks using styles.

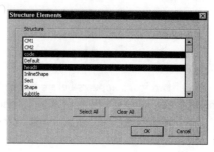

Figure 7.23 Select specific tags to convert to bookmarks.

Note

If you click an element by mistake, click it again while pressing the Ctrl/ Command key to deselect it. You can choose Select All to select the entire list. Click Clear All to deselect all the tags and start over.

4. Click OK to close the dialog. Acrobat takes the selected tags, converts them to bookmarks, and adds them to the Bookmarks pane in one collapsed basic bookmark named *Untitled* (**Figure 7.24**).

Figure 7.24 The converted tags are nested within one bookmark named *Untitled*.

5. Click the plus sign to the left of the bookmark's name to open the list. Only the Untitled bookmark uses the basic bookmark icon; the others use the tagged bookmark icon, as shown in **Figure 7.25**. The bookmarks aren't named using any content from the document; instead their names reflect their tag element's name.

Figure 7.25 The converted tags use the tagged bookmark icon and the style tag name.

6. Modify the bookmarks' appearance and view as desired. You can add and remove, rename, and relocate bookmarks in the Bookmarks pane. If you add new bookmarks, they will use the basic bookmark icon because they are *added* bookmarks and not part of the document structure.

Modifying Content with Tagged Bookmarks

Did you know you can modify the content of your document by using tagged bookmarks? Here's the scoop: First, select a bookmark or bookmarks from the list in the Bookmarks pane. Right-click/Control-click it to open a shortcut menu (or open the pane's Options menu); you see a number of document-modifying commands (**Figure 7.26**).

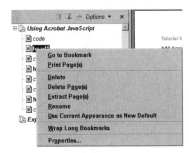

Figure 7.26 Tagged bookmarks allow you to modify document content.

Here's what you can do:

- Click Print Page(s) to print the pages containing the selected tag(s).

- Click Delete Page(s) to delete the pages containing the selected tag(s). If you choose this command, you'll see a warning dialog (**Figure 7.27**) telling you that you can't "undelete." Click Yes to proceed.

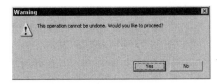

Figure 7.27 Acrobat warns you before a page is deleted.

Note

Even though Acrobat warns you that the action isn't reversible, it actually is. No, you can't choose Edit > Undo to undo the command. But you can choose File > Revert and revert to the last-saved version of the document (tricky, eh?).

- Click Extract Page(s) to extract the information from the pages containing the selected tag(s) and to create a new PDF document.

Web Tagged Bookmarks

If you convert a Web page, the tagged content is added to the Bookmarks pane and displays the Web tagged bookmark. You use this bookmark as you would any other tagged bookmarks. In addition, you can open the link in a Web browser or append other Web pages from the converted Web page's site.

TIP 67: Using Tagged Bookmarks

TIP 68 Working with a Layered Document

Acrobat 6 introduced the ability to work with layered documents created in Microsoft Visio and AutoCAD. Unfortunately, layered documents created in programs such as Adobe Photoshop are not supported.

This tip uses a four-layer document, created in Microsoft Visio XP, that has four named layers. Our document displays a logo for one company using four languages. Each language is on a separate layer. The default view (**Figure 7.28**) shows the content of all layers simultaneously (looks a bit messy, doesn't it?). If you come across a document like this, have a look at the bottom left of the Acrobat window. If you see a "layer cake" icon ▦, you know the document is layered. Click the Layers tab in the Navigation pane to open the Layers pane. If the Layers tab isn't visible in the Navigation pane, choose View > Navigation Tabs > Layers to open the tab.

Layer cake icon

Figure 7.28 You can use multilayered documents in Acrobat 6. If the document opens as a scrambled heap of text, look for a "layer cake" icon at the bottom left of the program window; it will confirm that the active document contains layers.

In **Figure 7.29**, you can see that our document has four named layers, each corresponding to the individual layer's language. The eye ◉ indicates that a layer is visible. You can toggle a layer's visibility on and off by clicking the eye icon. In **Figure 7.30**, only the Japanese layer is set to visible, and the content on the layer appears in the Document pane.

Different Types of Layers

What you see in the Layers pane depends on how the original document was constructed and converted. In some cases, a document is converted with *preserved* layers, as in our example. In other cases, the document layers may be *flattened* or *locked*. In a flattened document, you see a single layer (like a regular PDF document). A locked document, on the other hand, displays the layers individually, but they can't be edited in any way.

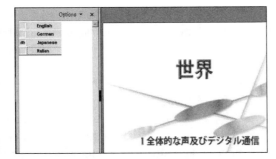

Figure 7.29 All layers are visible, indicated by the eye icons.

Figure 7.30 Toggle a layer's visibility on and off by clicking the eye icon. Here, just one layer is visible.

As with other documents, you may be able to make changes to the content (depending on the rights granted by the document's author). Our sample doesn't have security attached, so you can add comments to it or export it in another file format from Acrobat. To see what a layer contains, right-click it on the Layers pane and choose Layer Properties to open the dialog shown in **Figure 7.31**. The Layer Properties dialog lists information about the layer, including its original name, print status, and export status. Keep in mind that settings applied to the original layered document cannot be changed. For example, our sample document uses the Never Print setting; although you can use the File > Print command and send the page to the printer, only a blank page prints.

Figure 7.31 You can view each layer's properties.

TIP 89: Working with a Layered Document

TIP 69 Bookmarking a Layered Document

Acrobat lets you attach bookmarks to layers, which lets you, for example, distribute the same information using different languages without having to provide documents in different languages. You can use bookmarks in conjunction with layers to give readers control over what they see or print. Using *actions*, you can extend the functionality of a bookmark beyond just pointing to a location in your document. Using the Set Layer Visibility action attached to the bookmarks, readers can click one button to get to the document layer that they need. Refer to Chapter 8 for a look at other actions.

Our sample document has four layers, each using a different language along with a company's logo. In Acrobat 6, layers work only for AutoCAD files and Microsoft Visio files (used in the sample). Layered PDF documents from programs such as Adobe Photoshop and Illustrator are not yet supported.

Follow these steps to bookmark a layered document:

1. Open the Bookmarks pane and add four bookmarks (**Figure 7.32**). At this point, if you click any bookmark it displays the same location on the same page.

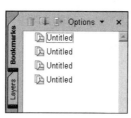

Figure 7.32 Create a set of bookmarks to use for displaying the layers in the document.

2. Select each bookmark and name it (**Figure 7.33**). To minimize confusion, name the bookmarks in the same order as the layers listed on the Layers pane.

Figure 7.33 For convenience, name the bookmarks in the same order as the layers.

Arranging Panes for Efficiency

Speed up your workflow when you're bookmarking layers: drag all but the Layers and Bookmarks tabs in the Navigation pane individually to the right to separate them from the list of tabs. Close them, and then reopen them as needed by choosing View > Navigation Tabs and selecting the pane you want.

3. On the Layers pane, toggle all layers but English to invisible (**Figure 7.34**). Set the destination view for the English title bookmark to display only the English layer.

Figure 7.34 Hide all layers but the English text layer.

4. On the Bookmarks pane, right-click the English bookmark to select it and open the shortcut menu. Choose Properties to open the Bookmark Properties dialog and then click the Actions tab.

5. From the Select Action pull-down menu select Set Layer Visibility (**Figure 7.35**). Then click Add. The action automatically appears in the Actions section at the bottom of the dialog.

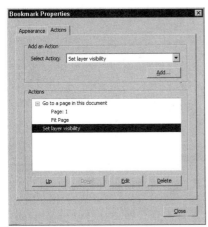

Figure 7.35 Choose the Set Layer Visibility action in the Actions tab.

Note

By default, a bookmark's action is to display a page number. This is shown in the bottom window in Figure 7.35. You can delete the action or leave it as is. In this case, it doesn't make any difference.

(Continued)

TIP 69: Bookmarking a Layered Document

6. A notification dialog appears (**Figure 7.36**) to tell you that the target layer state of the selected actions will be set to the current state. In other words, set the layer you want to see as a result of clicking a bookmark and leave the rest hidden. Click OK. The action is added to the Actions list.

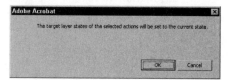

Figure 7.36 Read the notification dialog and click OK before applying the action.

7. Click OK to close the Bookmark Properties dialog.

8. Repeat with the other layers. Be sure to hide all layers except for the one you are attaching to the bookmark.

TIP 70 Where Did I See That Word?

Of course, the navigation feature we all use at one time or another is the dependable Search function. This function allows you to track down words or phrases within a single file or through all the PDF files in a folder, another drive, or even on the Internet. Let's take a look at how it works in Acrobat 6:

1. To begin, choose Edit > Search to open the Search PDF pane; use the shortcut Ctrl+F/Command+F; or click the Search tool **Search** on the File toolbar. The Search PDF panel opens on the right side of the Document window.

2. Type the word or words you want to find in the first field. You can specify either a word or a phrase (**Figure 7.37**).

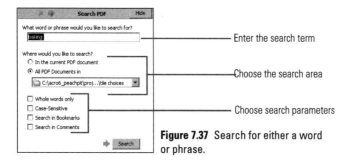

Enter the search term

Choose the search area

Choose search parameters

Figure 7.37 Search for either a word or phrase.

3. Select the file or folder you want to search. Click the first radio button to search the currently active file; click the second radio button to search in multiple files. Then, click the pull-down arrow and select the folder and drive location.

4. Click Search. You'll see the striped indicator bar as Acrobat searches. When the search is completed, Acrobat displays the results, as well as the locations where it found the search term, in the Results area (**Figure 7.38**).

(Continued)

Web Searches

Click the search PDF's on the internet line at the bottom of the search page to start a Web search. Acrobat's Internet searches are performed by Google, which means that your reach is virtually limitless. However, the breadth of the search means it can take a *very* long time to locate a particular phrase in an online PDF file.

Figure 7.38 You can see the number of occurrences, as well as the documents in which the search term appears.

You can see the number of instances of the word occurring in the set of files you searched, along with the number of documents containing the word.

5. Click the box to the left of the file path to open a list of the results' locations. As you move your mouse over a result, it displays the document page number (**Figure 7.39**).

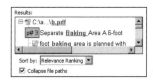

Figure 7.39 Click the box to the left of the file path to see the page on which the search term appears.

6. Click a result in the Results pane to jump to the location in the document. Acrobat obligingly highlights the term on the document for you (**Figure 7.40**).

Figure 7.40 Select a result on the Search Results dialog to highlight the term on the document.

Note
Shortcut keys allow you to work through a long list of search results. Open the first document, and then press F3 to jump to the next and subsequent hits. Press Ctrl+] to go to the next document; press Ctrl+[to go to the previous document. In a document, press Ctrl+G to go to the next result; press Ctrl+Shift+G to go to the previous result.

Zeroing In on Your Searches

Use the customization options when possible to cut down the number of search hits. The Case-Sensitive option can be used with a string of text. For example "My dog Betty" returns only those files containing the exact words in that exact sequence with the same capitalization. Searching for "dog" returns the text, but can also return hits for "my other dog Barnie".

Just a warning, though—searching for "my dog Betty" (with "my" all lowercase) provides no returns if you used "My" in the document.

CHAPTER EIGHT

Controlling Documents with Links

As shown in the last group of tips, bookmarks are a convenient way to link a label to content. But they are certainly not the only way. Another popular method for building an interactive document is to link content.

A PDF, with all its features, more closely resembles a Web site than an ordinary printed document. Would you go to a Web site and scroll through innumerable pages of content to find information? Would you be comfortable using a Web site that didn't have some sort of navigational structure? Of course not! You expect a Web site to come complete with a system of links that allows you to click through the site to find information.

Although people tend to use Acrobat just to convert documents to a common PDF format so they can be shared, that's only the tip of the iceberg. Once you have converted your masterpiece, you can easily add links to guide readers through your document.

In this collection of tips, we'll show you how links work. You can use a great variety of *actions* with links to do everything from jumping to another page in a document to opening another document to playing a movie clip. We'll show you two useful actions for creating links that print a document and send an email automatically.

We'll look at most of the available actions in this group of tips (we'll save the forms and media-related actions for Chapter 9 when we look at ways to use and create multimedia projects in Acrobat). We will also explain a specific type of link called a *destination* that's used with bookmarks to enable you to control content across documents. Destinations are covered in Tip 80.

TIP 71 Linking Content in a Document

You typically use links to connect information from one location in a document to another location in that document. Simple links are easy to add to a document and configure.

Follow these steps to add a basic link:

1. Choose Tools > Advanced Editing > Show Advanced Editing Toolbar (**Figure 8.1**). Drag the toolbar to dock it at the top or side of the Acrobat window.

Figure 8.1 The Link tool is on the Advanced Editing toolbar.

2. Click the Link tool 🔗. Then, click in the document and drag to draw a rectangle enclosing the text you want to use for the link. Once you release the mouse, the Create Link dialog opens (**Figure 8.2**).

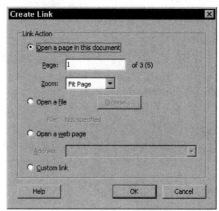

Figure 8.2 The Create Link dialog opens when you draw a link box.

3. Choose from one of four basic link options:

   • Open A Page In This Document is the default selection. Type a page number in the Page field, and choose a magnification level from the Zoom pull-down list.

   • Click Open A File to activate the Browse button. Click Browse and locate the file you want linked.

- Click Open A Web Page to activate the Address field. Type the Web address or click the pull-down arrow and select the page from the list of Web addresses you have used previously in the document.

- Click Custom Link to use other types of linking such as such as linking to actions. If you choose this option, the Link Properties dialog opens when you click OK. Choose an action and click Close to dismiss the dialog and set the link.

4. Once your link is drawn and you close the Create Link dialog, you'll see the red link box on the page (**Figure 8.3**). You can reposition the link if necessary. With the Link tool selected, move the pointer inside the link box and drag to the desired location. You can also resize the link box. Move the pointer over a resize handle on the edge of the link's box and drag to increase (or decrease) the link's dimensions.

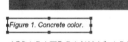

Figure 1. Concrete color.

SEPARATE BAKING AREA

Figure 8.3 A visible box shows where the link is located on the page.

Zooming Around

When you're creating a set of basic navigation links, use the same zoom setting for all of them if possible. That saves you one step per page as you are constructing the links. Also, it's easier on your reader if the view doesn't jump to different sizes from page to page.

5. You can't see the finished link as long as the Link tool is active. Click the Hand tool on the Basic toolbar. Now you can see the actual link (**Figure 8.4**). In this example, our link uses a custom appearance; read about custom link appearances in the next tip.

Figure 1. Concrete color.

SEPARATE BAKING /

Figure 8.4 You can't see a link's appearance when the Link tool is selected. Choose the Hand tool instead.

6. It's always a good idea to test the link. Using the Hand tool pointer, move over the link area. Click when the pointer turns to a finger pointing. The page you specified in the Create Link dialog should appear in the Document pane at the zoom setting you've selected.

TIP 71: Linking Content in a Document

TIP 72 — Setting Link Appearance and Action

You can modify a link's function and appearance to add features and to match the look of your document. Make sure the Link tool is selected, and then follow these steps:

1. Double-click the link on the page to open the Link Properties dialog.

2. Choose options for the link's appearance in the Appearance tab (**Figure 8.5**).

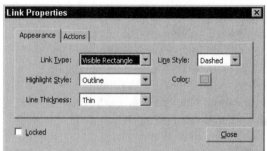

Figure 8.5 Use the Appearance tab to set the link's line style, color, and visibility.

There are a number of ways you can configure the appearance of a link. To start with, you can make the link—that is, the box around the text—visible or invisible. If you use a visible link, choose options for highlight style, line width, and line style (**Figure 8.6**). You can also specify colors and styles that coordinate with the rest of your document. Click the color button to choose a custom color for the link decoration.

Figure 8.6 You can choose your link's line colors and styles to coordinate with the rest of your document.

Note

*If your document had button shapes added to it in the source program (**Figure 8.7**), it's a good idea to use an invisible link. The buttons don't need any decoration or identification; they only need the functionality.*

Figure 8.7 If your document contains drawn buttons like these ones, use invisible links.

3. Click the Actions tab. Click the Select Action pull-down arrow in the Add An Action section to display a list of action types (**Figure 8.8**). Scroll through the list and make your selection. In this example, we're using the default "Go to a page in this document" action.

Figure 8.8 You can choose from a bunch of action types.

4. A dialog specific to the action displays; in this example, we see the dialog "Go to a page in this document" (**Figure 8.9**). In the example, we do the following:

Figure 8.9 You'll see a dialog with options specific to your chosen action.

(Continued)

Visible or Invisible?

When deciding on your link's appearance, how do you know what options to choose? Choose invisible if the link is visible to your readers in other ways. For example, if you write CLICK THIS LINK, the reader has a fairly good idea what to do! In that case, use an invisible link. You want the functionality, but you don't need any decoration to identify the active area on the page.

Use a visible link to identify active areas that aren't obvious link text. In our sample document, we created several links between descriptions and larger images. With the appearance options we choose, the link is a noticeable object on the page.

TIP 72: Setting Link Appearance and Action

- Click Use Page Number.

- Type the page number to use for the link (we used 3).

- Choose Fit Width from the Zoom pull-down list.

5. Click OK to close the dialog and return to the Actions tab.

6. Verify that the information in the window matches your settings. (**Figure 8.10**).

Figure 8.10 When you specify an action, you can read the settings before completing the link.

7. Click Close to close the Link Properties dialog box.

When you click the link with the Hand tool, page 3 should display in the Document pane.

TIP 73 Building a Series of Links

It may seem as though each link is independent from the others, and on the surface they are—click a link and you go to another page—but that's only half the story. You also have to consider how your readers are going to return to the location they started from. Your 500-page User Guide may have important links on the first page; your readers click a link and end up on page 287. Now what? Will you make them navigate manually through the document to return to the page they started from (if they can remember the page)? Good navigation design considers both the user's interests and probable method of navigation, in addition to presenting your carefully crafted words and material in a systematic way. A big document can have literally hundreds of links, and that's just for simple navigation. Add special kinds of links (such as opening files and reading articles), and you can have quite a complex job to organize. This tip shows you some of the features and settings you can use to get the job done efficiently and accurately.

Plan Before You Build

Start at the beginning. Plan how you want readers to navigate through the document. Often you use a combination of links and bookmarks. If you use a bookmark to jump to a topic heading, for example, and then have additional information on the topic in another part of the document (or even another document), use a link. Plan how you want the links to look as well. If your original document contains high-lighted or bold text, you can use that text and apply invisible links. On the other hand, you may wish to use visible text links for selected phrases or words in your document. You can also use a variety of objects, such as arrows, or the word *Back* or *Home* (**Figure 8.11**); you can even use a table containing text to attach links like you might find in a Web navigation table. If it sounds as if you're designing a Web site, you are right; the process and purposes of linking in a PDF document are virtually the same.

Figure 8.11 Use drawing and text commenting tools to create a button.

Who's Got the Button?

Sometimes you need a button on your document and it doesn't have one. You can create one in the source document and reconvert it, or you can fudge it in Acrobat.

The button in Figure 8.11 is composed of several elements. Using the drawing tools in the Advanced Commenting toolbar, we created two rectangles (using the cloud-style stroke), offset to create a shadow effect. The button's label is a text comment; the inner box is a link box. See the tips in Chapter 6 for information on using the commenting tools.

You can even reuse the button if need be. Click the Select Object tool and draw a marquee around the shapes. Copy and paste as needed.

Don't forget to provide a return path from your links. Forcing your reader to use a back button on a toolbar to return to the previous view isn't good design. If you link from a page to another document, insert a link on the second document to return your readers to their starting point. If you add a link from one page to another in the same document, be sure to add return links to significant points in the document, such as a section heading or a list of topics. Return links can be as simple as a Back button or an arrow, or as complex as a browser-like navigation bar on every page.

Building the First Link

Here's how to build the first link:

1. Once you've planned your link strategy, build your first link by dragging over text with the Link tool.
2. Set its appearance in the Link Properties bar (**Figure 8.12**).

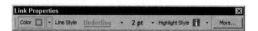

Figure 8.12 Open the Link Properties toolbar when you're configuring your links.

3. Set the action as described in Tip 72.
4. Click the Hand tool on the Basic toolbar, and then test the link.

Setting Link Properties

Use the Link Properties bar to quickly define your link settings. You can open the Properties bar in one of three ways:

- Press Ctrl+E/Command+E.
- Right-click/Control-click on the toolbar area at the top of the Acrobat window and choose Properties Bar.
- Choose View > Toolbars > Properties Bar.

Now that you've created your very first link, and gotten it looking the way you want it, place it in the correct location on the first page. **Figure 8.13** shows the example, which is the page number footer at the bottom of the page.

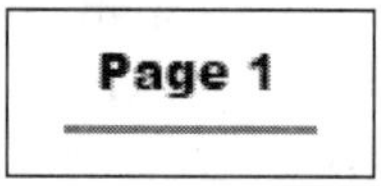

Figure 8.13 Check the layout and appearance of the finished link.

Adding a Series of Page Links

You can add a group of similar links quickly. Let's pick up where the last section left off and assume the first link is on the first page:

1. Click your link with the Link tool to select it; copy the link.

2. Click the Next Page arrow in the status bar under the Document pane (**Figure 8.14**) to display page 2.

Figure 8.14 Use the page controls in the status bar under the Document pane to quickly move through the document.

3. Paste the link. The link appears on the page, usually at the center (**Figure 8.15**).

Figure 8.15 The pasted link appears at the center of the page.

4. Drag the link to the location you want it to appear on page 2. We want ours on the page number in the lower-right corner.

5. Go to the next page, paste the link, and then position it again. Continue to the end of the document.

Another Page, Another Link

You add multiple links in one of two ways:

- Add one link at a time, position it, configure it, and test it.
- Add all the links, position and configure them, and then test them.

I strongly prefer the second option, particularly with a long document. It's much simpler to perform the same process, such as copying and pasting, 50 times than it is to completely finish one link and then start the next one.

TIP 74 Precisely Positioning a Series of Links

If you're copying and pasting a number of links, you'll discover that they don't paste into the same location from page to page. If you are using a visible link over text, such as a box or an underline, you want the text and frame to have a consistent layout throughout the document. You can position them accurately using the Info panel.

Let's look at a method for precisely aligning visual links; in this example, the links appear as underlines under a word. Use this method if you have a fairly small project, say 8 to 10 pages. If you were doing a 300-page manual and had to align links over that many pages, it would be better to go back to the source program and make some modifications.

Here are the steps:

1. Choose View > Navigation Tabs > Info to open the Info panel.

2. Depending on the page layouts, either dock the Info panel with the other Navigation tabs or leave it floating. In our example, the panel is floating (**Figure 8.16**).

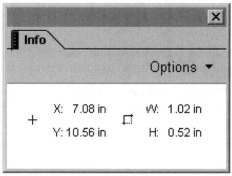

Figure 8.16 Leave the Info pane floating to keep the information close to where you are working.

To Float or Not to Float

When working with a variety of links in various locations on your pages, dock the Info panel. However, if your links are in the same location on all pages, such as a series of links on page numbers, leave it floating.

Figure 8.16 shows the benefit of a floating panel. The Info panel is in the same approximate area as the link. You click or adjust the link and read the Info panel's values without looking back and forth across the screen. When you go to the next page, the Info panel stays in the same position, you scroll the link into view, and you are ready to set the second page's link precisely.

3. Position the link over the first page's text. Click the Hand tool to see the visible link (**Figure 8.17**). In our example, in which the link is shown as an underline, it is important to see the position of the link without the red link box displayed.

Page 1

Figure 8.17 Select the Hand tool to see your visible link.

4. Note the values displayed in the Info panel. Be careful with the pointer location. As you move the pointer around the page, you see the values change in the x and y coordinates in the Info panel.

Note

Choose a consistent location for your pointer to use as a point of reference. I use the top-left corner of the link box. As I slowly move the pointer over the corner resize handle, the pointer changes to a double-ended arrow; that is the coordinate location I note. For subsequent pages, if the pointer is placed at the same location on the links, I know the positioning values are accurate.

5. Go to the next link. Position the link using the Info panel coordinates. Continue through the rest of the project.

Note

You can nudge a link box to position it precisely. Select the link box with the Link tool, and then use the arrow keys on the keyboard to move the link in the direction of the arrow.

6. Save the file. After you spend a considerable amount of time making sure visible links are aligned, it is more than annoying to have some sort of computer problem wipe out all your efforts.

7. Go back to page 1. Set the actions for each link and then test them.

Rebuilding a Document

If you rebuild a document in the source program to make linking simpler, be careful how you change the pages in the PDF document. If the content is nothing more than text and/or images, simply name the document using the original name. If you have other content, such as other types of links, comments, bookmarks, and so on, use the Document > Pages > Replace command and swap pages. This will leave the extra content in place.

TIP 75 Positioning a Group of Links on a Page

Many documents use a series of headings laid out in a table as a means of navigating. Adding the links and then positioning them evenly can be quite a chore. Fortunately, Acrobat's align/distribute tools, designed to make the positioning process simpler, are at your fingertips. Our sample document contains a table with links to nine pages. To show you how the link alignment/distribution process works, we are using a narrow line around the links; in an actual document using a table layout, we suggest you use invisible links.

To position a group of links on your page, follow these steps:

1. Click the Link tool, and then set the properties for your links. In the Link Properties toolbar, click the point size pull-down arrow and choose Thin.

2. Draw your first link over the first text label.

3. Ctrl/Option-click the link to copy it and drag the copy to the next text label. Click to deselect the new link box, and then Ctrl/Option-drag the original link box again for the third text label. Continue until you've created the whole set of links (**Figure 8.18**).

Lining Up Your Links

Regardless of whether you use visible or invisible links, it's simpler to use Acrobat's align/distribute tools to evenly space the links on your page than to drag them manually and eyeball their placement.

Click Links for More Information on Our Luxury Coach Tours:		
Atlanta	Nashville	Orlando
Boston	New Orleans	Phoenix
Chicago	New York	San Francisco

Figure 8.18 All the text labels have links pasted onto them.

4. Resize the links as necessary to fit over the text labels. In the example, the label "San Francisco" at the bottom right is larger than the link. Drag a resize handle to increase the width of the link.

5. Leave the link around the longest text label selected, and Ctrl-click/Command-click the other links on the table to select them all. Right-click/Control-click to open the shortcut menu; choose Size > Width (**Figure 8.19**).

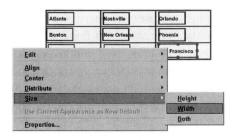

Figure 8.19 Use the shortcut menu to resize all the links.

Acrobat sizes the link boxes according to the first box you selected. In the example, we resized the box over the San Francisco label and selected it first. The set of links are now set to the same width, as shown in **Figure 8.20**.

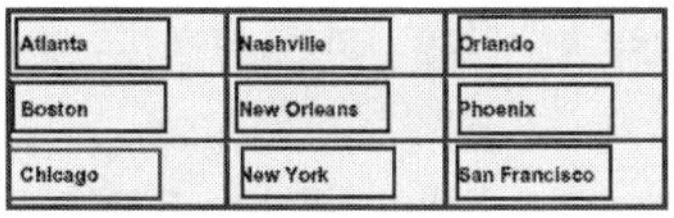

Figure 8.20 The links are all the same size, which is dictated by the largest one.

6. The boxes aren't aligned vertically or horizontally; that's next. Select the link that is in the correct position; in **Figure 8.21**, the top link is correctly placed, but we want to adjust the middle and bottom links. Ctrl-click/Command-click the remaining links in the same column.

Atlanta
Boston
Chicago

Figure 8.21 Align the links vertically and horizontally for consistency.

7. Right-click/Control-click to open the shortcut menu, then choose Align and an alignment option; you can choose from left, right, center, vertical, and horizontal alignment.

8. Repeat the selections horizontally and vertically until your set of links is distributed and aligned correctly.

9. Now that your links are positioned properly, click each link and set the page location as described in Tips 71 and 72.

TIP 75: Positioning a Group of Links on a Page

TIP 76 Linking One Document to Another

You can use links to connect content in separate documents. For example, a user manual may have links from terms to a glossary; a sales summary report may feature links to related spreadsheets. Creating inter-document linking is a quick and easy process. If your documents are very stable and you don't plan to make any changes over time, you can use the simple Link To Another Document action. If there is a possibility that you will change some of your document collection's content over time, we suggest you use destinations instead (see Tip 80).

To link one document to another:

1. Draw the link on the document. The Create Link dialog opens.

2. Click the Open A File radio button; the Browse button is activated. Click Browse to open a dialog; select the file you want to attach and click Select.

3. In the Specify Open Preference dialog (**Figure 8.22**), choose one of three options to specify how the user can view the linked document. You can force the linked document to open in a new window, in the current window, or according to user preference. Click OK to close the dialog and return to the Create Link dialog.

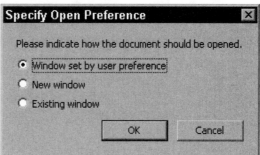

Figure 8.22 You can define how your users view linked documents.

Note

I usually leave the user preference setting enabled. People have their own way of working, and it can be confusing if a document suddenly replaces the document they were viewing or another window pops open.

4. The attached file's name appears in the Create Link dialog (**Figure 8.23**). Click OK to close the dialog. Then be sure to test your new link.

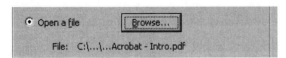

Figure 8.23 The Create Link dialog displays the attached file's name.

Setting an Open Window Preference

How do you want a linked document to open when you click an Acrobat link—in a new window or replacing the content in the current window? You can set a preference.

Choose Edit > Preferences (in Mac, Acrobat > Preferences) and click General in the left-hand list. Click Open Cross-Document Links In Same Window. When you view linked documents, the open document will be replaced by the document it is linked to in the same window. If you uncheck this option, each time you click a link to a different document, a new window opens.

TIP 77 Using Links for Viewing Snapshots or Articles

Did you know you can build a link in your document that displays the content from an image snapshot? You can also add a link that lets your readers view articles.

Linking to a Snapshot

Acrobat lets you build a series of links that connect to snapshots of the same image at varying degrees of magnification. In this example, we'll link a document to snapshots of a map in another document. The first document contains two text buttons: *full map* and *intersection*. The larger view of the map will be linked to the *full map* text; the magnified area, to the *intersection* text. We'll start with both documents open and arranged on the screen as shown in **Figure 8.24**.

A Snapshot is Worth a Thousand Words

Linking to snapshots is handy for showing image magnifications, like with maps. Rather than having to create a number of documents, each showing the map at different magnifications, you can use one page, take snapshots of the map at varying magnifications, and then build the set of links from the snapshots.

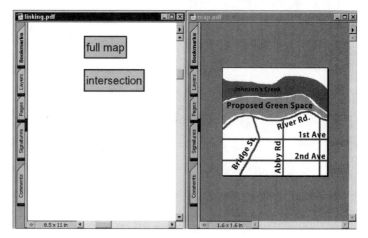

Figure 8.24 Tile windows when working with two documents at once.

1. Link the *full map* text to the entire page, as described in Tip 76.

2. Click the Snapshot tool on the Basic toolbar and click and drag to draw a marquee around the area of the page you want to capture. Acrobat copies the image to the clipboard.

   ### Note
   If you just click the page with the Snapshot tool, the visible page is captured in the snapshot.

3. Click the Link tool on the Advanced Editing toolbar and draw the link around the *intersection* text. The Create Link dialog opens. Click Custom Link (**Figure 8.25**), then click OK. The Link Properties dialog opens to the Actions tab.

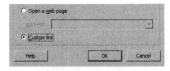

Figure 8.25 Use the Custom Link option to choose other link actions.

4. From the Select Action pull-down list, choose Go to snapshot view (**Figure 8.26**). Then click Add.

Figure 8.26 Choose Go to snapshot view to link to clipboard content.

The Create View From Snapshot dialog opens, informing you that the snapshot will be converted to a page. Click OK to close the dialog and return to the Actions tab.

5. The new action appears in the Actions tab (**Figure 8.27**). Click OK to close the dialog and finish the link.

Figure 8.27 Check the information about the action before completing the link.

6. As usual, be sure to test your link. The link labeled *intersection* opens the snapshot of the magnified area of the map in a new document (**Figure 8.28**).

(Continued)

TIP 77: Using Links for Viewing Snapshots or Articles

Figure 8.28 We've used a close-up of a map section converted from a clipboard snapshot as a link.

Linking to an Article

As you might expect, you need to have at least one article in the document you want to use for linking in order to use the action.

Here are the steps for linking to an article:

1. Click the Link tool and draw the link on the page. When the Create Link dialog opens, click Custom Link and click OK. The Link Properties dialog opens to the Actions tab.

2. From the Select Action pull-down list, choose Read An Article, then click Add.

3. The Select Article dialog opens (**Figure 8.29**). Choose one of the articles from the document and click OK. The Select Article dialog closes, and you return to the Link Properties dialog; the Read An Article action is now listed (**Figure 8.30**). Click Close to close the Link Properties dialog.

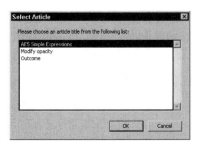

Figure 8.29 Choose one of the articles from the document for the link.

Figure 8.30 Check the information about the article link before completing your link.

4. Test the link by clicking the Hand tool on the Basic toolbar and clicking the link. The article displays in the Document pane.

Read an Article with Links

Using links to articles can be a convenient way to organize content for users who can't otherwise follow the flow of the document, like those reading a document using a high magnification or a handheld device.

TIP 77: Using Links for Viewing Snapshots or Articles

TIP 78 Linking to Menu Items

Did you know that you can control a program's function through a link? It sounds complicated, and you may wonder why you would do something like that. Here's a good example, and a terrific way to make a strong impression on your readers—provide a link that automatically prints your document.

1. Draw the link on the document. You can use a button image placed on the source document before you convert to a PDF, or you can draw the content using the drawing and text tools in Acrobat. **Figure 8.31** shows some examples of print button images created from symbols, clip art, and drawing tools.

Figure 8.31 Use a variety of different button images to serve as links to automatically print your document.

2. The Create Link dialog opens. Choose the Custom Link option and click OK. The Link Properties dialog opens to the Actions tab.

3. From the Select Action pull-down list, choose Execute A Menu Item (**Figure 8.32**). Click Add to open the Menu Item Selection dialog.

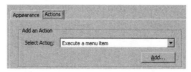

Figure 8.32 Choose Execute A Menu Item to add actions that use program commands.

4. Choose File > Print. The dialog displays the command (**Figure 8.33**). Click OK to close the dialog and return to the Actions tab of the Link Properties dialog.

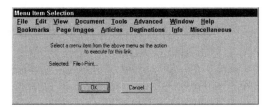

Figure 8.33 Select a command from the menu items.

5. The action now appears in the Actions window. Click Close to dismiss the Link Properties dialog and complete the link.

6. Click the Hand tool on the Basic toolbar and click the link to test it.

7. The Print dialog opens (**Figure 8.34**), which is the action you wanted. Close the dialog or click Print to print a copy of the document.

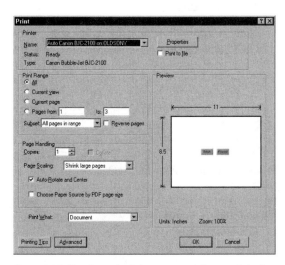

Figure 8.34 Check out the Print command that you linked from the button.

Jump into Action

Experiment with the options available in the Execute A Menu Item action. You may be surprised how interesting and functional your documents become. Here are a few of the things you can do:

- Send a document directly to a reviewer.

- Save the document as a certified/signed document.

- Open documents or eBooks.

- Zoom to various magnifications.

- Import or export forms data.

TIP 78: Linking to Menu Items

TIP 79 Using Links for JavaScript

If you are sending out your resume in PDF format, why not add an email link directly to the document? A recruiter just clicks the link to open her email program and a new message appears, already addressed to you. Now the eager recruiter can let you know how impressed she is with your Acrobat skills and set up an interview.

To construct the link's action, use Acrobat JavaScript. JavaScript lets you assign actions to links, bookmarks, and form fields. Unfortunately, an in-depth discussion on JavaScript is beyond the scope of this book. One very good book on the topic is *Extending Acrobat Forms with JavaScript*, by John Deubert, from Adobe Press; you should also check online resources at Adobe and other Web sites.

Follow these steps to create link text or a link image:

1. Using the Link tool, draw the link on your document. The Create Link dialog opens.

2. Click Custom Link and then click OK. The Link Properties dialog opens to the Actions tab.

3. From the Select Action pull-down list, choose Run A JavaScript (**Figure 8.35**). Click Add to open the JavaScript editor.

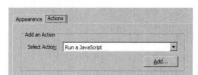

Figure 8.35 Select Run A JavaScript from the Select Action pull-down list.

4. Type the following email script in the JavaScript editor (**Figure 8.36**):

```
app.mailMsg(true, "name@address.com","", "", "Subject of
the E-mail");
```

Figure 8.36 Type the script in the JavaScript editor.

Click OK to close the JavaScript editor and return to the Link Properties dialog.

5. The JavaScript action is now listed in the Actions window. Click Close to close the Link Properties dialog and complete the link.

6. Click the Hand tool on the Basic toolbar and then click the link to test it.

7. Your email program opens, and you see the content from the script added to the blank email message, including the email address and the subject (**Figure 8.37**).

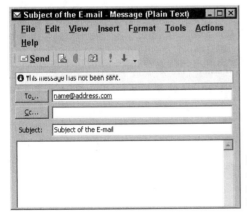

Figure 8.37 The content from the script displays in a new email message.

Customizing the JavaScript

The script we used in this tip is very simple. Make these changes to customize the script for your documents by changing the text:

- Rather than *name@address.com*, type your email address.
- Where it says `""`, `""`, you can include additional addresses for carbon copy (cc) and blind carbon copy (bcc).
- Replace *Subject of the E-mail* with text you want to display on the subject line of the email.

TIP 79: Using Links for JavaScript

TIP 80 Naming Destinations to Use for Navigation

Have you ever been to a Web site and clicked a link only to receive a message that the page can't be found? Everyone has. The same thing can happen in a group of PDF documents. If you make links in documents and then delete or replace pages in your linked documents, the links will be damaged or removed altogether. You can avoid that situation by using *destinations*. It takes more effort to build destinations, but in the long run it can save you a lot of time. Rather than simply linking to a document, you name each link separately from the general file's name. If you then change the document containing the destinations, as long as the named location is still present, the link won't be broken.

You need two documents to build destinations. In this tip, the document containing the link is called the *source* document; the one containing the named destination is called the *destination* document.

Naming the Destinations

The first step in the process is to name the destinations:

1. Open the destination document.

2. Choose View > Navigation Tabs > Destinations to open the Destinations pane (**Figure 8.38**). You can dock the pane with the other tabs in the Navigation pane or leave it floating. Note the message at the bottom of the pane telling you that the document isn't scanned. This means that the document hasn't been checked for destinations; unless you scan the document, you can't add any destinations.

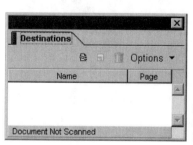

Figure 8.38 Destinations are defined and set in their own panel.

Link Marks the Spot

Use named destinations to link to a specific location on a page. In Acrobat 6, basic links take you to the top of a page. If you want to jump to a particular paragraph or section, create a named destination; you can define the location on the page as well as the page number and magnification.

3. Click Scan Document 📄 at the top of the Destinations pane. Acrobat looks through the document for any preexisting destinations. If the document contains any destinations, they appear in the pane. When the scan is complete, the Create New Destination command will be active.

4. Position the document in the window to display the content you want to use for the destination. Suppose you want the link to display the heading halfway down the page.

5. Click Create New Destination 🔲. A destination named *Untitled* is added to the pane, as shown in **Figure 8.39**.

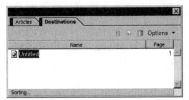

Figure 8.39 The new destination appears in the panel, as yet unnamed.

6. To rename a destination, right-click/Control-click it to open a shortcut menu, choose Rename, and type over the existing text (**Figure 8.40**). You can also double-click the destination and then overwrite the text to rename it.

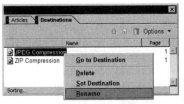

Figure 8.40 Right-click a destination to open a shortcut menu that lets you rename the destination.

7. Save the destination document.

Note
Each time you open a document that contains destinations, you must rescan it. To do that, click the Scan icon in the Destinations pane.

Plan Your Destination

Develop a practical method of naming that is recognizable and understandable, especially if you are working with similar material for different destinations. For example, if you are constructing a sales document that incorporates four regional reports into an overall report, preface each document's destinations with a key to the region, such as N (North) or M (Midwest). Then include another indicator from the individual document, such as a product line, and then the key to the individual destination. A destination with a name like *N-OP-I-Canon* could indicate the North sales region's report, the Office Products section, and the description of Canon Inkjet printers. Although selecting a document is part of choosing named destinations to link to, adding a prefix referring to the document is a simple safeguard. This can be especially useful if you are working with a large number of destinations over a large number of documents.

Completing the Links

Once you've set the destinations in the destination document, go to the source document to create the links to the named locations:

1. In the source document, click the Link tool and draw the link on the page. The Create Link dialog opens.

2. Click Custom Link, then click OK. The Link Properties dialog opens to the Actions tab.

3. Click the pull-down arrow and choose Go To A Page In Another Document from the Select Action list (**Figure 8.41**). Click Add.

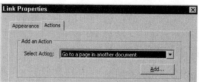

Figure 8.41 Use the Go To A Page In Another Document action to set a destination link.

4. In the Target Document section of the resulting dialog, click Browse. Locate the destination document on your hard drive and select it. The dialog displays the filename (**Figure 8.42**).

Figure 8.42 Choose the document to use for the link and it will be listed in the dialog.

Note

Set the user view if you want. The default is the user's preference. If you want to change that, click the pull-down arrow and choose Existing Window or New Window. See Tip 76 for more information.

5. Click Named Destination in the Options section of the dialog; the message "Name: Not specified" appears below the selected option (**Figure 8.43**). Click Browse to open the Choose Destination dialog.

Figure 8.43 Once you choose to use a named destination, you have to specify it.

6. Select the destination to use for the link and click OK to close the dialog (**Figure 8.44**). You'll return to the Go To A Page In Another Document dialog.

Figure 8.44 Select a destination from the list.

The named destination appears in the Options area of the dialog. Click OK to return to the Create Link dialog.

7. You can check out the new link information in the Actions window of the Create Link dialog (**Figure 8.45**). Click Close to close the Create Link dialog and complete the link.

Figure 8.45 The Actions panel displays the link information.

8. Save the source document. Click the Hand tool and test the link. The portion of the page defined in the destination document loads in the Document pane.

Set Up a System

When you are working with several documents and several destinations, it is simpler to work through one phase of the process after the other rather than one destination at a time.

1. Open your destination documents first.

2. Scan and then create all the destinations.

3. Then open the first document you want to link the destinations to, and create the set of bookmarks you want to work with.

4. Set the destinations for that document's bookmarks.

5. Then go on to the next document until you are finished.

It is much quicker to work in a batched way—you are less prone to making errors, and are more likely to name the destinations consistently (see the Plan Your Destination sidebar).

CHAPTER NINE

Using Multimedia, eBooks, and Other Content

Acrobat 5 let you add sound and movie files to a document, use transitions for projects converted from Microsoft PowerPoint files, or even program transitions in Acrobat using JavaScript. In Acrobat 6 the repertoire of materials you can work with has been expanded even more: Flash files, material imported from Photoshop Album, and you can also use Picture Tasks that activate with certain image types. You can create presentations from within Acrobat, and include transitions and other effects.

This set of tips covers a lot of ground; we focus on working with a variety of media, objects, and functions. Acrobat 6 includes a number of special actions called *triggers* that let you control how media is played in a document; the same processes also apply to form fields. We also show you how to download free eBooks, which in Acrobat 6 you can read using the Adobe Reader, the same reader used for other PDF documents.

TIP
81 Using Media in Documents

You can't embed media files directly into PDF documents within Acrobat 6 Standard (with the exception of audio files). You have to add the media to a source document—such as a Word document or a Web page—and then convert the file.

To set general multimedia preferences, begin by choosing Edit > Preferences > Multimedia. Then follow these steps:

1. In the upper section of the dialog, click the pull-down arrow and choose a player option (**Figure 9.1**).

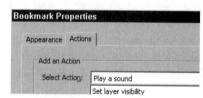

Figure 9.1 Choose a media player in the Multimedia preferences.

Note

The preferences do not identify the versions of the chosen players. For example, the latest Flash player is version 6; if users choose Flash as their player option but have version 4 installed on their computer, they won't be able to see your work unless it is playable on a version 4 player.

2. At the lower portion of the dialog are the Accessibility Options (**Figure 9.2**). If you use assistive devices, enable the appropriate options.

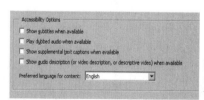

Figure 9.2 You can set accessibility preferences for multimedia use.

3. Click OK to close the Preferences dialog.

Different versions of Acrobat support different media. For instance, Acrobat 5 let you insert movies in QuickTime or AVI formats into a document. You can't do that with Acrobat 6 Standard, but you can with Acrobat 6 Professional.

Play to Your Audience

When working with multimedia in a project, you have to take your audience into account. If you're targeting the cutting-edge design crowd, you can safely work with the latest and greatest in terms of media formats. This group is likely to have the most recent versions of media players, and they're also more likely to have a high-bandwidth Internet connection. On the other hand, if you are designing for a much more generic audience, you shouldn't assume that they have the latest Flash player, for example, and design material specifically for that player. Some functionality requires Flash 6, but a simple animated logo for example, doesn't.

Using Multimedia, eBooks, and Other Content

Three types of actions apply to using media:

- Play Media (Acrobat 5 Compatible)—Plays a specified Quick-Time or AVI movie that you created as Acrobat 5 compatible. A media file must already be embedded in the PDF document in order for you to be able to select it.

- Play a Sound—Plays a specified sound file. The sound is embedded into the PDF document in a cross-platform format that plays in Microsoft Windows and the Mac OS.

- Play Media (Acrobat 6 Compatible)—Plays a specified movie that you created as Acrobat 6 compatible. Again, a media object must already be embedded in the PDF document for you to be able to select it.

Acrobat includes a set of functions called *triggers*, which are used to control the activity of media clips and form fields in your document (referred to as *actions*). Navigation buttons on a Web page are simple examples of triggers. If you click a button, the mouse click is the trigger, and the display of a new page is the action. As **Figure 9.3** shows, you can set a page opening or closing, a bookmark, or a link as a trigger for an action, such as playing a sound clip or loading a Flash movie.

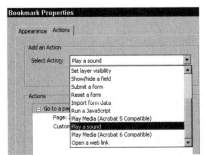

Figure 9.3 You can attach a sound action to a bookmark or a link.

You use the same triggers for both media and form fields; in addition, several other triggers are available that are specific to forms. (You must create the forms themselves in Acrobat 6 Professional.)

Make It Accessible

One of the cornerstones of designing accessible content is including alternate versions of visual content. For users working with screen readers or other assistive devices, you have to provide the text equivalent of your visual content and captioning (if required). The media you're using determines your ability to embed text, verbal commentary, and captions, and you can't control this ability from within Acrobat.

TIP 82 Controlling Animation with Triggers

One common use for triggers is to control animation in a document. Keep in mind that the document must already have the media embedded in it. In our example, the document is converted from a Web page, and the page contains a Flash animation (**Figure 9.4**).

Figure 9.4 Convert a Web page to PDF and use an embedded Flash movie.

Note

If you have programmed buttons or other types of JavaScript on your Web page, they are not converted along with the Web page to PDF.

Say we have three buttons that need actions. We want buttons that start and stop the animation and that go to the previous page of the document.

Note

If your document doesn't include buttons, you can easily build them in Acrobat using the drawing and text tools described in Tip 61, "Using Advanced Commenting Tools."

Attaching an Action to Start the Animation

The actions for the animation are attached to links. You use the Link tool on the Advanced Editing toolbar, along with the Create Link and Link Properties dialogs, to set the action:

1. Select the Link tool ![link tool icon] in the Advanced Editing toolbar and draw the link over the Start button (**Figure 9.5**). The Create Link dialog opens.

Figure 9.5 Draw a link over the Start button image on the page.

Note

If your animation is running when you open the page, it disappears when the Link tool is selected. Don't worry—the actions set with the Link tool restore its function. If you change your mind about using the link, click the Hand tool on the Basic toolbar. Move the pointer over the area on the page where the animation is located; when the hand changes to a pointing finger cursor, click to restore your animation to view.

2. Click the Custom Link option at the bottom of the Create Link dialog (**Figure 9.6**) and click OK. The Link Properties dialog opens.

Figure 9.6 Click Custom Link and then click OK to open a dialog for attaching media actions.

3. Set the Link Type to Invisible Rectangle on the Appearance tab (**Figure 9.7**).

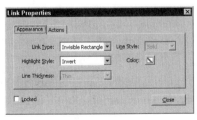

Figure 9.7 When you use a button image, set the link's appearance to invisible.

(Continued)

TIP 82: Controlling Animation with Triggers

Match Media to Player

Make sure the media is compatible with the version of Acrobat you are targeting. The sample document in this tip has a Flash movie embedded; Flash is compatible with Acrobat 6 but not with 5. If we choose Play Media (Acrobat 5 Compatible) in the Link Properties dialog, you'll see a warning message shown.

Note

If you don't have a button shape to overlay the link, draw a visible link instead.

4. On the Actions tab, click the pull-down arrow and choose Play Media (Acrobat 6 Compatible) from the Select Action dropdown menu (**Figure 9.8**).

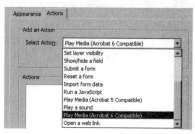

Figure 9.8 Choose media that is compatible with the Acrobat version you are designing for.

5. Click the Add button (**Figure 9.9**). The Play Media dialog opens.

Figure 9.9 Click Add to open the Play Media dialog.

6. Choose an operation from the Operation to Perform pull-down list; in this example, choose Play (**Figure 9.10**).

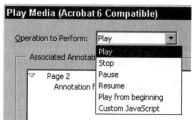

Figure 9.10 Choose an operation from the pull-down list.

The Associated Annotation (a description of the embedded object) is listed in the dialog. If several objects are embedded, each is listed along with its page number.

7. Click the object shown in the Associated Annotation list; that is, click Annotation from *<embedded object>* to select it (**Figure 9.11**). If you don't click the object's description, you can't

Stopping the Animation

As you might expect, attaching a link to a Stop button uses the same process as for a Play button. You can repeat steps 1 through 5 as described in the tip. The action isn't automatically transferred from one link to another; you have to choose the Stop function in step 6.

click OK to set the action. Now, Click OK to close the dialog and return to the Link Properties dialog.

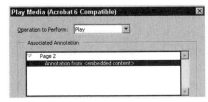

Figure 9.11 You must select the object in order to activate it in the dialog.

8. The action is now listed in the Actions window of the Link Properties dialog (**Figure 9.12**). Click Close to close the Link Properties dialog box and set the link.

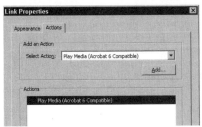

Figure 9.12 The action is listed in the Actions window of the Link Properties dialog.

9. Click the Hand tool  on the Basic toolbar to deselect the Link tool. Move the pointer over the Start button; you see the Hand tool change to a pointing finger cursor (**Figure 9.13**). Click the link to launch the animation.

Figure 9.13 Click the new link to start the animation.

TIP 82: Controlling Animation with Triggers

To finish the navigation for the animation's page, attach an action to the Back button. In this case, in a three-page document, the animation is on page 2, and the Back button should return to page 1. Add a simple link; then draw the link box over the Back button. When the Create Link dialog opens, select the Open a page in this document radio button, enter the page number, and click OK (**Figure 9.14**).

Figure 9.14 Enter the page number in the Create Link dialog.

Controlling the View

As you can see in Figure 9.14, we selected the Inherit Zoom option. The sample document doesn't have much content; each page merely contains titles and buttons. The animation's page displays in a magnified view, showing the animation and the control buttons.

If we left the default zoom option, Fit Page, when setting the Back button's action, the Document pane would show all of page 1 (**Figure 9.15**).

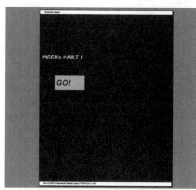

Figure 9.15 The default zoom option is Fit Page, which shows all the content on page 1.

Instead, with the Inherit Zoom option, the magnification of the first page matches that of the animation page, making for a more professional-looking document since the blank black space is cropped out (**Figure 9.16**).

Figure 9.16 When we use the Inherit Zoom option, the magnification of the first page matches the animation's page zoom.

If the pages contain varying amounts of content, such as an animation on one page and a full-page block of text on another, use a different option, such as Fit Page.

TIP 82: Controlling Animation with Triggers

TIP 83
Adding a Sound Action Using a Bookmark

As you know, some documents, especially those that require user input, can be quite complex. You can guide the user with sound cues just as you can with messages. Suppose you create a catalog order form that includes a front page for customer information, such as name and address. Before proceeding to the order page, the user is required to complete that information. When users click the Next button without supplying all the required information, you must tell them to enter all the information before proceeding. An interesting way to accomplish that is to create sound files that serve as cues for the reader, or add a sound like a chime to the Next button that rings when it is clicked. If the information is complete, a message says something like "Thank you. Please place your order." and the catalog ordering page displays. (To be safe, you should create both message pop-ups and sound files since there is no guarantee that all readers will have their computer sound turned on.)

If your document uses a lot of links, don't use sound for each link unless you are designing an accessible page with sound cues—it becomes quite irritating.

You attach actions to objects or pages in your document using either links or bookmarks; both offer the same list of actions. These steps describe adding a sound to a bookmark. The process for adding the sound to a link is very similar; you just select the link instead of the bookmark. Follow these steps to add a sound action to a page:

1. Right-click/Control-click the bookmark you want to attach sound to (**Figure 9.17**) and choose Properties from the shortcut menu. The Bookmark Properties dialog opens.

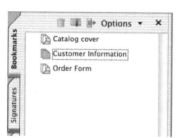

Figure 9.17 Right-click/Control-click the bookmark to open the shortcut menu.

Sound Comment or Sound Action?

Sound attached to a file using a trigger is not the same as sound attached to a file using a Comment tool (see Tip 61). The sound comment is a file attachment; using a sound action actually embeds the sound into the document. Use a sound comment if you've dictated a message to accompany a document or other comment, for example. Your readers have to click the Sound Comment icon on the page to activate their computer's audio utility program to play the message. The sound action should be part of a multimedia presentation, such as a background score, music that plays as a page loads, or sounds you hear as a button is clicked. A sound is commonly used in a document to accompany page loading—you click a bookmark and a sound plays as the new page loads. There are also many other ways you can use sound, such as attaching sound cues to buttons and links.

Note

You can also click the Options menu in the Bookmarks pane and choose Properties from the menu list.

2. Click the Actions tab. The original action attached to the book-mark, Go to a page in this document, appears in the Actions list (**Figure 9.18**). Choose Play a Sound from the Select Action pull-down menu, and then click Add. The Select Sound File dialog opens.

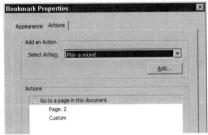

Figure 9.18 Choose Play a Sound from the Select Action pull-down menu.

3. Locate the sound file on your computer you want to use for the action. You can choose from WAV sounds (*.wav, *.wave) or AIFF sounds (*.aif, *.aiff, *.aifc).

4. Click Select to close the dialog and attach the sound.

    In the Bookmark Properties dialog, you'll see that Acrobat has added the new action to the Actions list (**Figure 9.19**). By default, each new action appears at the bottom of the list. Click Close to close the Bookmark Properties dialog.

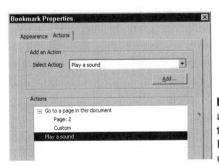

Figure 9.19 The sound action is added to the Actions list in the Bookmark Properties dialog.

Ordering Actions

Acrobat places new actions at the end of the Actions list in the Book-marks or Links Properties Action dialog by default. Usually, the order isn't important since the actions apply to the same location and take place at pretty much the same time. In this tip's example, playing a sound and viewing a page occur almost simultaneously, so ordering the actions doesn't matter.

In other circumstances, you may need to reorder the actions. In our earlier example, the user goes to page 3, fills out a form, clicks the Submit button to send the form, and then a voice message says Thank you. Logically, you want users to complete the form before you thank them for doing it. To reorder the action sequence, click the Submit a form action in the list, then click the Up button to move the action higher in the list.

TIP 83: Adding a Sound Action Using a Bookmark

Completing a Form and Setting Forms Preferences

In Acrobat 6 Standard, users can fill in a form and submit the actual form (or just the data it contains) to a database, Web site, or email address. Acrobat lets users save the completed form, save the content to reuse another time, and print it as well. You can even set preferences to have Acrobat assist your users by suggesting information used in similar form fields. If you fill out the same type of form numerous times, such as health or dental insurance, reusing the information saves a lot of time.

When you start filling out a new form, you'll see a dialog that tells you you can use Acrobat's Auto-Complete feature to help fill in the form fields more quickly. When you use this feature, as soon as you type the first few characters of a word in a form field, if the characters match what you have entered in another form, Acrobat automatically enters the rest of the text (**Figure 9.20**). The automatic text is selected; you can easily delete or change it if you need to.

Filling Out Forms

To fill out an Acrobat PDF form, you move the pointer inside a field on the form and click. You'll see the I-beam, which tells you that the form is active and that you can start to type. Other types of fields use buttons, checkmarks, and so on. Click an option to select it, and then press Tab (or Shift+Tab) to go to the next (or previous) field.

Figure 9.20 The Auto-Complete feature displays a probable entry as soon as you type the first few characters.

To enable this feature, choose Edit > Preferences (Windows) or Acrobat > Preferences (Mac OS), and choose Forms from the Preferences list. At the lower part of the window, you see the Auto-Complete options. Click the pull-down arrow and choose an option (**Figure 9.21**). Your choices are Off, Basic, and Advanced. Make your selection and click OK to close the dialog.

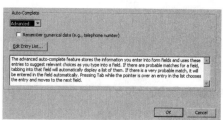

Figure 9.21 Choose an Auto-Complete option from the pull-down list.

The Basic Auto-Complete process suggests choices when you start typing an entry. A drop-down list shows probable choices; the option listed first appears in the field automatically. In the example shown in **Figure 9.22**, the names starting with *D* are displayed as soon as I type the letter *D*; as you can see, Acrobat places the first name from the list in the field automatically. If you want to choose another name, click that name to select it from the list.

Name:

Figure 9.22 As soon as you type the first character in a field, a list of possible matches appears.

The Advanced Auto-Complete feature takes the process one step further. Once you start typing and see the auto-entry list, simply move your pointer over the choice you want to use and press Tab. Acrobat fills the field with the selection you specified and moves the pointer to the next field.

Note

You can remove entries from the auto-entry listing. Just click Edit Entry List below the Auto-Complete options in the Forms preferences dialog to open the Edit Entry List dialog. Select the entries you don't want on the list, click Remove to delete them (Figure 9.23).

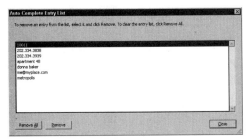

Figure 9.23 You can edit the Auto-Entry listings.

TIP 84: Completing a Form and Setting Forms Preferences

Other Preferences for Forms

Acrobat provides several other preferences for forms. Try some of the options—you may find that they increase your form's processing speed and make working with forms simpler.

Choose Edit > Preferences > Forms. The top portion of the dialog contains a set of forms preferences:

- Automatically Calculate Field Values—Calculates the content of numerical fields when you enter the data. Often this feature is programmed into the form.

- Show Focus Rectangle—Shows which form field is currently active (or has focus). This is a very useful preference especially in forms that have narrow fields or a great deal of information on one page (**Figure 9.24**).

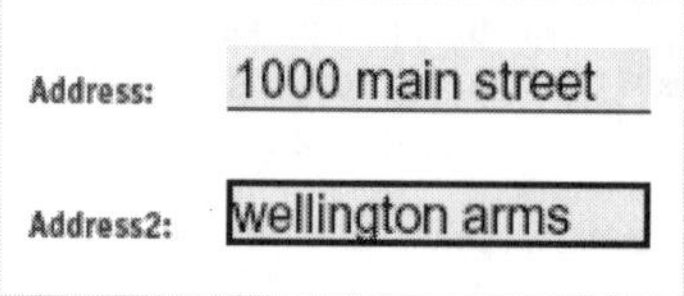

Address: 1000 main street

Address2: wellington arms

Figure 9.24 Use the Show Focus Rectangle option to clearly see the active field on a form.

- Keep Forms Data Temporarily Available on Disk—Retains the information you add to a form online. This is a useful preference if you fill in forms over the Internet; you can't store the data permanently, but you can reuse it during a session.

- Show Text Field Overflow Indicator—Displays a plus sign when you try to type too much text into a text field. The number of characters allowed in a field is defined by the form's designer.

- Show Background Color for Form Fields—Displays a color for form field backgrounds. This is a useful preference when you work with a lot of forms and find screen glare hard on your eyes, or when you work with large forms and want to see how much work you have to do! You can use colored backgrounds for the form fields regardless of how the form is designed; the form's designer doesn't have to assign a color.

TIP 85 Exporting and Importing Form Data

Forms consist of two components: the fields and the content. The fields are constant and remain part of the document; the content changes each time the form is reset or someone else starts to add content. If you complete a form once, you can save the content and reuse it the next time you fill out the form.

When you have completed a form, choose Advanced > Forms > Export Forms Data to open the Export Form Data As dialog. Browse to the location on your hard drive where you want to store the file. Acrobat names the file using the form's name; the file format is FDF. To complete the process, click Save.

Note

If you work with a lot of forms, leave the default file name. That way, you know which data file belongs to which form.

The next time you need to add information to a form that you've filled in at least once and stored data from, instead of typing the content for the fields just import the data file. To do so, choose Advanced > Forms > Import Forms Data. When the Select File Containing Form Data dialog opens, locate the data file on your hard drive. Select the file, and then click Select (**Figure 9.25**). The dialog closes, and Acrobat fills in the form fields for you.

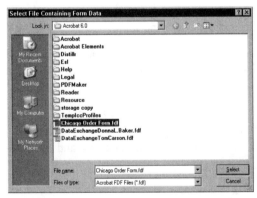

Figure 9.25 Import saved data from your hard drive to use in another form.

Storing Forms Data

There is no specific place on your hard drive to store FDF and other data files. If you fill out forms on a regular basis, decide on a location and use it consistently. That way, you can keep track of the files you have stored, and will be able to find them easily when you need them. I store data files in the main Acrobat 6 folder in the Program Files folder.

TIP 86 Customizing Form Activity Using Actions

You can't create a form in Acrobat 6 Standard; you must have Acrobat 6 Professional. But if you receive a form from someone and want to customize it, Standard gives you that power. **Figure 9.26** shows a sample order form from a fictitious art glass company. Let's say I am a frequent buyer and want to modify the form to suit the way I work.

Figure 9.26 You can modify some form functions to suit the way you work.

I want to make three changes to the form using the following actions, available in Acrobat 6 Standard:

- Import Form Data—Brings data from another form and adds it to the form open in Acrobat. I can click a bookmark and have the form data I use repeatedly added to the form automatically without having to choose any menu items.

- Reset a Form—Deletes content added to a form. I can click a bookmark and have the content of the fields removed so I can start over, again without having to choose any menu items.

- Submit a form—Sends data to a specified address. Instead of having to open my email program, start a new message, and then attach the file, I simply click a bookmark and have the information sent automatically.

Using Bookmarks for Actions

Most often, actions on a form are triggered by buttons. You may have buttons added by the initial form's creator, or you can add buttons using the drawing and text tools. However, bookmarks are even simpler to use than buttons; you just have to specify some text, and you don't have to draw any objects. To begin, open the Bookmarks pane and display the desired page in the Document pane. Click Create New Bookmark  on the Bookmarks toolbar. Then, add one bookmark for each action you want to use (**Figure 9.27**).

Figure 9.27 Add one bookmark for each action you want to use.

Attach the actions to the bookmarks (described below). Before you save the document, be sure to check the Document properties to make sure the bookmarks will be displayed. Choose File > Document Properties > Initial View. Set the Show option to display both bookmarks and the page, and then click OK to set the properties (**Figure 9.28**). Save the file.

Figure 9.28 Set the initial view to display both bookmarks and the page.

Accepting Your Limitations

Regardless of how you configure a form in Acrobat 6 Standard, you are governed by how the original form was created; this might cause a glitch if you try to set up an automatic form-submission action. For example, a form's designer can designate fields as required, meaning that the form cannot be submitted without data in the required fields. If you construct a Submit a form action, you have to include the form fields required by the original design. If you fail to do that, you'll see an error message informing you about empty fields.

(Continued)

TIP 86: Customizing Form Activity Using Actions

Sending a Form Automatically

Sometimes forms have their own Submit button or action. If not, here's a quick way to add one of your own:

1. Select the object you want to attach the action to—in this example, a bookmark named Submit the Form (**Figure 9.29**).

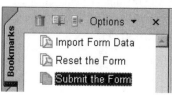

Figure 9.29 We'll attach a submit action to a bookmark named Submit the Form.

2. Right-click/Control-click the bookmark and choose Properties from the contextual menu. The Bookmark Properties dialog opens. Click the Actions tab.

3. Select the Submit a form action from the Select Action pull-down list (**Figure 9.30**). Click Add, and the Submit Form Selections dialog opens.

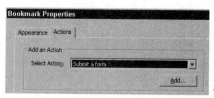

Figure 9.30 Select the Submit a form action from the pull-down list.

4. Enter an address for submission. The address can be a URL, an FTP address, or an email address (**Figure 9.31**).

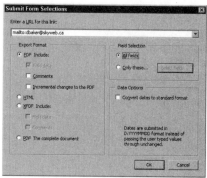

Figure 9.31 You can submit form data to a URL, an FTP address, or an email address.

Note

When you type the address, be sure to type the entire URL, including the protocol—that is, http or ftp.

5. Choose submission options. You can send the form data, the PDF document itself, or the content as HTML, and also specify what content is sent.

6. If you want to define only a specific number of fields, click Only these in the Field Selection section of the dialog (**Figure 9.32**). Click the Select fields button. The Field Selection dialog opens (**Figure 9.33**).

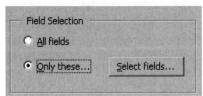

Figure 9.32 You can use all the fields or only specific fields in the form.

Figure 9.33 Select the fields you want to use in the Field Selection section of this dialog.

7. Choose the fields for export and click OK to return to the Submit Form Selections dialog. Click OK to close the Submit Form Selections dialog and return to the Bookmark Properties dialog.

8. The Submit a form action now appears in the bookmark's Actions list. Click Close to close the Bookmark Properties dialog and apply the action.

9. Click the bookmark to test the action.

Note

Once you've set up a bookmark using a Submit form action, if you want to modify its properties, be sure to click the bookmark's icon, not the text of the bookmark.

TIP 86: Customizing Form Activity Using Actions

Other Form Actions

Once a form is filled in, either manually or by using imported form data, you can add an action to reset it. You can reset all or only a selected portion of the information in a form. These steps start with the assumption that you've created a bookmark for each action you wish to attach to the form. See the previous tip for information.

1. Select the bookmark, right-click/Control-click, and choose Properties to open the Bookmark Properties dialog. Click the Actions tab.

2. Select the Reset a form action from the Select Action pull-down list (**Figure 9.34**). Click Add, and the Reset a Form dialog opens.

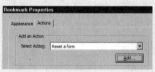

Figure 9.34 Select the Reset a form action from the Select Action pull-down list.

3. All the fields in the document are listed in the Reset a Form dialog and are selected by default (**Figure 9.35**). Deselect fields that you don't want reset and click OK to close the dialog.

Figure 9.35 All the fields in the document are selected by default; click to select or deselect the fields.

4. Click Close to dismiss the Bookmark Properties dialog and apply the action. Acrobat removes the content in the fields according to the selections you made in step 3.

There are times when you may not want to reset all the data in a form. For example, if you use the same form for ordering supplies for several people or departments, you likely use most of the same data; perhaps the only changes are to a contact name and number. In that case, it may be simpler to use a partial reset of the form and type in the person's name rather than resetting the entire form and then importing a different FDF file to fill the form's fields.

You can also use an action to import form data. Choose the bookmark you want to use for the action. Right-click/Control-click the bookmark, choose Properties, and then click the Actions tab in the Bookmark Properties dialog. Select the Import form data action and specify the FDF file you want to use for the form. Save the file and then test the action by clicking the bookmark. The fields in the form automatically fill using your information. What a timesaver!

TIP 87 Making Your Document Responsive

Actions can be applied to individual fields, or to an entire document. You can use actions applied to your document for a variety of purposes. For example, you may want to display instructions or thank visitors for completing a form.

Document actions are set using JavaScript, a relatively simple (read: not frightening!) scripting language that's native to Acrobat.

1. To start a document action, choose Advanced > JavaScript > Set Document Actions. The Document Actions dialog opens (**Figure 9.36**), showing a list of actions that refer to different states of a document. There are five states:

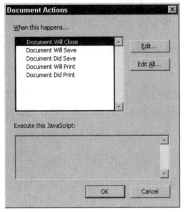

Figure 9.36 Use this dialog to control the behavior of the entire document.

Document Will Close—When a document closes

Document Will Save—Before a document is saved

Document Did Save—After a document is saved

Document Will Print—Before a document is printed

Document Did Print—After a document is printed

Take note of the different states. For example, an action used in the Document Will Save state means that the action takes place before the document is saved, whereas the Document Did Save action occurs after the document is saved.

(Continued)

TIP 87: Making Your Document Responsive

2. Select an action from the list at the left of the dialog. Then click Edit to open the JavaScript editor.

3. Type in the following JavaScript (**Figure 9.37**):
app.alert("Thanks for visiting. Come back again.",4);

Figure 9.37 Type your JavaScript in the JavaScript Editor.

Click OK to close the JavaScript Editor.

The script now appears in the Document Actions dialog (**Figure 9.38**). The selected document action now has a green circle beside it, indicating that it has an active script. Click OK to close the Document Actions dialog.

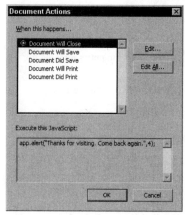

Figure 9.38 The Document Actions dialog displays the script.

What's in a Number?

In this tip's JavaScript, note the 4 before the closing bracket. The number refers to the type of alert icon displayed with the message. If you don't add a number, the default dialog displays the error icon; Alert 4 shows no icon, only the message. Other numbers produce different icons, such as for warning, question, or halt. These icons differ slightly in Windows and Macintosh, but they convey pretty much the same idea. Tailoring your alert icon to your message is a great way to add a touch of professionalism to your document.

4. Save the document.

The script is called an *application alert*, which refers to the type of dialogs that give you information when you perform actions in a program; they pop up on your screen all the time. The script loads the information dialog—in this case, the thank-you message. The text is enclosed within quotation marks.

5. To test the script, close the document. Before it closes, the message appears, as shown in **Figure 9.39**.

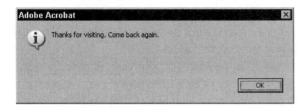

Figure 9.39 Close the document to test the script; the custom message displays.

Creating a Presentation with Page Transitions

One of the strengths of presentation software is the ability to display content and control movement through a document. Did you know you can do the same thing with Acrobat? Using page transitions and some page view settings, you can create a presentation of a PDF document in Acrobat. The material you use for a presentation can come from a number of sources. You can use files from a range of programs converted to a PDF (see tips in Chapter 2 for conversion information for various types of source materials), or assemble a binder using any number of file types (described in Tip 14).

Acrobat provides a number of transition effects. You can apply them to selected pages or to all the pages in a document. In addition, you can configure the speed of the transition and specify whether the pages advance automatically or require keyboard or mouse actions.

Note

If you use documents converted from Microsoft PowerPoint presentations, the transitions are preserved. Bullet fly-in animations are also transferred to the PDF document.

Follow these steps to add transitions:

1. Choose Document > Pages > Set Page Transitions to open the Set Transitions dialog.

2. In the Set Transitions dialog box, choose a transition effect from the Effect pull-down menu (**Figure 9.40**). You can choose among several dozen effects.

Varying Effects

Instead of applying the same transition throughout your presentation, you can quickly choose individual pages or groups of pages to display a particular effect. Select the pages using the page thumbnail view in the Pages panel (shift-click to select a group; Ctrl-click to select pages in different locations in the document.) From the Options menu, choose Set Page Transitions to open the Set Transitions dialog.

Use different transitions to identify different segments of a document. For example, I use a PDF presentation as a resume/portfolio. The document contains several pages of artwork samples. To differentiate the artwork from other elements of the document, the pages use a different transition.

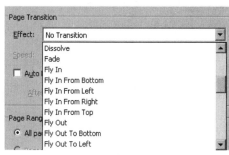

Figure 9.40 Choose a transition effect from the pull-down menu.

Using Multimedia, eBooks, and Other Content

Note
The effects options in the Set Transitions dialog are the same as those in the Preferences dialog. Choose Edit > Preferences > Full Screen, and click the Default Transition pull-down arrow to open the same list of options. If you set a transition preference, it overrides any document's settings. Also, if you choose Ignore All Transitions, transitions added to a document aren't played.

3. Select a speed for the effect: Slow, Medium, or Fast.

4. Set the navigation method. Select Auto Flip and choose the number of seconds between automatic page turning. You can choose a range of time options from 1 to 30 seconds. If you leave the Auto Flip setting deselected, the user moves through the document using keyboard commands or mouse clicks.

5. Select the page range you want to apply the transitions to (**Figure 9.41**).

Figure 9.41 Select other options for the effect, including transition speed and page range.

6. Click OK to close the Set Transitions dialog.

7. You'll see the transitions only when the document uses Full Screen view. To set this view, choose File > Document Properties > Initial View. Click Open in Full Screen mode in the Window Options section.

8. To test the presentation, save the file, close it and reopen it.

Tips for Using Transitions

As anyone who has sat through a mind-numbing presentation can tell you, transitions can be overused, or used poorly. Although transitions are not the main part of your presentation, your audience receives visual cues from them, just as they will from other page elements like fonts and colors. Here are some tips for using transitions in a document:

- Pick transitions that relate to the content. If the document is a collection of images set against a pale background, it might look good using a glittery transition. For a document discussing business losses over the past quarter, a more somber transition is more appropriate.

- Test timed pages. If you use the Auto Flip option, be sure to test the pages. The content determines how long a page should be visible. If the user has a lot of content to read, specify a longer display time.

TIP 88: Creating a Presentation with Page Transitions

TIP 89 Using Photoshop Album Slideshows and Picture Tasks

If you've forgotten to get a birthday card in the mail to your best friend, don't despair. You can use Adobe Photoshop Album, or other Photoshop products, to create interesting slideshows and email greetings called *eCards*. Content can be exported from Photoshop Album in PDF format. Once you open that PDF document in Acrobat, two plug-ins are activated, and a new item is added to the Task Button toolbar named Picture Tasks. The Image Viewer plug-in displays the slideshow or eCard content; the Picture Tasks plug-in provides some new commands that let you work with the files' content. The first time you open a document created in Photoshop Album, you'll see the message dialog pops-up to tell you that you can export, edit, and print the pictures embedded in the document, as well as send them to an online print shop for developing. Once you've read the message, click Don't Show Again at the bottom left of the dialog to hide it in future sessions.

Picture Tasks

With your file open, click the Picture Tasks [Picture Tasks ▾] button's pull-down arrow to display its menu Then click the Picture Tasks task button to check out its How To pane (**Figure 9.42**).

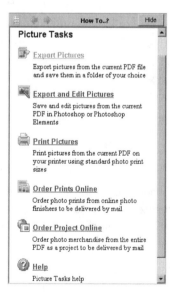

Figure 9.42 Click the Picture Tasks task button to display its How To pane.

Picture Tasks offer you several options for using the content in your documents:

- You can export images to use in other documents. Click Export Pictures to open the dialog shown in **Figure 9.43**. Select the images for export, and then choose a folder for storage. You can also assign a common name to the images. Just click Export to export the images from the document.

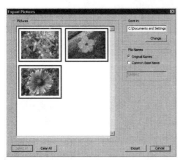

Figure 9.43 Select images for export in this dialog.

- You can export images and modify them before using them elsewhere. Click Export and Edit Pictures to open the Export and Edit dialog. It's the same as the Export Pictures dialog, with an additional option to open the images in your image-editing program.

- Print the images in a wide variety of sizes and arrangements. Click Print Pictures to open the Select Picture dialog (**Figure 9.44**). Choose the images you want to print and click Next; the Print Pictures dialog opens.

Figure 9.44 Choose pictures for printing in the Select Picture dialog.

Modifying Photoshop Album Slideshows in Acrobat

Among the great options offered by Adobe Photoshop Album is the ability to create and share a slideshow of your images. This is a handy way to share both personal photos and business-related shots. Although Photoshop Album handles the images flawlessly, it might not be the best tool for adding text to the slideshow. If you want to modify your slideshow, first open it in Acrobat. Select the TouchUp Text tool 𝕋 on the Advanced Editing toolbar and Ctrl-click to start a new line of text. You can add captions, titles, bullet lists, and so on. You can also select caption text that you added in Photoshop Album and modify it using the TouchUp Text tool.

TIP 89: Using Photoshop Album Slideshows and Picture Tasks

Acrobat offers an interesting collection of printing options (**Figure 9.45**). For example, you can print sets of wallet-sized images or larger portrait-sized images. Be sure to specify the number of copies you want to print.

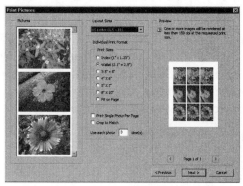

Figure 9.45 You can print images in a variety of sizes.

- You can order prints of your photos online. Click Order Prints Online to launch a dialog connecting you to an online printer (**Figure 9.46**). Follow the prompts in the Online Services Wizard (called an Online Services Assistant in Mac OS) and the specific upload and payment instructions for the online service.

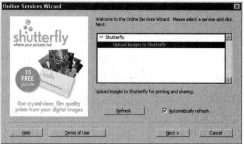

Figure 9.46 Use the Online Services Wizard (or Assistant on the Mac) to connect to an online printer.

- There's even an option for ordering projects from the Web. Click Order Project Online to connect to an online printing service to produce Photoshop Album template-based material, such as calendars and photobooks.

TIP 90 Downloading and Reading eBooks

Prior to Acrobat 6 and the Adobe Reader, you viewed general PDFs using Acrobat Reader, and you used the Adobe eBook Reader for viewing eBooks. Adobe Reader 6 combines both viewers into one package. You can organize and control eBook material through Acrobat 6 or through Adobe Reader. This tip shows you how to download free eBooks and build your own eBook library.

Downloading Free eBooks

Let's look at the download process in Adobe Reader 6:

1. Choose View > Task Buttons > eBooks to display the Task Button toolbar.

2. On the toolbar, click the eBooks ![eBooks] task's pull-down arrow to open the menu shown in **Figure 9.47**. Click Get eBooks Online.

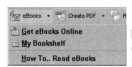

Figure 9.47 Access the eBook menu from the Task Bar button.

Note

If you have never used the eBook options in Acrobat 6 or Adobe Reader 6, you must first activate an account. See the sidebar "Activating the DRM Process" for information.

The program's link leads you to Adobe's eBook Mall. From the Web site, you can choose from dozens of booksellers in a variety of languages. Select a book to purchase from a bookseller, and follow the prompts for payment and download.

Note

You can find plenty of free eBooks in other online venues as well. For example, PlanetPDF (www.planetpdf.com) offers dozens of classics you can download and read, and its library is growing. Search online for other great sources.

(Continued)

Storing eBooks

To save time, store all of your eBooks in the same location. It makes it easier to find them to add to the collection, and it certainly makes it easier to delete books from the collection. You can't delete books from within Acrobat but must delete them directly from your hard drive location.

Follow these steps to download a free eBook from PlanetPDF:

1. Click an eBook to open it. The PDF displays in Adobe Reader 6 when you are online. You can read the book online or download it for future use.

2. Click Save a Copy ![Save a Copy] on the File toolbar to open the Save a Copy dialog. Browse to the storage location you want to use, change the title if you wish, and click Save to save the PDF document (**Figure 9.48**).

Figure 9.48
Save eBooks on your hard drive.

3. Close your browser when you have finished downloading your book(s).

Viewing Your eBook Collection

In Acrobat, you can use the My Bookshelf dialog to organize your eBook content. Open the My Bookshelf dialog in one of two ways:

- Choose File > My Bookshelf.

- Click the eBook task button's arrow and select My Bookshelf from the menu.

Note
If you download purchased books, they are automatically added to the My Bookshelf dialog. This tip shows how to use free eBooks, which are downloaded to your hard drive and stored like any PDF document.

The My Bookshelf dialog opens, and except for any eBooks you've purchased, the listing is blank.

1. Click Add File ![Add File button]. The Add File dialog automatically opens the My eBooks folder on your hard drive.

2. Select the book or books you want to add to the My Bookshelf listing and click Add. The dialog closes.

3. The selected books now appear in the My Bookshelf dialog (**Figure 9.49**).

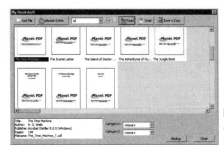

Figure 9.49 eBooks are added to the My Bookshelf dialog's list.

Modifying eBooks

eBooks are the same as other PDF files—you can add comments, links, export images, and so on, depending on the permissions granted in the security settings. Many free eBooks, such as those from PlanetPDF, have no security applied.

By default, books are organized using large thumbnails. eBooks use cover images; in our example, the books are all from one source, and use the Web site's generic cover.

4. Click a thumbnail. At the bottom left of the dialog, you'll see information about the book, including its author, title, and filename. You can click the List toggle ![List toggle] to display the book information in a list form instead of thumbnails (**Figure 9.50**).

Figure 9.50 Click the list toggle to display the book information in a list form instead of thumbnails.

5. Finally, to read a book, double-click its name in the list or the thumbnail view, or select the book and click Read on the My Bookshelf toolbar.

TIP 90: Downloading and Reading eBooks

TIP 91
Organizing and Managing Your eBook Collection

The problem with eBooks is that, since they are so easy to get and to use, you can end up with dozens or even hundreds of files. Fortunately, the My Bookshelf dialog lets you organize and categorize your collection for easy access.

1. Start by defining categories. Click the pull-down arrow at the top of the My Bookshelf dialog to open a list (**Figure 9.51**).

Figure 9.51 Click the pull-down arrow at the top of the My Bookshelf dialog to open a categories list.

The categories include Romance, History, Reference, Travel, and so on. However, in my collection, there isn't much in the way of romance or reference material. Click Edit Categories to open the Bookshelf Categories dialog.

2. Delete listings that are not useful to you. Click a heading in the right column, and click Delete to remove the entry.

In this example, we've deleted all categories except Fiction and Travel (**Figure 9.52**).

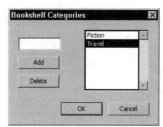

Figure 9.52 Customize the list by removing categories you won't use.

3. Add categories that are meaningful to your collection. Type the name of a new category in the top left of the Bookshelf Categories dialog, and then click Add. You can add categories according to any method you choose. For example, based on genre or author. Click OK to close the dialog.

Sharing eBooks

You can send out eBooks right from the My Bookshelf dialog (unless they are rights-protected). Select the book you want to mail from the booklist. Click Email [Email] at the top of the My Bookshelf dialog to open an email message, which will include the subject line "A document for you" as well as instructions for how to read it and how to download the Adobe Reader. The eBook is attached to the email message. Simply enter the recipient's name and send the file.

4. Back in the My Bookshelf dialog, click a book to select it from the listings at the top of the dialog (**Figure 9.53**).

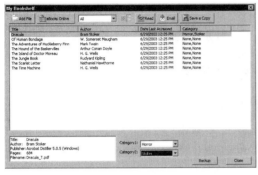

Figure 9.53
Click a book to select it from the listings at the top of the dialog.

5. At the bottom of the dialog, click the Category 1 pull-down menu and choose a category for the book.

Note

You can assign two categories to eBooks, so if you accumulate 100 fiction titles, for example, you might also assign them to romance, mystery, or travel subcategories.

6. Click the Close button to close My Bookshelf.

As you continue to add books to your collection, categorize them in the My Bookshelf dialog (**Figure 9.54**). You can sort the collection using the list view. Simply click any of the list headings (Title, Author, Access Date, Categories) to sort the list alphabetically.

Title	Author	Date Last Accessed	Category
The Scarlet Letter	Nathaniel Hawthorne	6/29/2003 12:25 PM	Fiction, <None>
Of Human Bondage	W. Somerset Maugham	6/29/2003 12:25 PM	Fiction, <None>
The Adventures of Huckleberry Finn	Mark Twain	6/29/2003 12:25 PM	Fiction, <None>
The Jungle Book	Rudyard Kipling	6/29/2003 12:25 PM	Fiction, <None>
Dracula	Bram Stoker	6/29/2003 12:25 PM	Horror, Stoker
The Time Machine	H. G. Wells	6/29/2003 12:25 PM	Horror, Wells
The Island of Doctor Moreau	H. G. Wells	6/29/2003 12:25 PM	Horror, Wells
The Hound of the Baskervilles	Arthur Conan Doyle	6/29/2003 12:25 PM	Mystery, <None>

Figure 9.54
Categorize and sort your books in the My Bookshelf dialog.

You can also display lists of books based on the categories. Click the category pull-down list at the top of the dialog and choose a category. Only those books assigned to the named category will appear in the My Bookshelf dialog.

TIP 91: Organizing and Managing Your eBook Collection

Backing Up and Deleting eBooks

Even if you download them for free, you may want to back up your eBooks. It may not be a problem if you lost your copy of *Dracula* to some sort of computer failure; however, if you are using *Dracula* as part of a thesis and have added a huge number of comments and bookmarks to the document, losing the file could be a little frustrating.

At the bottom of the My Bookshelf dialog, click Backup [Backup]. When the Backup and Restore Bookshelf dialog opens, choose the categories you want to back up from the pull-down list (**Figure 9.55**).

Figure 9.55 Select catagories of books for backup.

The option to back up comments and markup is selected by default. Click OK. The Browse For Folder dialog opens, where you must select the folder you want to use to store the backup (**Figure 9.56**).

Figure 9.56 Select a storage location for your backup files.

Click OK and then Close to close dialogs. Now copies of the Horror book category are stored in your backup folder (**Figure 9.57**).

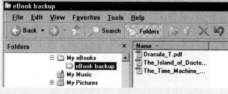

Figure 9.57 Remember where your backup files are stored!

If something goes wrong with your system, you can use your backup file. In the My Bookshelf dialog, click Backup. The Backup and Restore Bookshelf dialog opens. Click Restore and then OK. Locate the backup file in the Browse For Folder dialog, and then click OK. The files will be restored to your My Bookshelf collection.

Deleting an eBook from the My Bookshelf dialog isn't quite so easy; Acrobat doesn't provide a command or dialog for deleting. Locate the folder where you stored the book file. By default, purchased books are stored in the My Documents > My eBooks directory in Windows 2000 and later; in Mac they are stored in the Documents > My eBooks folder. Delete or move the eBook PDF file out of the storage folder, then open My Bookshelf in Acrobat. Double-click the name of the book in the list, or click the title and click Read 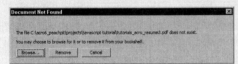. A message opens saying your book can't be located (**Figure 9.58**). Click Remove to remove the book from the My Bookshelf listing.

Figure 9.58 Delete a file from the storage folder to remove it from the My Bookshelf dialog.

TIP 92 Creating eBooks

Is an eBook really just a PDF in fancy literary clothes? Aside from the name, what differentiates an eBook from a regular PDF document is primarily related to layout. eBooks are designed for onscreen use. The main issues to consider are the page size, fonts used, navigation, and presentation. eBooks can be created in any source program used to create other types of PDF documents. Let's look at some tips to get you started building your own eBooks:

- Use a smaller page size for an eBook than a traditional document. An average document is 8 1/2 x 11 inches and uses 1-inch margins. Change the size of the page to approximately 5 or 6 inches by 7 or 8 inches. The smaller page size makes it easier for the page to be viewed on a variety of screen sizes and still lets the viewer print on a standard-sized page (**Figure 9.59**).

Figure 9.59 Use a smaller page size for easier viewing of an eBook page.

Note
My personal preference is a page sized at 5.5 x 7 inches. This is large enough to provide a considerable amount of content on the page, and still allows the reader using Acrobat or Adobe Reader to see the contents clearly when the page view is set to full width.

- Leave the margins at approximately 1 inch all around. The content can be clearly displayed, and there is still enough room for a page number and other header and footer material.

- Use a clear font that will work well for online use. A simple serif font such as Times or Palatino looks good on an eBook page (**Figure 9.60**). Don't use a heavy or bolded font. The added weight doesn't contribute to a clearer page. Make sure you embed the fonts used in your eBook project.

A simple serif font such as Times or Palatino looks good on an eBook page.

Don't use a heavy or bolded font. The added weight doesn't contribute to a more legible page.

12 point font is sufficiently large for the reader to see the content clearly in a full width page view.

Figure 9.60 Use clear, regular-weight serif fonts for easy reading.

- Don't use too large a font; it wastes screen and page space. I usually use a 12-point font. That is large enough for the reader to see the content clearly in a full-width page view.

- Don't use a colored background for an eBook. The color is very distracting, and unnecessary. If you want to inject a bit of color into your eBook, use it in the pages' header/footer sections. Add a logo, a colored horizontal line, or another small graphic element.

Note
The noncolored background is especially important if any of your readers use custom screen colors or high-contrast color schemes. A colored background often inverts when viewed in a high-contrast scheme, and that makes the content very difficult to view.

- Be sure to use bookmarks for each chapter heading. Make the bookmarks descriptive when necessary. For example, *Chapter 9* doesn't provide as much information for the reader as *Constructing the Framework* for a technical eBook. On the other hand, a chapter number is usually sufficient in a novel unless chapter titles are an integral part of the book's design (**Figure 9.61**).

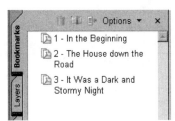

Figure 9.61 Use descriptive chapter titles when necessary.

- Provide navigational cues in the eBook itself. You can use page numbering such as *page 2 of 50,* or include a header or footer containing the chapter number and name.

Note

Depending on the structure of your eBook, add the navigation items such as headers and footers in the source program or in Acrobat. If the content comes from a single Word document, for example, add the section breaks and headers/footers in Word before converting the document to a PDF. If you are combining content from a variety of sources, add the headers/footers and page numbers in Acrobat.

- Take advantage of the power of Acrobat when designing an eBook. Include links to additional sources of information, material, user groups, Web sites, and so on.

- An interesting cover image can add a lot of character to your book. You can create the image in any image-processing or illustration program and add it to the source document before conversion, or you can add it as a PDF document to the converted eBook file. When the eBook appears in the My Bookshelf dialog listing, you'll see a thumbnail of the first page (**Figure 9.62**).

Figure 9.62 The cover page of an eBook displays as a thumbnail in the My Bookshelf dialog.

Note

If you distribute your book using an online distributor, you generally need to provide a JPEG thumbnail of the first page for advertising and selection purposes as well as building the full-size image for the eBook itself.

More Tips for eBook Creation

eBooks are a special hybrid of a traditional book and an online document. Here are some more tips for building interesting and useful eBooks:

- Set the Document properties before finishing the eBook project. Set the initial view to open with both the bookmarks and the page, and set the magnification to view page width. When your readers open your book, they immediately see all of the first page and the bookmark list as well.

- Tag the document. Your viewers read eBooks on a wide range of devices, ranging from computer screens to handheld devices. If a document is tagged, readers can use a reflow view if necessary for clear viewing.

CHAPTER TEN

Making Your Documents Secure

Once you have completed building, configuring, and tweaking your document, you are almost finished. But there's one important final step: guaranteeing your document's security. It isn't necessary to secure every document you create. I don't bother with security for any material I use and store on my own computers. On the other hand, if I want to have someone review my work, or am putting documents on a Web site for general distribution, I usually protect the document's content in some way.

As you'll learn in this set of tips, you can add security to your documents in several ways. Which option you choose depends on the material involved, as well as on your intended audience:

- You can protect the content of your document with a password, and further restrict any types of changes with another password.

- You can certify your document, which restricts editing of the document's contents.

- You can restrict access to your document to a specific user list.

- You can change permissions for movies and sound clips.

A user list or certification is based on digital signatures. *A digital signature* can be part of a third-party system, which is an appropriate option for large organizations or for distribution to a large number of people; or you can use *self-sign security*, which we also discuss in this set of tips.

TIP 93 Choosing a Security Level for a Document

You can add password security to a document in source programs that use a PDFMaker macro (Microsoft Office programs), change the options in Distiller, or add the security when you get the document into Acrobat.

Note

The only time I add security before a document gets into Acrobat is when I plan to convert and email a document directly from Microsoft Word. Not only are extra steps involved in setting the passwords in the source program, but once the document opens in Acrobat, I have to enter the passwords before I can do any work.

Changing the Compatibility Settings

Acrobat 6's default setting is a high level of security that's compatible with Acrobat 5 and Acrobat 6. When you open Distiller, you see the Compatibility level listed on the dialog below the Default Settings box (**Figure 10.1**). To change to a lower level of security (so that you can share your document with readers using older versions of Acrobat), you have to first modify the Compatibility level.

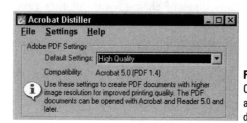

Figure 10.1 The Compatibility level appears below the default settings.

In Distiller, choose Settings > Edit PDF Settings to open the Adobe PDF Settings dialog with the General tab displayed. Then, choose a version option from the Compatibility pull-down list (**Figure 10.2**). If you plan to use the settings repeatedly, click Save As and save the settings as a custom .joboptions file.

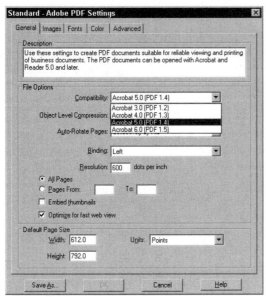

Figure 10.2 Choose a version compatibility option in this dialog.

Note

You can end up with quite a few custom files. For example, the standard conversion options include High Quality, Press Quality, Standard, and Lowest File Size. If you select the Standard settings and then reset compatibility to Acrobat 4, you save one custom set of options; if you set compatibility to Acrobat 6, you save another custom set of options, and so on.

You can also change the setting in a program such as Word that uses the PDFMaker macro. Choose Adobe PDF > Change Conversion Settings > Advanced Settings. The same dialog shown in Figure 10.2 opens, and you can select a compatibility level.

TIP 93: Choosing a Security Level for a Document

The Difference in Encryption Levels

The only difference between the Acrobat 5 and 6 levels of encryption is the ability to export metadata as text from Acrobat 6. Unless you need to do this, use the Acrobat 5 setting—that level of security is accessible by many more people.

The differences in security options between the versions relate primarily to printing and the types of changes users are allowed to make. Acrobat 3 and 4 allowed either high-resolution or no printing at all. Versions 5 and 6 expand the options to allow low-resolution printing (150 dpi) as well.

In earlier versions of the program, specific types of changes were allowed, such as filling in form fields, commenting, and signing. Those options are available in versions 5 and 6 as well. You can also choose various combinations of options and allow specific text access for screen readers used by the visually impaired.

TIP 94 Adding Password Security to a Document

Two levels of passwords are available. The user level, or *Document Open* password, is a traditional type of password that requires the user to type the correct characters in order to open the file. The master level password, or *Permissions* password, allows you to modify the document restrictions. You can use one or both of the password options in the same document.

Adding Passwords in a Source Document

To access the Security tab in a program using the PDFMaker macro, such as Microsoft Word, choose Adobe PDF > Change Conversion Settings > Security. You see the encryption level at the top of the dialog (**Figure 10.3**). To add a password:

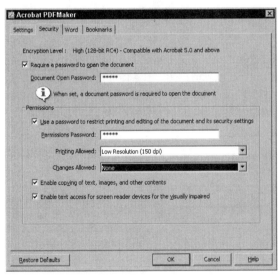

Figure 10.3 Set passwords and restrictions on the Security tab.

- Click the "Require a password to open the document" check box to activate the field. Type in the password.

- Click the "Use a password to restrict printing and editing of the document and its security settings" check box. Type in the password. Then specify the restrictions you want to add to the document.

When you add one or both passwords and click OK to close the Security dialog, you see a confirmation dialog, shown in **Figure 10.4**. Retype the password and click OK. If you set both passwords, you must confirm both; each opens in a separate dialog.

Figure 10.4 Confirm the passwords you added to your document.

After you convert the document to a PDF, you must enter the password to open it in Acrobat (**Figure 10.5**). Simply type the password and click OK to open the document.

Figure 10.5 After a document is converted to a PDF, you must enter the password to open it in Acrobat.

When the document opens, you see a security icon at the bottom left of the Document pane. Click the icon to open the Document Status dialog, which explains that the document has been encrypted and has attached security features (**Figure 10.6**). Click Close to dismiss the dialog.

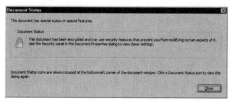

Figure 10.6 The Document Status dialog explains the security features attached to the document.

Modifying Passwords in Acrobat

You can modify, add, or remove password security from within Acrobat.

1. Choose File > Document Properties > Security to open the Security pane in the Document Properties dialog (**Figure 10.7**).

Some Words about Passwords

Here are a few things to remember about Acrobat passwords:

- A PDF file with both Document Open and Permissions passwords can be opened by using either password.

- Passwords can use any characters, but they are case sensitive.

- You can't use the same characters for both Document Open and Permissions passwords.

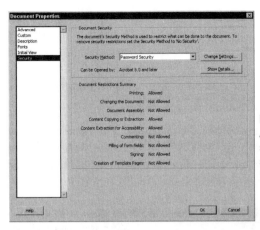

Figure 10.7
A document's security settings are listed in the Document Properties dialog.

You can also click the Secure task button arrow, and choose Restrict Opening and Editing to open the Password Security Settings dialog.

Note

If the Secure task button isn't visible, choose View > Task Buttons > Secure to display it in the toolbar area.

2. The security type appears at the top of the dialog—in this case, Password Security. The dialog summarizes the security restrictions. Click Show Details to open a Document Security dialog that lists the restrictions as well as encryption information (**Figure 10.8**). Click OK to close the dialog.

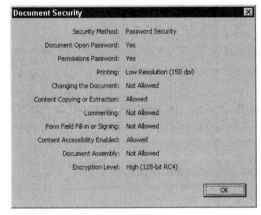

Figure 10.8
This Document Security dialog lists the restrictions and encryption information.

TIP 94: Adding Password Security to a Document

3. You can change the password security settings if you logged into the document using the Permissions password. In the Document Security pane, click Change Settings  to open the Password Security Settings dialog, which gives you the same options as those shown in Figure 10.3. Make the desired changes and click OK.

If you logged in with the Document Open password, when you click Change Settings you'll instead see the dialog shown in **Figure 10.9**. Enter the Permissions password and click OK to open the Password Security Settings dialog, then make your changes.

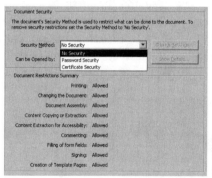

Figure 10.9 Enter the master password and click OK to open the Password Security Settings dialog.

You can delete the password protection in Acrobat as well.

1. In the Document Security pane, click the Security Method pull-down arrow and choose No Security (**Figure 10.10**). Click OK to close the Document Properties dialog.

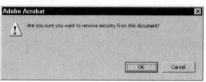

Figure 10.10 Choose No Security to remove password protection.

2. The confirmation dialog shown in **Figure 10.11** opens. Click OK to confirm that you want to delete the security and remove the passwords from the document.

Figure 10.11 Confirm that you want to delete the security options and remove the passwords.

TIP 95 Creating a Digital ID Profile

The key to document security (pun intended) is a *key encryption process*. In order for you to share secure documents with others, and for others to share secure documents with you, you need to use *digital signatures*. A digital signature is based on a digital ID, just as your handwritten signature represents you.

Note
A digital signature, digital ID, and digital profile are the same thing.

You can either create default signatures or design custom signatures. To create a new signature:

1. Choose Advanced > Manage Digital IDs > My Digital IDs > Select My Digital ID File to open the Select My Digital ID File dialog (**Figure 10.12**). Any existing signatures appear in the Digital ID File pull-down list.

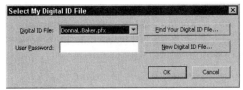

Figure 10.12 Existing signatures are listed in the Digital ID File pull-down list.

2. To build a new signature, click the New Digital ID File button. The Self-Signed Digital ID Disclaimer dialog opens, describing the types of situations in which a self-sign security system isn't the best choice. Click Continue to close the disclaimer. The Create Self-Signed Digital ID dialog opens.

Note
If you are designing digital signatures to use for sharing secure material with a workgroup, for instance, a self-sign security system is appropriate. Each person who wants to access a secure document using a self-sign security option has to contact you directly for permission to use the document. If you want to share material at an enterprise or public level, use a third-party security system.

(Continued)

How a Digital Signature Works

A digital signature is composed of two parts: a *public* key and a *private* key. You have a signature that contains two keys. The private key is yours alone, and you share the public key with others. Your colleague's signature also contains a pair of keys; the private key is hers alone, and she shares the public key with you. If your colleague has your public key listed in her document, she can share the information with you; if you have her public key listed in a document, you can share with her. You can use a number of keys for the same document and share it with a group.

3. Fill in the information for the digital signature (**Figure 10.13**). You can specify a password to protect the content of the signature. Click Create, and the New Self-Sign Digital ID File dialog opens.

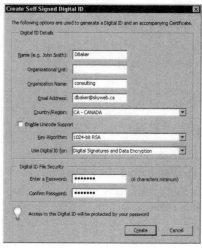

Figure 10.13 Supply the information to create a new digital signature.

4. The file uses the name you entered in the previous dialog. The self-sign security ID files are stored on your hard drive. Choose a folder to store the files, or leave the default location. Then click Save to save the new ID and close the dialog.

Customizing the Digital ID

Acrobat gives you the choice of using the default signature appearance or customizing the appearance by using a PDF document image.

1. Choose Edit > Preferences (on Macs, Acrobat > Preferences) to open the Preferences dialog; and choose Digital Signatures from the list on the left. The Appearance window at the top of the dialog lists existing signature appearances (**Figure 10.14**). Click the New button.

Figure 10.14 The Appearance window lists existing signature appearances.

Note

If you want to modify a signature appearance, select it in the list and click Edit; to remove the signature appearance, click Delete; click Duplicate to create another copy.

2. The Configure Signature dialog opens (**Figure 10.15**); enter the new signature's description and information.

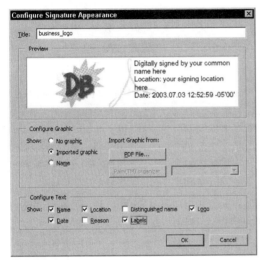

Figure 10.15
Enter your new signature's description and information.

- Assign a name to the appearance by typing it in the Title text box. This name is used in the Appearance list, so be sure to select a descriptive name if you use several signatures.

- Specify a Configure Graphic option. You can choose to use no graphic at all, to include an image, or to use your name as it appears in the program. If you want to use a graphic, it must be a PDF file. Click PDF File to open the Select Picture dialog (**Figure 10.16**). Locate the PDF file you want to use, and then click OK. The Select Picture dialog closes, and you return to the Configure Signature Appearance dialog.

(Continued)

TIP 95: Creating a Digital ID Profile

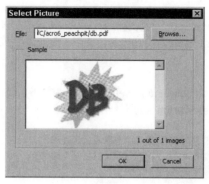

Figure 10.16 Choose a PDF image file to use as a graphic element for your signature.

Signature Preferences

In Figure 10.17, you can see other digital signature preferences below the Appearance list:

- Signing Method—The default is to ask for a signature. You can also select Default Certificate Security; in Windows, you can choose Windows Security.

- Verifying Signatures—The default option is to verify signatures when the document is opened.

- Advanced Properties—This button opens a dialog that lets you choose more options for certificate verification and Microsoft Windows Certificate Security settings.

- In the Configure Text section, specify the options that you want to display on the signature. All options are selected by default. Click those you don't want to include in the signature appearance to deselect them. When you later sign a document using the signature, you can add details (such as the reason for signing); other details (such as the date) are automatically displayed (if you chose the appropriate options).

3. The appearance now displays in the Appearance list (**Figure 10.17**). Click OK to close the Preferences dialog.

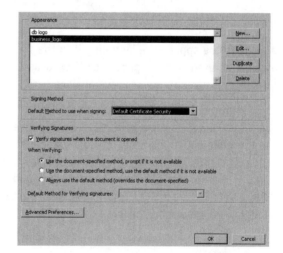

Figure 10.17 The Appearance list now displays the new signature appearance. This dialog also lets you choose from a number of options for signing and verifying signatures.

TIP 96 Certifying a Document

One way to maintain a PDF document as a legally correct document is to *certify* it. When you certify a PDF document, you're certifying the contents and specifying the types of changes allowed that maintain the certification. For example, a form may be certified and allow the user to fill in the fields; however, if the user tries to delete or replace pages, the document will no longer be certified. Certification is one way of using digital signatures. Make sure you have finished modifying your document before certifying it. Otherwise, changes you make may violate the certification settings and corrupt the signature.

Choose File > Save as Certified Document and follow the wizard-like screens, starting with the introduction (**Figure 10.18**). If you want to use a third-party security company click Get Digital ID from Adobe Partner on the introductory screen. Otherwise, proceed through the dialogs defining the type of certification and what actions you want to allow your users to take. You also define the visual characteristics of the signature, including its location on the page.

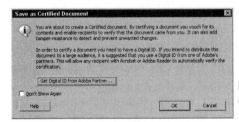

Figure 10.18 This dialog describes the document-certification process.

Some tips for making the certification process smoother:

- In the Choose Allowable Actions dialog (**Figure 10.19**), specify the options you want the user to be able to change. The pull-down list offers three options: you can prevent any changes from being made, allow users to fill out forms, or allow users to both comment and fill out forms.

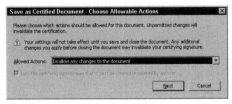

Figure 10.19 Specify the actions you want to allow users to make in the certified document.

- In the Sign dialog, choose options for the actual signature used in the certification process (**Figure 10.20**). You can choose the signature appearance, reason for signing, and other options (see the previous tip).

Signing and Saving

- If you aren't completely sure the document is finished, don't click Sign and Save; instead, click Sign and Save As. Save the document with another name, and preserve the original unsigned in case you decide to make changes before distributing the document.

- Don't try to save the document with another name after the certification is complete. Saving is disallowed.

- You cannot encrypt a document if it already contains signatures. If you want to share a document that has been signed, either use an unsigned copy or remove the signatures. To delete the signatures, click the Options menu in the Signatures pane and click Clear All Signature Fields.

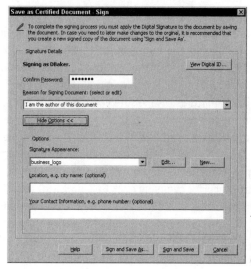

Figure 10.20 Choose options for the signature used to certify the document.

Certification Information

Once a document is certified, you can find out certification information from the document itself. When the document is opened, you'll see a Certified Document icon at the left of the status bar. Hold your pointer over the icon, and a message displays telling you that the document is certified. Keep the pointer over the icon a bit longer, and a larger message appears, describing the certification process—the author, date, and its status (**Figure 10.21**). You can also click the certified document icon to open a dialog that describes the document's status. The dialog contains the information shown in Figure 10.21; it also explains that the document has special security features, and has buttons for accessing legal and signature information.

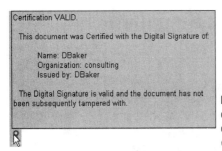

Figure 10.21 A tool tip describes the author, date, and status of the certified document.

You can also find information about the document's status in the Signature pane. Click the Signatures tab on the Navigation tab to open the pane (**Figure 10.22**). Information about the document, its status, signature dates, encryption method, and so on are listed in the pane.

Figure 10.22 Information on the document's status is listed in the Signatures pane.

Sharing a Certified Document

In order to use a document in a review process, you should certify the document to allow commenting and form fill-in.

A document that can be modified is potentially dangerous. The document is said to have "malicious potential." In the Signatures pane, information about the potential problems is included with other signature information (**Figure 10.23**).

Figure 10.23 Information about potential problems is included with other signature information.

TIP 97 Adding a Signature Field and Signing a Document

If you are the creator of a document, you can certify it with a digital signature, as shown in the previous tip. You can also sign a document as part of a review process, specifying whether you are the author or have reviewed the document, and so on.

Instead of adding a single certifying signature, you add a blank signature field, and you use the same field for collecting signatures from others.

To add a signature field, follow these steps:

1. Activate the Digital Signature Field tool. You can choose a menu option or select the tool directly:

   • Click the Sign ![pen icon] task button to display its menu. (To display the Sign task button, choose View > Task Buttons > Sign.) Choose Sign this Document from the menu (**Figure 10.24**), and Acrobat activates the Digital Signature Field tool.

   Sign this Document...
   Validate All Signatures in Document
   Create a Blank Signature Field
   How To...Sign

Figure 10.24 Click the Sign button to display its menu.

   • Open the Advanced Editing toolbar (Tools > Advanced Editing > Show Advanced Editing Toolbar), and select the Digital Signature Field tool ![icon].

2. Next, draw a signature field on your document (**Figure 10.25**). The Digital Signatures Properties dialog opens to the General tab.

Figure 10.25 Draw a signature field on your document.

Who Are You Today?

Acrobat lets you have any number of signatures, but keep in mind that it's easy to become confused by working with one signature and thinking you are working with another. Before you start a signature process, check your digital ID status from the menu listings. Choose Advanced > Manage Digital IDs > My Digital ID Files. The second command, Close My Digital ID File <name> shows the name currently active. Check the name of the digital ID to make sure it is the ID you want to work with. If it isn't, click Open Another Digital ID File and select a different digital ID.

3. Type a name for your field in the Name text box (**Figure 10.26**). Then specify whether you want the field to be visible or invisible. Click Locked at the bottom left of the dialog if you want to lock the signature field to prevent changes after you sign the document.

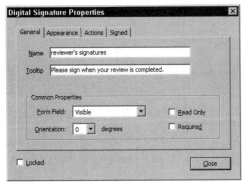

Figure 10.26 Name the signature field on the General tab of this dialog.

Note

I always supply a tool tip as well. When recipients move their mouse over the field, they see a prompt to sign the document. Tool tips serve as good reminders.

4. Click the Appearance tab. If you are using a visible field, choose color, line thickness, and so on (**Figure 10.27**).

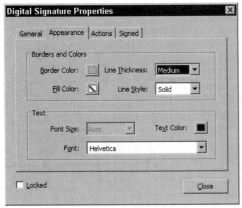

Figure 10.27 Choose color and line settings for visible fields.

(Continued)

More Digital Signatures Properties

The Digital Signatures Properties dialog includes two more tabs, Actions and Signed. The Actions tab lets you add mouse actions to the signature field. For example, you can set an action to have the user go to another page in the document when he or she clicks the signature field. (See Chapters 7 and 8 for tips on using triggers and actions.) The Signed tab includes options that let you reset fields as read-only or execute a custom JavaScript. The options on this tab are compatible with Acrobat 6 only.

TIP 97: Adding a Signature Field and Signing a Document

5. Click Close to dismiss the dialog and complete the signature field.

6. Check the contents of the Signature pane. The new signature field and its characteristics (it is empty at this point) are listed here (**Figure 10.28**).

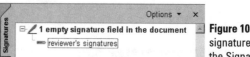

Figure 10.28 The new signature field is listed in the Signatures pane.

7. Save the document with its signature field.

If you've created and originated the document, sign it as well. You can use a certification process (covered in Tip 97), or you can use the blank signature field and sign it. Click the field on the document and follow the signature prompts. When the process is complete, your signature appears in the field. Also, the information in the Signatures panel will expand to include the information about your signature (**Figure 10.29**).

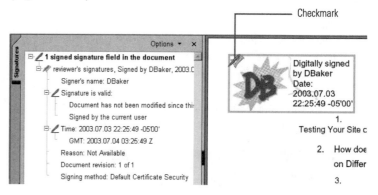

Figure 10.29 Your signature displays on the document and information is listed in the Signatures pane.

Notice the checkmark at the top left of the signature appearance. This checkmark indicates that the signature is valid. At the bottom left of the document status bar, you see a signed document icon ⬚. Hold the pointer over the icon to read the tool tips. The first tool tip states that the document is signed; hold the pointer a little longer, and the more complete tool tip appears, as shown in **Figure 10.30**.

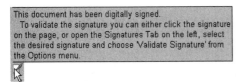

This document has been digitally signed.
  To validate the signature you can either click the signature on the page, or open the Signatures Tab on the left, select the desired signature and choose 'Validate Signature' from the Options menu.

Figure 10.30 Move the pointer over the signed document icon see the tool tip.

When you close and reopen the document, the signature information as well as its appearance will change, as you can see in **Figure 10.31**. Instead of the checkmark at the upper left of the signature, you now see a question mark. In the Signatures pane, Acrobat tells you that the reviewer's signature is of unknown validity.

Question Mark

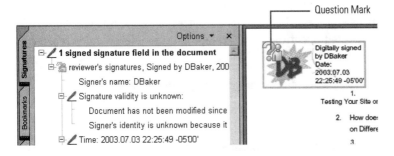

Figure 10.31 When you reopen a document, the signature information changes.

To check the validity of your signature (and that of others, coming up in Tip 98):

1. Select a signature in the Signatures pane. Right-click/Control-click the signature or click the Signatures menu to open it.

2. Choose Validate Signature. The signature is tested, and Acrobat displays the results in a dialog (**Figure 10.32**).

Figure 10.32 Information about the signature's validity appears in a dialog.

3. Click Close to dismiss the dialog, or click Legal Notice or Signature Properties to read more about the signature.

Validating Yourself

Sometimes when you start work on a document that you originally signed and want to check the validation of your signatures and those of other reviewers, you don't see a simple change from an unknown validity to a valid signature. Instead, you see a dialog with a rather confusing message: "The signer's identity is unknown because it has not been included in your list of Trusted Identities and none of its parent Certificates are Trusted Identities." How's that for complicated?

The solution is actually quite simple. Check that you are signed in with a signature by choosing Advanced > Manage Digital IDs > My Digital ID Files and checking the option selected. If you are signed in using a different profile that you used to create the document security, you'll see the message. If you aren't signed in at all, choose Advanced > Manage Digital IDs > My Digital ID Files > Select My Digital ID File and choose the profile you used to create the security.

TIP 97: Adding a Signature Field and Signing a Document

TIP 98 Sharing and Importing Certificates

You can't open a document that has been signed by someone unless you have a copy of that individual's certificate. (Read about creating and customizing certificates in Tip 95.) Certificates you share with others are referred to as *trusted identities*.

Sharing Your Certificates

You can share your certificates with others working in a group or review process. Begin by choosing Advanced > Manage Digital IDs > Trusted Identities. The Manage Trusted Identities dialog opens (**Figure 10.33**).

Figure 10.33
Display the contents of your identities list as either contacts or certificates.

Acrobat lets you display the contents of your identities list in one of two ways: by using contacts or by displaying certificates. *Contacts* are formal FDF files you exchange with someone else. You request an FDF (signature) file by email, and your contact sends back his or her FDF file.

A contact is secure as you go through a formal data exchange process, but an *extracted certificate* is much quicker. Rather than having to email people and request their certificate, you just extract it from a document they have sent to you.

1. Select a certificate or contact from the list to send that person your certificate information, or to save a copy of your certificate to your hard drive or other storage location, and then click Export. The Data Exchange File - Export Options dialog opens (**Figure 10.34**).

Figure 10.34
You can ask for someone's certificate automatically.

2. Choose the email radio button to export the data file.

3. To export the content of the certificate to a file, choose "Save the data to a file." In either case, a series of wizard screens will walk you through the process.

Note
Store all your certificates and data exchange files in the same location. That way, you can keep track of your contacts and access them easily.

Requesting Certificates

You can also ask others to share their certificates with you. Start the process in a similar way to the sharing process:

1. Choose Advanced > Manage Digital IDs > Trusted Identities. The Manage Trusted Identities dialog opens.

2. Click Request Contact (**Figure 10.35**). The Email a Request dialog opens.

Request Contact Button

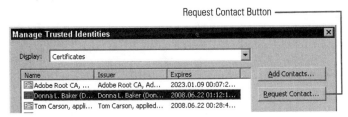

Figure 10.35 Add names to your recipient list.

(Continued)

Certify It or Sign It?

Decide when you need to certify a document and when you need to sign it. If you create a lot of documents for secure distribution, you may want to certify each document as you generate it.

However, be aware of the restrictions added to a document when you certify it. If you intend any of your recipients to make changes, such as additions or deletions, sign it and specify a reason (such as *I am the author*) rather than certifying it.

TIP 98: Sharing and Importing Certificates

Sending and Receiving Certificates

You can automatically include your certificates to add to your contact's list of trusted identities. Just click Include My Certificates. If you click this option, you have to choose a signature profile and enter your password in order to include the information in the email.

3. Type your name and email address (**Figure 10.36**). You can choose to email the request or save it as a file to send later. Click Next and proceed through the wizard-like dialogs.

Figure 10.36 Email a request for your contacts' certificates.

TIP 99 Building a Recipient List

Acrobat combines the certificates you share with and receive from others into a *recipient list* that you can use to share documents securely:

1. Choose Document > Security > Encrypt for Certain Identities Using Certificates. The Document Security - Digital ID Selection dialog opens.

2. Click the digital ID you want to use; click OK (**Figure 10.37**). The Restrict Opening and Editing to Certain Identities dialog opens.

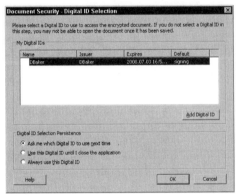

Figure 10.37 Select the digital ID you want to use for managing the list.

3. Select names for your recipient list. Click Add to Recipient List to move the name to the Recipients list (**Figure 10.38**).

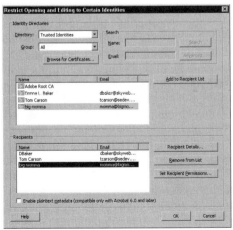

Figure 10.38 Add recipient's names to your list.

(Continued)

TIP 99: Building a Recipient List

Setting and Changing Permissions

If you don't set permissions, your recipients will have full rights to the document by default. You can change a recipient's settings at any time. Select Document > Security > Encrypt for Certain Identities Using Certificates to open the dialog, select the recipient's name, and click Set Recipient Permissions. Reset the permissions in the Recipient Permission Settings dialog. You can delete a recipient from your list altogether; select the name in the Recipients list of the Restrict Opening and Editing to Certain Identities dialog, and click Remove from List (refer to Figure 10.38).

4. Set or modify permissions for the recipients if required. Select the name or names and click Set Recipient Permissions. The Recipient Permission Settings dialog opens.

5. Choose the restrictions for the recipient (**Figure 10.39**). Click OK to close the dialog and return to the Restrict Opening and Editing to Certain Identities dialog. When you have finished setting permissions, click OK to close the dialog.

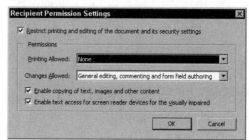

Figure 10.39
Choose the restrictions for each recipient.

TIP 100
Troubleshooting Self-Sign Security

Working with digital signatures can be confusing at first. It gets easier the more you work with them, like everything else. To help you along the way, here are some troubleshooting tips:

- Let's say you create a document and sign it. At a later date, you open the document—or at least you *try* to open it. Instead of seeing the document, you see an alert message that says you don't have access rights. This usually occurs if you are working with a digital ID different from the one you were using when you created the document. Remember that you can have any number of profiles, and you are always logged into the program using a profile. Choose Advanced > Manage Digital IDs > My Digital ID Files, and check the name with which you are logged into the Acrobat session. If it isn't the name you used to create the original security on the document, choose Advanced > Manage Digital IDs > My Digital ID Files > Open Another Digital ID File to open the dialog shown in **Figure 10.40**. Select the correct name from the list, enter the password, and click OK. Now try to open the document again.

Figure 10.40
Choose the identity you used when creating the security for the document.

- Whenever possible, plan ahead. If you create a recipient list and sign your document, before you can modify the list you have to remove your initial signatures. You can't select the initial signature and delete it outright. Instead, select the signature and choose Clear All Signatures from the Signatures pane menu. The content is removed, and you have one empty signature field left in the document.

Don't Sign that Document

When certifying or signing a document for the first time, save the signed version as a copy; don't certify or sign the original. You never know whether you'll have to make changes to an original document before distributing. Using a copy doesn't affect the original; make the changes and reapply the security.

Seeing into the Past

You can see what a document looked like when any of its recipients signed it. Click the signer's name in the Signatures pane. Then choose View Signed Version from the Signatures pane's Options menu. Acrobat displays the document as it existed at the time of signing.

You can display a list of the changes made to a document after the last signed version. Select the signature in the Signatures tab, and choose Compare Signed Version to Current Version from the Option menu. Right-click/Control-click the signature in the Signatures pane or in the Document pane, and choose Compare Signed Version to Current Version.

- Be careful setting digital signature preferences. If your signatures don't look right and don't work correctly, take a look at the preferences. There are many options available in a number of locations. If you get confused, reset the defaults. Choose Edit > Preferences > Digital Signatures. Click Advanced Preferences at the bottom left of the dialog to open the Digital Signature Advanced Preferences dialog (**Figure 10.41**). Click Reset at the lower left of the dialog, and Acrobat resets all your preferences to their default settings.

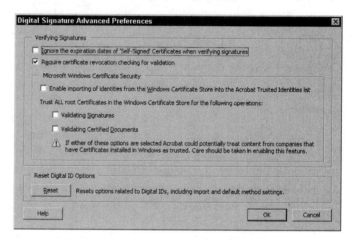

Figure 10.41 Reset the digital signatures settings and preferences.

- If you have numerous signatures in your document, collapse their information listings in the Signatures pane. Move the pointer over a signature to display a tool tip listing the basic information about the signature (**Figure 10.42**).

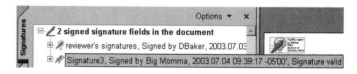

Figure 10.42 Collapse the signature information in the Signatures pane to save room. A tool tip will display basic information about the signature.

- Make sure the members of a review group all have the same sets of certificates. If not, a missing certificate results in an invalid signature. You can get certificate information directly from a signature to use to validate that signature. Verify that the reason the signature isn't validating is not simply that the certificate is missing. Right-click/Control-click the signature appearance on the document and choose Validate Signature. The Signature Validation Status dialog opens, describing why the signature is invalid (**Figure 10.43**). Click Signature Properties to open the Signature Properties dialog. At the right of the dialog next to the signature name, click Trust Identity (**Figure 10.44**). Follow the prompts to add the certificate to your list.

Figure 10.43 The Signature Validation Status dialog describes why the signature is invalid.

Figure 10.44 Use the Signature Properties dialog to add a certificate if necessary.

Note

Don't make a habit of using the certificates from signatures. If you have to use one, such as when you are offline, get the person to send you a certificate file as soon as it is convenient or practical.

- Don't always expect signatures to be valid. If you sign a document and someone makes changes to the document and returns it to you, your original signature will no longer be valid.

- You can sign a document in a browser, but it is stored differently than a signed document on your hard drive. Click Sign to sign a document in your browser; only the portion of the document that changed from the previous signature until you signed it is automatically saved to your hard drive. If you want the entire document, sign the document, and then click Save a Copy on the Acrobat toolbar.

What's in a Name?

Be careful naming signatures and choosing passwords. Name the signature in a form that is recognizable to both you and any recipients you may share the profile with. For example, *dbaker* is understandable to me (it's my name!) and to those I share the certificate with. On the other hand, naming a profile *General or Magazine* isn't useful to anyone but me. If you use certificates for different workgroups or situations, develop a naming system. *dbaker_basic* is useful both to me and to my recipients, although the name is a little lengthy. Use the same caution with passwords, and be sure to use character strings you can easily remember.

Who Can You Trust?

You can decide which of your readers can access media (such as movies and sound) based on their status. For example, if you send a document containing a Flash animation to a colleague who has your name included in his list of trusted authors, he can play the movie. If you are not on his list, the movie can be blocked. Trusted documents and authors are used regularly for products such as downloaded files and updates from different hardware and software manufacturers.

Use the Trust Manager preferences to change your security settings. Choose Edit > Preferences > Trust Manager (**Figure 10.45**). Choose from a number of options that range from allowing documents to open other files and other applications to blocking permissions.

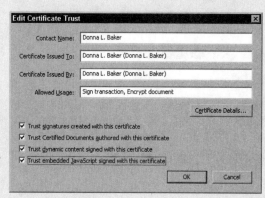

Figure 10.45 You can set options for both trusted and non-trusted documents.

Choose Advanced > Manage Digital IDs > Manage Trusted Identities, and click the Edit Trust button in the dialog to open the dialog in **Figure 10.46**. Evaluate the trust options for multimedia as you would any other type of material coming into your computer. If it's from a source you trust (such as a business partner), choose all the options. If you are on a large mailing list, you might want to restrict the options to choosing only the certificate or certified documents.

Figure 10.46 Choose from a range of settings for multimedia security in the Trust Manager preferences.

APPENDIX A

Other Sources of Information

This appendix contains a list of URLs referenced in this book, as well as other sources of information you may find useful in your work.

Adobe Sites

These URLs link to information/resource sites at Adobe:

- **Adobe Studio (requires login and ID):**
  http://studio.adobe.com/expertcenter/acrobat/main.html

- **Acrobat Support Knowledgebase:**
  www.adobe.com/support/products/acrobat.html

- **User-to-User Forum/Macintosh:**
  www.adobeforums.com/cgi-bin/webx?14@@.ee6b2ed

- **User-to-User Forum/Windows:**
  www.adobeforums.com/cgi-bin/webx?14@@.ee6b2f2

- **Downloads for Windows and Macintosh:**
  www.adobe.com/support/downloads/main.html

Information Sites

These sites offer valuable information on the PDF file format.

- **PlanetPDF:** Information on all things PDF; offers a very active user-to-user forum.
  www.planetpdf.com

- **PDFzone:** Another large PDF and document management site.
  www.pdfzone.com

- **Creativepro**.com: Offers articles, reviews, and other information for designers.
  www.creativepro.com

System Requirements

Make sure your computer meets the minimum system requirements for operating Acrobat 6.0 Standard.

Windows

The minimum and recommended system requirements for using Acrobat 6.0 Standard on Windows systems:

- Intel Pentium processor
- Microsoft Windows 98 Second Edition, Windows NT 4.0 with Service Pack 6, Windows 2000 Professional with Service Pack 2, Windows XP Professional or Home Edition, or Windows XP Tablet PC Edition
- Microsoft Internet Explorer 5.01
- 64MB of RAM (128MB recommended)
- 220MB of available hard-disk space
- 800x600 screen resolution monitor
- CD-ROM drive

Macintosh

The minimum and recommended system requirements for using Acrobat 6.0 Standard on Macintosh systems:

- PowerPC G3 processor
- Mac OS X v.10.2.2
- 64MB of RAM (128MB recommended)
- 370MB of available hard-disk space
- 800x600 screen resolution monitor
- CD-ROM drive

APPENDIX C

Shortcut Keys

Nearly all Acrobat 6.0 program functions can be controlled using keyboard shortcuts. This appendix lists Acrobat's standard shortcuts.

Table C.1 Moving Through a Document

Use the document navigation shortcuts to move through an open document.

Action	Windows	Mac OS
Previous screen	Page Up	Page Up
Next screen	Page Down	Page Down
First page	Home or Shift+Ctrl+Page Up or Shift+Ctrl+Up Arrow	Home or Shift+Command+Page Up or Option+Shift+Up Arrow
Last page	End or Shift+Ctrl+Page Down or Shift+Ctrl+Down Arrow	End or Shift+Command+Page Down or Option+Shift+Down Arrow
Scroll up	Up Arrow	Up Arrow
Scroll down	Down Arrow	Down Arrow
Scroll (when Hand tool is selected)	Spacebar	
Zoom in	Ctrl+plus sign	Command+plus sign
Zoom out	Ctrl+minus sign	Command+minus sign
Zoom in temporarily	Ctrl+Spacebar, then click	Command+Spacebar, then click

Table C.2 **Navigating in the Program**

Use the navigation shortcuts to move through menus and dialogs in the program.

Action	Windows	Mac OS
Show/hide menu bar	F9	F9
Move focus to menus	F10 or Alt, then arrow keys	
Move focus to toolbar area	Alt, then Ctrl+Tab	
Move focus to next toolbar	Ctrl+Tab	
Move focus to toolbar in browser or Help window	Shift+F8	
Open Properties toolbar or Properties dialog	Ctrl+I	Command+I
Cycle through open documents (focus on document pane)	Ctrl+F6	Command+ ~
Move focus to next floating panel or open dialog	Alt+F6	
Move focus to next item in document pane	Tab or Right Arrow	Tab or Right Arrow
Move focus to previous item in document pane	Shift+Tab or Left Arrow	Shift+Tab or Left Arrow
Activate selected tool/ item/command	Spacebar or Enter	Spacebar or Return
Open/close context menu	Shift+F10	Control+click
Close an open menu, context menu, or dialog	Esc	Esc
Close all windows	Shift+Ctrl+W	Shift+Command+W
Move focus to next tab in a tabbed dialog	Ctrl+Tab	
Move highlight to next search result in document	F3	
Select text (with Select Text tool active)	Shift+arrow keys	Shift+arrow keys
Select previous/next word (Select Text tool active)	Shift+Ctrl+Right Arrow or Left Arrow	Shift+Control+Right Arrow or Left Arrow
Move cursor to next/ previous word (Select Text tool active)	Ctrl+Right Arrow or Left Arrow	Command+Right Arrow or Left Arrow

Table C.3 Selecting Tools

Change a preference setting to use the Selecting Tool shortcuts.
Choose Edit > Preferences > General (on Mac, Acrobat > Preferences
> General) and click Use Single-Key Accelerators to Access Tools.

Tool	Windows	Mac OS
Article tool	A	A
Crop tool	C	C
Hand tool	H	H
Link tool	L	L
Select Object tool	R	R
Snapshot tool	G	G
Touch Up Text tool	T	T
Hand tool temporarily	Spacebar	Spacebar
Current selection tool	V	V
Cycle through selection tools: Text/Image/Table	Shift+V	Shift+V
Cycle through zoom tools: Zoom In/Out/Dynamic	Shift+Z	Shift+Z
Current zoom tool	Z	Z
Select Zoom In tool temporarily	Ctrl+Spacebar	Command+Spacebar
Select Dynamic Zoom tool temporarily(Zoom In/Zoom Out active)	Shift	Shift

TABLE C.3: Selecting Tools

Table C.4 Using Comments

Change a preference setting to use the Commenting Tool shortcuts. Choose Edit > Preferences > General (on Mac, Acrobat > Preferences > General) and click Use Single-Key Accelerators to Access Tools.

Action/Tool Selected	Windows	Mac OS
Note tool	S	S
Text Edits tool	E	E
Stamp tool	K	K
Text Box tool	X	X
Pencil tool	N	N
Pencil Eraser tool	Shift+N	Shift+N
Current attach tool	J	J
Cycle through attach tools	Shift+J	Shift+J
Current drawing tool	D	D
Cycle through drawing tools	Shift+D	Shift+D
Current highlighting tool	U	U
Cycle through highlighting tools	Shift+U	Shift+U
Move focus to comment	Tab	Tab
Open pop-up for comment that has focus	Spacebar	Spacebar
Send comments	Q	Q
Send and receive comments in browser-based review	O	O
Mark document status as complete in browser-based review	W	W
Save document and work off line (browser-based review)	Y	Y
Go back online	I	I

Table C.5 Using the Navigation Tabs

Use shortcut keys to move among the tabs in the Navigation pane. Use several key combinations in the Bookmarks panel.

Action	Windows	Mac OS
Open/close navigation pane	F6	F6
Move focus between navigation and document panes	Shift+F6	
Move focus to next element of the active navigation tab	Tab	Tab
Move to next navigation tab and make it active (focus on the tab)	Up Arrow or Down Arrow	
Move to next navigation tab and make it active (focus anywhere in navigation pane)	Ctrl+Tab	
Move focus to next item in a navigation tab	Tab or Down Arrow	Down Arrow
Move focus to previous item in a navigation tab	Shift+Tab or Up Arrow	Up Arrow
Expand current bookmark (focus on Bookmarks tab)	Right Arrow or Shift+plus sign	Right Arrow or Shift+plus sign
Collapse current bookmark (focus on Bookmarks tab)	Left Arrow or minus sign	
Rename selected bookmark	F2	F2
Expand all bookmarks	Shift+*	Shift+*
Collapse selected bookmark	Forward Slash (/)	Forward Slash (/)

TABLE C.5: Using the Navigation Tabs

Table C.6 **Using the How To and Help Windows**

Use shortcut keys to work in the How To window and the Complete Help file.

Action	Windows	Mac OS
Open window	F4	F4
Close window	F4 or Esc	F4 or Esc
Move focus between How To window and document pane	Shift+F4	Shift+F4
Go to home page	Home	Home
Move focus among How To window elements	Shift+Ctrl+Tab	Shift+Control+Tab
Go to next page	Right Arrow	
Go to previous page	Left Arrow	
Open/close Help window	F1	F1
Move focus to Help window toolbar	Shift+F8	Shift+F8
Move focus through Help menu tabs	Right Arrow or Left Arrow	Right Arrow or Left Arrow
Toggle focus between active tab and tab contents	Tab	Tab
Move to next element in active tab	Up Arrow or Down Arrow	Up Arrow or Down Arrow
Reflow the Help document	Shift+F4	Shift+F4

Index

R

ranges. *See* page ranges
RC4 encryption, 276
"Read an article" action, 226–227
Read Out Loud feature, 92–94
readers, screen, 92, 97, 239
Reading Order options, 96
Receive Comments button, 178
recipient document, 111
recipient lists, certificate, 297–298
redraw speed, 14
Reflow feature, 100–101
Remove White Margins option, 119
Replace command, 219
Replace Pages dialog, 116
resampling options, 18
"Reset a form" action, 252, 256
resolution, exported image, 68
Restore Defaults button, 24
reusing
    images, 135–136
    page elements, 133–136
    table information, 142–143
    text, 134, 136
Revert command, 114
Review & Comment taskbar, 146, 154
review process, 170–180
    browser-based, 178–180
    collecting feedback from, 176–177
    controlling, 175
    and document certification, 289, 300–301
    initiating, 170
    responding to request for, 172–173
    sending out documents for, 170–171
    tracking, 174–175
Review Tracker, 174–175, 180
RGB color space, 36, 73
rich text format. *See* RTF files
Rotate Pages dialog, 120
RSA encryption, 276
RTF files, 67, 142, 143
"Run a JavaScript" action, 230
run-length compression, 19

S

Save As Certified Document dialog, 287
Save As command/dialog, 17–18, 67, 71
Save As Doc Settings dialog, 67
Save As HTML dialog, 69
Save As JPEG Settings dialog, 71
Save PDF File As dialog, 17
saving. *See also* exporting
    conversion settings, 38
    as images, 71–73
    job options, 38
    as PDFs, 17–18
    as text-based files, 67–68
Scan Document icon, 233
scanned documents
    capturing content of, 51–52
    creating PDFs from, 48–50
    fixing incorrect characters in, 52–53
    identifying PDFs created from, 50
    importing editable text from, 51–53
    increasing clarity of, 49
screen
    modifying items displayed on, 3
    reducing clutter on, 10–11
Screen job options, 23
screen readers, 92, 97, 239
scripting language, 257. *See also* JavaScript
scrolling, automatic, 86–87
Search PDF pane, 207
Search tab, Help menu, 7
searching
    Comments list, 168–169
    Help file, 7–9
    PDF files, 207–208
    Web, 207
security, 275–302
    and Acrobat versions, 278
    with digital signatures. *See* digital signatures
    with document certification, 287–289, 294–298
    and key encryption process, 283
    with passwords. *See* passwords
    and reuse of page elements, 133

Index